# T. C. Murray, *Dramatist*

Sanford Sternlicht, *Series Editor*

T. C. Murray, n.d.
Photographic portrait; 8 x 10 in. (photographer unknown).
Courtesy of the John J. Burns Library, Boston College.

# T. C. MURRAY,
## *Dramatist*

### *Voice of Rural Ireland*

Albert J. DeGiacomo

Syracuse University Press

Permission to reprint from the following sources is gratefully acknowledged: From the Frank
O'Connor Collection, Department of Special Collections, Boston University; from the Berg
Collection of English and American Literature, New York Public Library, Astor, Lenox, and
Tilden Foundations; from the Council of Trustees of the National Library of Ireland; for the
Yeats letters—by permission of Oxford University Press on behalf of Michael B. Yeats; for
HTC Clipping Files—courtesy of Harvard Theatre Collection, Houghton Library, Harvard
University; for the photograph of T. C. Murray—courtesy of John J. Burns Library,
Boston College.

**Library of Congress Cataloging-in-Publication Data**

DeGiacomo, Albert J.
T.C. Murray, dramatist : voice of rural Ireland / Albert J. DeGiacomo.—
      1st ed. p. cm.—(Irish studies)
ISBN 0–8156–2945–1 (hardcover (cloth) : alk. paper)
1. Murray, T. C. (Thomas Cornelius), 1873–1959—Criticism and interpretation. 2. Cork
(Ireland : County)—In literature. 3. Rural conditions in literature. 4. Ireland—In literature. 5.
Drama—Technique. I. Title. II. Irish studies (Syracuse, N.Y.) PR6025.U75 Z64 2002
822'.912—dc21
2002014408

For Adele M. Dalsimer
and
for John B. Sturrock

*May Their Memories Be Blessed*

**Albert J. DeGiacomo** is an assistant professor in the English and Theatre Department at Berea College in Kentucky, where he teaches courses in English, theater, and general studies and directs productions in the Berea College Theatre Laboratory. He has published articles in the *Irish University Review* and *Éire-Ireland*. This is his first book.

# Contents

**Illustrations**

# Abbreviations for Collections and Depositories

AT, NLI      Abbey Theatre. Papers. National Library of Ireland, Dublin.

BC, NYPL      Berg Collection. New York Public Library.

FJHO'D, NLI      O'Donnell, Frank J. Hugh. Papers. National Library of Ireland, Dublin.

HTC      Harvard Theatre Collection. Nathan Marsh Pusey Library, Cambridge, Mass.

JH, NLI      Holloway, Joseph. Papers. National Library of Ireland, Dublin.

MJMC, JJBL      MacManus, M. J. Collection. The John J. Burns Library, Boston College, Chestnut Hill, Mass.

MOM, NLI      O'Mahony, Mathew. Papers. National Library of Ireland, Dublin.

NLI      National Library of Ireland, Dublin.

TCD      Trinity College Library, Dublin.

TCM, NLI      Murray, T. C. Papers. National Library of Ireland, Dublin.

TLC, JJBL      Connolly, The Rev. Terence L. Papers. The John J. Burns Library, Boston College, Chestnut Hill, Mass.

# Preface

"I REMEMBER SEEING F. J. McCormick in *Autumn Fire* at the Abbey, and he tore my heart out," said a Dublin woman at the mention of Murray's name. T. C. Murray (1873–1959), a second-generation dramatist of the Abbey Theatre, was well known to Irish theater audiences at one time. *The New York Times* obituary, "Thomas Murray, Playwright, Dies," described him as "a playwright associated with the earliest and most distinguished days of the Abbey Theatre." Murray wrote plays that were regular features of the Abbey repertoire from 1910 to 1940 and were standards for many years more in Irish amateur dramatic societies; the best of them continue to appear in their repertoire to the present day.

Murray produced a dramatic body of seventeen plays in one, two, and three acts. In addition, he penned a series of poems, short stories, book reviews, essays on educational methods, occasional pieces on travel and one autobiographical novel, *Spring Horizon* (1937). Despite Murray's accomplishments, no book-length study of his life and work has ever been published. The publication of *Selected Plays of T. C. Murray* (1998) makes seven of the plays newly available and will hopefully engender new interest in his work.

In critical estimation, the artistic height of Murray's playwriting career was the period between 1912 and 1924—between *Maurice Harte* and *Autumn Fire*. In 1929, Andrew E. Malone, one of the first scholarly critics to write on Murray, called him "one of the best of the Irish dramatists" (1965, 194). More recently, Desmond Maxwell wrote that Murray's work, though "of its time," has "a life beyond its contemporary relevance" (1984, 77). In 1980, the late Augustine Martin stated emphatically: "This remarkable Corkman . . . managed to shape out of the materials of daily rural experience a series of tragic dramas which have not yet had their critical due" (1980, 40).

Martin thus provides the present study with its rationale: to highlight Murray's singular contribution as dramatist to the Irish dramatic movement. I also hope to illustrate Murray's life as lecturer and essayist and to support Robert Welch's claim for Murray as "one of the country's leading Catholic intellectuals" (1999, 99).

Alone among the Abbey dramatists, Murray dedicated his writing career almost exclusively to the exploration of the tragic genre. No one would argue that Murray was one of the greatest of Irish dramatists, but his plays spoke strongly to Irish people from 1910 well into the 1950s, helping them interpret their own experience. Recalling Murray in a letter to the author, John B. Keane reflected on his formative years, "I remember seeing *Birthright* in a village near here [Listowel]. I was struck by its intensity and passion. I also regarded and still do regard *Autumn Fire* as one of the great Irish plays" (Keane 1992).

The recurring theme in Murray's plays is the cry for freedom. His characters yearn to throw off the oppression of land, family, and religion, and to create a life true to their unique natures. Although domineering priests and parents, arranged marriages, and broken dreams fill Murray's dramatic landscape, Murray's heroes succeed progressively in creating independent lives. In 1925, Dorothy Macardle wrote in the *Dublin Magazine* that Murray's work presents "the claim of each new generation to free, sweet, natural life" (2:394). All of Murray's heroes, especially Maurice Harte, Morgan in *The Briery Gap*, Myles O'Regan in *Aftermath*, Peter Keville in *The Pipe in the Fields*, and Brian Egan in *Illumination*, are in the process of creating authentic lives, with varying degrees of success. Brian Egan comes nearest to the goal, completing the progressive march from the submission of Maurice Harte to the bitter freedom of Myles O'Regan in *Aftermath*.

As political events in the struggle for Irish independence appear very rarely in Murray's plays, it might seem initially that Murray was an apolitical writer who contributed little to the cause of cultural nationalism. But this is not true. Principally a writer of rural life, Murray seldom adverts to political upheavals, but he shows his country people struggling to survive. Daniel Corkery in *Synge and Anglo-Irish Literature* (1931) decried the predominance of English models presented to Irish readers as experience worthy of emulation, both in the art of writing and, at least implicitly, in the struggle of living. Corkery maintained that reading English fiction was debilitating to the Irish reader "for he cannot find in these surroundings what his reading has taught him is matter worth coming upon" (15). Murray, in his realistic portraits, created an indigenous dramatic literature that helped Irish people see and understand their own lived experience without reference to English art or politics. This was precisely Murray's contribution to cultural nationalism.

The Irish dramatic movement was an integral part of the Irish literary renaissance. Murray's unique voice in the dramatic movement lay in his use of religion. In 1908, one year before Murray began writing plays, Horace Plunkett wrote, "In no other country in the world, probably, is religion so dominant an element in the daily life of the people as in Ireland" (94). Murray's people, most characteristically, are the peasants of West Cork, "the most ostentatiously religious in Ireland," says Malone, who "make parade of their religious beliefs and practices" (1965, 186). Their intense Catholicism is both a shaping influence and an oppressive force. Murray's sustained exploration of this dimension of their lives distinguishes his work from that of others, notably Padraic Colum, his closest contemporary in style and subject matter.

In certain ways, T. C. Murray was a successor to Colum, another Catholic known for his ability to create faithful presentations of peasant speech and customs (Sternlicht 1985, 23). Yet Murray was distinct from Colum, Lennox Robinson, and other Irish dramatists in depicting the peasants' religious instinct as manifested in the vicissitudes of daily life. Murray's best dramas succeeded because of his own acute religious sensibility, which enabled him to reveal the religious interior of his characters and to illuminate their daily round, grounded in religious values which Murray also held dear. Like Colum before him and O'Casey after him, Murray faltered as dramatist when he turned from the world and the people he best knew.

In his declining years, Murray realized that his dramatic day had passed, acknowledging, in a letter to Mathew O'Mahony on 27 January 1954, "I belong to the past and not to the atomic age" (MS. 24,902, folder x, MOM, NLI). Yet in a critical appreciation of Murray's work, broadcast on 19 November 1952, Daniel Corkery described audiences of the teens, twenties, thirties, and forties as held rapt by Murray's tragic drama: "They sit in an appalled silence—still, almost rigid; they are looking not at themselves but into themselves" (Corkery, quoted by O.G.D., Ms. 23,514, TCM, NLI). This silence speaks of the intensity of Murray's best work, creating for Irish audiences an authentically Irish *seeing place*—a *theatron* in the Greek sense—where the theater mirrored rural life with accuracy and found peasant lives eminently stageworthy, indeed, "matter worth coming upon." Whether they lived in the country or the city, Irish audiences were never far removed from their roots in the land. Murray, in his tragic vision, helped Irish people recognize the pattern of their often tragic lives.

I present this study chronologically with the exception of Murray's experimental plays, which I have grouped in one chapter for reasons of thematic unity. The work is essentially one of theater history. I present little discussion of the plays as they might work on stage today. I have never seen a Murray play performed, except for a production of *The Briery Gap* which I directed so that I might have a sense of how a Murray drama might play and how it might be received by an audience, albeit an American academic one.

For their pioneering work on T. C. Murray, I am much indebted to Tadhg Murray (unrelated to the playwright), Mathew O'Mahony, and the Rev. Matthew T. Conlin, O.F.M. Tadhg Murray was a professional actor and director who came from Macroom, the playwright's hometown. O'Mahony, a civil servant, was an amateur actor and director and a friend to Murray for close to thirty years, who corresponded with him for the duration of their friendship. Both O'Mahony and Tadhg Murray acted in and directed T. C. Murray's plays. Both delivered memorial lectures on the playwright, Murray in 1974 in Macroom, Co. Cork (Ms. 24,879, TCM, NLI), and O'Mahony in 1982 at Newman House in Dublin (Ms. 23,976, MOM, NLI). These lectures, plus an interview of O'Mahony by the author, provided initial biographical information. Especially helpful was the correspondence between Murray and the Rev. Terence L. Connolly, S.J., of Boston College. Connolly, who was English Department chair, university librarian, and founder of the Irish collection, met Murray in Dublin at the 1938 Abbey Theatre Festival; they remained friends for the next twenty years. Their correspondence and Murray's gift of a typescript of *Illumination*, both of which are housed in the John J. Burns Library of Boston College, precipitated my initial study of Murray in 1990. Incorporating components of theater history, the present enterprise draws upon Matthew T. Conlin's 1952 doctoral dissertation, a literary study completed when the playwright was still living. I am also indebted to Mícheál ÓhAodha and Gerald Fitzgibbon for the important critical work they completed on Murray in the 1970s.

For hospitality and advice while in County Cork I am exceedingly grateful to Finola O'Donovan, T. C. Murray's grandniece, who introduced me to several persons who guided me on my way. Mary Murray, the playwright's niece, led me through her home: the playwright's place of birth, his home, and the setting of his novel and many of his plays. Donal Ó Mathúna, principal emeritus of Bishop McEgan College in Macroom, and John Martin Fitz-Gerald of Macroom led me on tours of Murray's hometown. Humphrey Twomey, retired secondary teacher, read all my early drafts, provided insight into the Irish National School system, and shepherded me through many locales in County Cork associated with Murray. Tadhg and Christine Ó Mathúna, current principal and teacher, respectively, of Murray's Rathduff National School, opened to me Murray's old schoolrooms, as well as the records kept by the master. Together with Humphrey Twomey, they organized an evening of lecture and reminiscence in the Rathduff school that enabled me to interview some surviving Murray pupils, exchange insights with locals, and come to understand more deeply Murray's life in Rathduff, so crucial to his plays.

I wish to thank Professors Sherwood Collins and Laurence Senelick of Tufts University, who supported this project first as a seminar paper, later as a doctoral thesis, and then as a developing book. So, too, John Atteberry and Thomas Desmond, Senior Reference Librarians, the John J. Burns Library of Boston College and the National Library of Ireland respectively, offered much appreciated assistance from first to last. I also wish to thank Sean Anthony Platt, Matthew Jonas Friddle, Brooke Kaiser, and Nathaniel Green, my students at Berea College, who helped to prepare the manuscript and served as the book's first undergraduate audience. Jonas Friddle, in particular, assisted me from editing the final draft, through editing copy, to reading the final proofs. Linda Smith, also of Berea College, offered invaluable computer assistance. John Bolin, Dean of the Faculty of Berea College and Jacqueline Burnside, Associate Dean, also supported the project through the Professional Growth Fund. All these persons of good will have my gratitude and affection.

Finally, I never would have begun this project except for the late Adele M. Dalsimer, one of my professors at Boston College, who suggested that I investigate the plays of T. C. Murray. The late John B. Sturrock, an important life mentor also of Boston College, saw the plays of T. C. Murray performed during his student years at Oxford. He was keenly interested in the progress of this book and looked forward to its publication. It is in gratitude for their enthusiastic counsel through the years that I dedicate this book to their memories.

Berea College
26 February 2001

T. C. Murray, *Dramatist*

Father Mangan : Have sense, man. Have sense.

Owen : She wont Father. Never.

*Maurice is seen to* ~~stand up~~ *rise from the chair abstractedly. With his eyes deep in the book, and still reading fragments of his office half* ~~audibly~~ aloud*, he goes out the open door very slowly*

Father Mangan : (in a low voice) Follow him, Michael.

*Michael goes out*

Mrs Harte : (tottering towards a seat)
My God ! My God ! My God !

*The priest looks at her with a pained sense of his own helplessness. The Curtain comes down slowly*

## The End

J. C. Murray.
Woodville
Rathduff Blarney
Co Cork

16·2·12

Final autograph manuscript page, *The Levite (Maurice Harte)*, 1912.

# 1

# The Schoolmaster Dramatist

IN THE LATTER HALF of the nineteenth century, a young couple of County Cork married and settled in the growing market town of Macroom. Determined to escape the vagaries of tenant farming, Cornelius Murray of Killnamartyra and Honora Kelleher of Coolavokig were eager to become merchants in Ireland's growing middle class. To this end, they opened a meal and flour shop in a large three-story building on Pound Lane, now called New Street. Prospering on Macroom's main thoroughfare, connecting Killarney with Cork City, the couple added a grocery and bar, housing their burgeoning family on the upper levels. Macroom is located in the province of Munster on the edge of the Irish speaking Gaeltacht in the southwest of Ireland. Con and Nora, both native Irish speakers, succeeded in their enterprise, in part, because they were fluent in English and were willing to transact business in this emerging language of commerce.

Thomas Cornelius Murray was born in Macroom on 17 January 1873, seventh of Con and Nora's eleven children. According to Murray, his father was stern and somewhat distant. In "Myself and Caesar," an article published in *The Irish Press* on 11 June 1943, Murray wrote of his father's firmness in refusing to indulge his boyhood wish to own a dog (Ms. 23,513, 2:149, TCM, NLI). He drew upon his father's characteristics in creating both the unbending father in *Birthright* and the caring yet remote father in *Spring Horizon*. According to Mathew O'Mahony, Con Murray was "no different from the average father of the time," asserting that "the children dutifully obeyed their father; but loved their gentle mother" (Ms. 23,976, 2, MOM, NLI).

In his parents' shop, close to the town square, young Murray observed a cross section of local life. Most of their customers were farmers. "It was through the friendly traffic with these," Murray wrote, "that I knew at first hand the peasant mind and the peasant's way of life" (Murray 1951, 126). More quiet and reflective than the average boy, he possessed a keen intelligence and a responsive imagination. Remembering many of the sights and events of his native Macroom, he recorded them years later in his plays and in his novel.

Murray was raised in a highly politicized climate. A symbol of England's dominance was daily offered to his mind by the castle that stood in the center of Macroom town. Though the absentee landlord resided in England, the castle's expansive wooded estate, surrounding the Sullane River, was off limits to the local citizens, and any boy who ventured to trespass was set upon by the warden. "Such cool, green fields as invited a boy to kick off his shoes and run freely on the grass," Murray recalled years later in "Tale of a Town," an article he wrote for the 3 June 1940 issue of *The Irish Press*. "By man-made laws," he lamented,"fields and woods, the gifts of Providence, were sacrosanct. From summer to summer you looked on them with a boy's hungry longing, but to venture into field or wood was to be a lawbreaker" (Ms. 24,891, TCM, NLI). From this unnatural restriction, he learned early lessons about oppressive foreign bondage that he transmuted into the themes of his plays.

Educated in Macroom's National School, Murray loved books from his youth. Reared in a home run by successful merchants, he had access to a set of Shakespeare's plays. Well into old age he remarked on his boyhood fascination with the captioned woodcut illustrations in these volumes. Other reading material included novels from the library in the Macroom Convent of Mercy. Nationalistic periodicals and newspapers were also available to him. Early in *Spring Horizon,* Murray reveals, in the character of Stephen Mangan, a glimpse of himself, aspiring to be a writer: "The Supplement, with its melange of story, sketch, and rhyme, reprinted mostly from the periodicals of the day, gave a sprinkle of color on Sunday afternoons to many households in Carberymore. Deep within him, Stephen nursed a secret ambition to see his name on its pages" (1937, 147).

From reading the burgeoning newspapers and periodicals of the day, Murray became interested, in his late teens, in Ireland's changing political climate. He was aware of the rise of literary societies and of the Gaelic Athletic

Association, which encouraged the playing of distinctly Irish sports, as opposed to English games. Most especially, he was conscious of the surge toward Home Rule under the leadership of the protestant nationalist leader, Charles Stewart Parnell. According to Mathew O'Mahoney, as Murray did not speak Irish at this time, his parents discussed Parnell's political fall, occasioned by an adulterous affair with his mistress, Kitty O'Shea, only in the native tongue (Ms. 23,976, 2, MOM, NLI).

In 1891, at the age of eighteen, Murray traveled to Dublin on a Queen's Scholarship to attend St. Patrick's Training College, Drumcondra, where he prepared for a teaching career. Six of Murray's ten siblings also became schoolteachers, a fact that Murray attributed to the economic security offered by this vocation, as opposed to the intrinsic uncertainty of farming, dependent on the way "the wind do be blowing" (Conlin 1952, 2). Shortly after young Murray's arrival in Dublin, he came face to face with the swirling political life of Ireland as he encountered the funeral cortege of Charles Stewart Parnell, an event he remembered to the end of his days. Indeed, it was an exciting time for a youth with a literary bent to be a student in Dublin City, for with the death of Parnell, the movement toward Home Rule and the drive for nationalism shifted from the political arena to the literary. It was clear that the impulse of political nationalism could be aided and abetted by the emerging Irish Literary Renaissance, which aimed both to recover the Celtic roots of Irish culture and to create an indigenous Irish literature. On 28 November 1892, Douglas Hyde delivered a momentous address on this subject, "On the Necessity for De-Anglicising the Irish Nation," at a meeting of the National Literary Society, founded in May of that year. Murray, who devoured Irish literary periodicals and who loved the theater, must have been stimulated, following the rising cultural movement and attending Dublin's theaters—the Gaiety and the Queens—whenever his student budget allowed. It was not the rising cries for Ireland's political freedom, however, that would feature in his plays, but a yearning for spiritual freedom. During his student days Murray responded strongly to Jean Racine's verse drama, *Athalia*. "The play touched some inner chord in my being," he recalled years later, "and directly on leaving college I read with absorbed interest most of Racine's works. . . . The appeal of Racine was an early indication of my feelings for literature as expressed in drama" (Murray 1951). Based on the Hebrew scriptures, *Athalia* must have stirred Murray's religious imagination, for Eliakim, the story's young hero, anticipates many of the young, oppressed heroes in Murray's plays.

Certified by the National Board of Education, Murray became a national teacher at the age of twenty. Upon his return to County Cork in 1893, he served as assistant teacher, first at Carrignavar in the country and later at Saint Francis National School in a poverty-stricken district of Cork City, where he came to know fellow teacher Daniel Corkery. As his health was endangered by the overcrowding and other conditions in this school, Murray accepted advice to move on to Carrigtwohill where he "breathed more freely" (Conlin 1952, 3). While teaching at St. Mary's School there, Murray met his future spouse, Christina Moylan, a colleague teacher and daughter of the principal. During their courtship, they would walk along the Mardyke by the River Lee; they married on 31 July 1903 at the Franciscan church of the Holy Trinity in Cork City. In 1900 Murray was appointed principal of the national school in Rathduff, another country town, near Blarney. Christina—or "Nina" as Murray called her—joined him at the Rathduff school in June 1907 when a teaching position became vacant. They lived with their children, Nora and Niall, near the railway station. As their family grew, they moved to Woodville, a house situated on a gentle hill sloping down to a small river. Their union, according to O'Mahony, was a marriage of true minds. If Murray was not attending a literary meeting in Cork, he and Nina spent their evenings reading "either separately or to each other" (Ms. 23,976:3–4, MOM, NLI).

Murray described Rathduff as "a rather dreary district of scattered farmhouses midway between Cork and Mallow," yet for his family's security he remained there for fifteen years. "Were it not that Rathduff was a short run to the city by rail, it would have been desolation" (Conlin 1952, 6). Murray's reputation as a schoolmaster was exceptionally high; yearly visits of the inspectors record the highest commendations. The first Inspector's Summary Report on Murray's tenure in Rathduff, written in 1900 by Robert Browne and F. Flannery, recorded the mark "very good," commenting on the very noticeable improvement in the children's attendance, demeanor, and performance since Murray took charge: "We cannot . . . commend too highly the exertions of the young Principal and his steady zeal to discharge well and faithfully the important duties of his office" (Browne and Flanery 1900–1906). Beginning in 1901, Murray's efforts earned the mark of "excellent" for the school for four of the next six years—1901, 1903, 1905, and 1906 (Browne and Flannery 1900–1906).

The Rathduff school was hardly ideal from an educational standpoint. Comprised of two small rooms of 1,120 square feet, it housed one hundred pupils. Murray wrote in the *The Irish School Weekly* that the students walked from one to three miles "through boreens, and heavy stubble and bad roads" to reach their master" (1909, 259). Though Rathduff locals remember Christina Murray as a lovely woman who staged operettas with the school children, Murray, they recall, was so exacting—and given to sarcasm—that some parents sent their children to schools in neighboring towns rather than expose them to Murray's tongue. Seano Walsh, a former Murray pupil, recalls that the master once got into trouble with a child's parents when the child came home to announce that the master had called her "a brass monkey" because she made a spelling error. The enraged parents confronted Murray in the school, telling him, "We brought you here to teach our children, not to christen them" (Walsh 1996). On another occasion, a farmer was driving past the Rathduff school when his donkey halted and would go no further. The farmer's remonstrations with his stubborn charge yielded to curses, provoking Murray in his role as schoolmaster, to emerge from his classroom to admonish the man for giving offense to the children within. The exasperated farmer urged on his donkey again, rechristening the animal "Mary Pauline," the name of one of Murray's daughters. The incident, according to Patrick O'Riordan, became part of local lore (1996).

Murray did not mix with the locals. Owing to the elevated status of his profession and to his own reserved nature, Murray never strolled down to the local pub to enjoy "the craic" (social conversation). Rather he drove his pony and trap six miles to Blarney on Saturdays "if the weather was fine." Here he would visit one of his sisters or "meet with some of his butties" (Walsh 1996).

Murray sought diversion in the activities of the Gaelic League, founded in 1893 to promote the learning of the Irish language and the recovery of Irish traditions. Murray's introduction to the league occurred on one momentous Blarney trip occurring the second Sunday in November 1901. Wandering into the village on a beautifully mild afternoon, he was surprised by the sight of a large crowd gathered to hear the Rev. O'Quigley, a Dominican priest, who had come to Blarney to launch a new branch of the league and to promote the spread of the Irish language. "The man and his words were to me very little short of a revelation," Murray wrote soon after this event in "Impressions," an article for *The Leader* of 7 December 1901 (Ms. 24,870, TCM, NLI). "An Irish Ireland was what he would wish us to yearn for and strive for. No man . . . who is continually absorbed in another's business can successfully perform his own. Waste, therefore—pitiful intellectual waste, all those hours devoted by so many of us to continental affairs." Murray was enthralled, writing "I felt stirred to my inmost depths" (Ms. 24,870, TCM, NLI). By nature, Murray was not a political or social revolutionary. Though he was residing in Dublin by the time of the 1916 Easter Rising, he would never have joined fellow school men and litterateurs such as Padraig Pearse, Joseph Plunkett, or Thomas MacDonagh. Even if he were inclined to such action, prudence and circumspection would have governed his behavior, needing as he did to retain his civil servant status in His Majesty's government. The Irish Renaissance offered Murray the perfect opportunity to engage in the spiritual and literary quest for cultural nationalism. Murray made frequent trips into Cork City to see plays, to study Irish, and to hear lectures sponsored by the Gaelic League and the Catholic Young Men's Society. In addition, he delivered papers on educational subjects at the Cork Literary and Scientific Society in the Crawford Municipal Library. In one such paper, delivered on 17 January 1913, Murray presented a history of the young Irish National Theatre Society. The text of this address was published in the *Cork Constitution* (Murray 1913, 8).

Murray began writing in 1893 at the start of his schoolmaster career. Some of his poems and stories appeared in *The Cork Examiner, The Irish Weekly,* and the nationalist papers *The Leader* and *Shan Van Vocht*. Two early poems, "Since Maggie Died" and "Dark Niall Mor," were also featured in W. J. Paul's 1897 book *Modern Irish Poets*. Murray was also gaining a reputation as an essayist and earning a guinea a week (Conlin 1952, 6). He submitted educational essays to Father T. A. Finlay's *New Ireland Review*. From June 1898 through April 1899, Murray sparked some controversy there by sparring with an anonymous member of the Inspectorate in a series of dueling essays, "Our Primary Schools and their Inspectors," in which Murray defended his fellow teachers from the charges of idleness and inordinate free time (1898; 1899). Over part of that period, Murray also engaged in an epistolary debate about the nature of Irish literature in *An Claideam Soluis,* a weekly newspaper published by the Gaelic League. In these pages, from 24 June to 16 September 1899, he argued with D. P. Moran and C. J. Murphy, asserting that Irish literature could be written in English.

Amid these educational and literary wars, the theater was beckoning. During the 1890s Murray was inspired by the annual visits of Sir Frank Benson's acting company to the Cork Opera House, where he witnessed Benson's troupe perform Shakespeare's plays. Preparing weeks in advance of their visit, the "high tide" of the year's theatrical events in his mind, Murray carried a pocket edition of Shakespeare's plays. "So completely did I know the text of most of the great tragedies that I could almost be prompted to step on to the stage and fill his [Benson's] part." The stage-struck Murray saw Benson in *Hamlet, Othello,* and *Macbeth* and witnessed him playing Romeo, Richard III, Antony in *Julius Caesar,* and, said Murray, "the most memorable of his studies," Richard II. "All this noble feast of drama at its finest seemed to nourish some elemental need in my mind." Remembering himself in his twenties, Murray remarked in an article in *The Capuchin Annual,* "I lived in a world remote from the humdrum of the common day" (1948, 18:171–72). His formation as a dramatist was under way.

The call to write drama came in 1909 when Murray's friend Daniel Corkery—playwright, short story writer, novelist, and fellow teacher—asked Murray to write a play for the newly formed Cork Dramatic Society, of which Corkery was the manager. Inspired by the Cork visits of the Abbey Theatre company in 1907 and 1909, Corkery founded the theater with fellow Corkmen Terence J. MacSwiney and Tom O'Gorman, in order to encourage playwriting among Cork writers. Corkery happened upon him on a Cork city street where the central bus station now stands. Murray recalled, "Here by the art shop he unfolded to me a project that had been long absorbing his mind." Corkery prodded, "Murray, you are always scribbling. We are trying to establish a theatre. Could you not write something for us?" (Conlin 1961, 126).

It is not surprising that Murray yielded to Corkery's request. His sheer love for the theater was sufficient motivation to render him sympathetic to the aims of the Cork enterprise. Corkery, for his part, had evidence of Murray's potential as a playwright. Murray had written two satirical verse plays. The first was *Edward VII and "A Famous Irish Author" or The Hob-A Nobbing of the*

*Gods* by "Rory," a spoof occasioned by the accession of Edward VII, which appeared on 19 October 1901 in *The Leader* (Ms. 24,870, TCM, NLI); the second was *Dawn—an Oratorio* (1905) by "Ernest Joker" with music by "Professor Mangood," a sendup of the Irish educational inspectorate published in a Cork newspaper on 23 September 1905 (Ms. 24,870, TCM, NLI). More importantly, Murray had attended every program that the Abbey Theatre had offered during its 1909 Cork visit. Lennox Robinson's *The Clancy Name* (1908) and *The Cross Roads* (1909), with their thoroughly Irish situations and characters, had proved a revelation to Murray, who wrote, "In their way of thought, their speech, their accent, the people he [Robinson] created were the people I knew. From the field, the farmhouse, the shop, the wayside tavern, they seemed to have wandered on to his stage" (Murray 1939b, 123).

In response to Corkery's entreaty and Robinson's example, Murray wrote *The Wheel of Fortune,* a one-act comedy dealing with an arranged marriage that would become one of his iterative themes. He struggled to teach himself the dramatic form. O'Mahony states: "His inside knowledge of country folk over the years helped in the creation of characters; writing the dialogue came naturally; the big problem was that of slotting the various sections of action into a natural and workable sequence" (Ms. 23,976, 2, MOM, NLI). Ironically, it was the artful structure of his plays for which Murray would become most recognized.

Rehearsals were a revelation for Murray; in "My First Play," an article he wrote for the 20 February 1941 issue of *The Irish Press,* he remembered: "There was first the strange thrill of watching the airy creatures of one's imagination taking on life and movement on the stage and of listening to one's written words coming in living accents from the players' lips" (Ms. 23,513, 2:128, TCM, NLI). The finished *Wheel* was produced on 2 December 1909 by the Cork Dramatic Society at the Dun Theatre in the Gaelic League Hall on Queen Street, now Father Matthew Street; it was first on a bill of one-acts that included Corkery's *The Hermit and the King* and Lennox Robinson's *The Lesson of His Life.* Murray watched Robinson direct his own *Lesson,* "wring[ing] from speech and gesture their own dramatic values," leaving the play "a transformed thing" (Ms. 23,513, 2:128, TCM, NLI). This comment, also from "My First Play," presages not only Murray's future as a playwright, but also his long association with Lennox Robinson. From then on, Murray expediently bypassed Corkery's little Cork theater and submitted all his plays to the Abbey Theatre in Dublin.

At the age of thirty-seven, Murray blazed upon the Dublin scene with *Birthright*. Robinson, managing director of the Abbey, shelved plans for Ibsen's *Little Eyolf*, already in rehearsal, and put the Murray piece into production at once. A melodrama about two brothers who fight to the death over the right to inherit their father's farm, *Birthright* created a sensation at its premiere on 27 October 1910. Joseph Holloway, the celebrated architect and diarist of the Dublin theatrical and social scene, gave his impressions of Murray following the premiere: "As the curtains divided, Mr. Murray bowed hurriedly and fled. He held a program in his hand. He is a young man with a boyish expression of face, and in speaking shows his gums and teeth abundantly" (Holloway 1967, 144). After the ecstatic curtain call, George Moore asked to see Murray in the Abbey green room. In the article "Confessional," published in *Inisfail* in 1933, Murray recalled the meeting years later, confessing: "The gesture was a salute from a high peak to a man struggling to gain the first foothold far below. . . . He was a man more than cordial in his appreciation of the play" (Ms. 23,513:20–21, TCM, NLI). Holloway returned the following afternoon and encountered the author. This meeting marked the beginning a friendship that lasted until Holloway's death in 1944.

From 1910 to 1912, Murray read the plays of the modern European dramatists. He told American critic Barrett Clark: "I had devoured all that was significant in modern dramatic literature, making a study of the Russian, Norwegian, Swedish, and German schools of drama" (qtd. in Malone 1965, 192). Sequestered in Rathduff, Murray also recorded the speech of the West Cork peasants for incorporation into his plays (Conlin 1952, 13). He jotted into pocket notebooks scenarios for future dramatization. Murray never kept a private study, and he never used a typewriter. Using fountain pen or pencil, he wrote his plays in foolscap copybooks while sitting at the breakfast or dining room table (Ms. 23,976, 18, MOM, NLI). Murray wrote in the midst of domestic activity, able to block out most distractions. In a letter to Terence Connolly, S.J., written 26 June 1959, Murray's daughter Pauline (then Sister Mary Alphonsus, O.S.C.) reported that her father often needed to rise from writing to referee his children's disputes, chiding them with the recurrent admonition "Will you not have the Grace of God about you?" (Cat. 112,

MJMC, JJBL). On 26 February 1911, after *Birthright* was produced, Murray confided in a letter to W. A. Henderson, managing director at the Abbey: "I have another play written for the Abbey—in my mind. When I shall be able to transfer it to paper is another matter. With a crowded nest—there are four ranging from six years to six weeks—opportunities of writing after the day's work are few" (BC, NYPL). Pauline further reflected: "It is difficult to understand how he managed to write so much as there was no such thing as leaving him at peace at home. He was always ready to greet us at our frequent interruptions, but would occasionally say, 'It is impossible to concentrate on writing here' " (Cat. 112, MJMC, JJBL).

Murray's artistic life between 1912 and 1915 was filled with tension of various kinds. Life in a rural backwater like Rathduff failed to provide the converse with other writers for which he yearned. On one occasion Murray delivered a lecture to the National Literary Society in Dublin in the presence of the Rev. George O'Neill, S. J., Padraic Colum, William O'Leary Curtis, and Seumas O'Kelly, literary luminaries of the day. Later, in a letter to Holloway dated only 1913, Murray extolled the stimulation of the city and lamented its loss. "I felt I was being cheated in being obliged to leave the capital so soon, and the breath of excitement was so grateful after the 'mists that do be on the bog' down here" (Ms. 13,267, NLI).

*Maurice Harte,* a play about a Maynooth seminarian who does not succeed to ordination, was a critical success in London and Dublin and won both popular and critical acclaim during the 1913–1914 Abbey Theatre tour of America. After the Dublin opening, Murray was surprised to learn that some regarded the play as anticlerical. Despite his desire to please the Dublin clergy, Murray experienced the displeasure of Father Lawrence Murphy, the cleric central to his life: "On the production of *Maurice Harte,* the Parish Priest and School Manager, with whom I had been on most friendly terms, turned sour. Some ill-informed person represented to him that the play was a reflection on the Irish priesthood! Things became difficult" (Conlin 1961, 128). Seano Walsh recalls it as "a terrible row with the priest" (1996). Murray endured a prolonged period of strained relations with this clerical school manager until 1915, when like a dramatic *deus ex machina,* the National Board of Education offered Murray an appointment by to be headmaster of the Model Schools at Inchicore in Dublin. On 9 September 1915, when word of his nomination became public, Murray wrote to Holloway, "It was a stroke of real luck. My official life has not been too happy here for some years. You see I was guilty of writing *Maurice Harte*" (Ms. 22,404, folder 13, JH, NLI). Having written *Birthright, Maurice Harte, Sovereign Love,* and *The Briery Gap,* Murray accepted the position and left Rathduff behind him, but he carried with him the memory of its oppression. Moving to Dublin with his son Niall, Murray took up the headmaster's post in September 1915; Christina followed later with their four daughters: Mary Pauline, Nora, Agnes Christine (Rena), and Eva. The family's first residence there, Gortbeg, stood at 136 South Circular Road, Kilmainham.

Teaching was a burden to Murray. On 3 February 1954 he wrote to O'Mahony, "The awareness that the work spelled my bread and butter was I think the source of that consuming 'energy' which burned in me from nine to three" (Ms. 24,902, folder 10, MOM, NLI). As an artist, Murray chafed under the rigid regimen of schoolmastering, foisted upon teachers by an exacting examining inspector. In his letter of 29 June 1926 to Frank J. Hugh O'Donnell in London, Murray lamented the "annual nightmare" of statistical compilations at the school year's end: "And you are doing Pall Mall, Picadilly [sic] and dancing gaily through life while I sit with the mill stone round my neck" (Ms. 21,715, folder 10, FJHO'D, NLI). In lines crossed out of the typescript of a 1937 radio broadcast entitled, "Myself—As A Schoolmaster," Murray complained against what appeared to be the clerical management of schools: "From the first day on which you enter upon your duties to the last day in the service of the Department of Education you have to work against an oppressive background of officialdom" (Ms. 24,874:3, TCM, NLI). He also found the Irish system of education unnecessarily hidebound in its conformity to British methods and argued for a native model. As early as 1905, Murray wrote, "While [John] Bull compels us to accept his code of civil legislation, he is not stupid enough, or bull enough, to force on us his educational codes. And yet—and yet—though the noise of our clamor for nationhood has been heard through centuries, we will not use that important measure of freedom which is permitted us" (Murray 1905).

The confinement of his teaching position under clerical management and his turn-of-the-century scuffle with the anonymous member of the Inspectorate in the pages of the *New Ireland Review* led him to use his dramatic art to write his way to personal freedom. These experiences formed in him a keen sense of the need of the individual to breathe free. "Very early in my career," he stated in the 1937 radio typescript "Myself—As a Schoolmaster," "I realized that a system which produced an atmosphere bred of suspicion on one side and of fear on the other was the negation of what a wise system should be" (Ms. 24,874:4, TCM, NLI). In addition, the rigidly prescribed curriculum and its methods were marked by lock-step memorization. For the pupils, "the wells of enchantment are poisoned at the source" (3). Such a system, Murray thought, should foster the growth and development of the student and the teacher: "The contact of mind with mind, the leading forward of a boy step by step the way he should go, the evidence of his growing intellectual strength, the consciousness of your influence as an instrument in shaping his destiny— all are deeply satisfying to the mind and heart" (3). Murray regretted that even with the coming of the Free State in 1921, the educational system was not reformed. The Irish language movement, he complained, caused even more tension: "The breakneck pace into which the teachers were stampeded on the introduction of Irish as an essential subject ill served the language cause. The threat of censure, or of possible dismissal, hung like a thundercloud over the schools" (5–6). The example of the language movement offers an insight into Murray's theory of human growth and development. Growth of any kind is fostered "not by coercive violence, but by a spirit of good will bred of a wise understanding of the nature of the human mind" (7).

In "A Pedagogue's Confessions," written c. 1909, Murray recalled his own retrograde experience as a national school student. He remembered that his teacher taught everything "through a castiron formula" (Ms. 24,874:3, TCM, NLI). The growth of the thinking faculty, Murray recognized, nurtures the unfolding of the individual. Regretting his own lack of a university education, he urged that university studies be made available to national teachers in training. In the early 1900s, during the days of "the university question," he had championed culture "as the end itself," extolling the formation of "a full mind made rich and expansive by wide and liberal studies" (4). He argued that such a mind would inevitably result in a more affecting teacher: "Every good influence to which your soul is subject reaches in some degree the souls of those with whom you are in direct and active contact from year's end to year's end" (4).

Murray also pleaded for "a large measure of civil freedom for the teacher" (Ms. 24,874:5, TCM, NLI). National teachers were subject to 214 rules that, among other things, prevented them from attending political meetings or voting for members of Parliament. Murray criticized these rules as restrictive, and also condemned as unjust the ban forbidding women to vote, especially as it applied to his teaching colleagues. He addressed this issue in his classroom more than once in the early 1900s, as he recalled in the 1937 typescript "Myself—As a Schoolmaster": " 'Here is Sally O'Brien,' I used to say, 'a very star of knowledge, yet while some day she may become a teacher, a doctor, a lawyer, a University professor, she is foredoomed to silence when it comes to a question affecting her own interest and that of the nation" (Ms. 24,874:9, TCM, NLI).

Though Murray attributed his own success as an educator to "the surrender of one's soul to a system," he was successful in the classroom (Ms. 24,874:10, TCM, NLI). The same imaginative gift that served him in writing plays, likewise enabled him, he claimed, to hold the attention of his students: "The forces acting within the mind of the playwright and the schoolmaster are virtually identical. You will see that your schoolmaster is really as much the creative artist as the playwright or the novelist. In the nebulous void of the child's mind he sets out to create a world in being; his materials being those latent forces inherent in the child's nature and which it is his function to call into action" (1). To support his claim, Murray pointed to the example of other playwrights and sometime teachers: Daniel Corkery, Robert Farran, Paul Vincent Carroll, and Francis (Frank) MacManus (1).

Once settled in Dublin, he began drafts of *The Serf* (initially entitled *The Cloud*) in 1916 and completed *Spring* in 1917, publishing it with *Sovereign Love* and *The Briery Gap* in 1918. Present in Dublin at the time of the 1916 Easter Rising, he made no reference to it in his personal correspondence. Once, in "The Call of the Sun: A Sunday in the Park," a column he wrote under the name "Tomas" for the *Irish Independent* of 8 September 1920, Murray reflected on the serenity of Phoenix Park after a Sunday afternoon concert: "What stranger in our midst would think that this Ireland—is Dublin itself, the heart of a nation in its hour of travail?" (Ms. 24,875, TCM, NLI). A nationalist, he expected Home Rule but not a republic; in a lecture he delivered to the Literary and Scientific Society on 17 January 1913, he opined:

"With the advent of Home Rule must come a new spiritual birth, and a sense of nationhood and of national dignity to which our generation has been strangers" (1913, 8). Though, like many Dubliners, he may have been surprised by the Easter Rising, he supported its aims, making oblique references to it in *The Serf* (1920) and in *The Last Hostel* (c. 1921).

Murray was a devout Catholic. A regular communicant who frequented Dublin's St. Andrew's Church in Westland Row, Murray took great solace in his religious values and practices. Precisely because of his Catholicism, he often felt the odd man out in his dealings with the members of the Abbey Directorate raised in the Protestant Ascendancy tradition, such as W. B. Yeats, Augusta Gregory, AE, and Lennox Robinson. Murray learned this lesson early in his career. Remembering George Moore's support after the *Birthright* premiere, Murray wrote to him about a proposed tragedy concerning a married man, keenly wishing to have children, who finds himself in a childless union. Moore replied that the theme was utterly unsuited to tragedy as the man's solution—an extramarital affair—was patently obvious. In his essay "Confessional," published in the periodical *Inisfail* in 1933, Murray reflected: "Bred as I am in the Catholic tradition, Moore's frank enunciation of his easy moral code crashed in upon my mind" (Ms. 23,513, TCM, NLI). Murray felt, moreover, that his newfound Ascendancy colleagues "moved in a social world to which I was alien" (Conlin 1952, 15). Despite Murray's feelings, Gregory and AE were in fact very gracious to him, and Robinson and Yeats, in particular, recognized the truth of Murray's dramatic world, imbued as it was with his own religious ethos.

Gregory also appreciated the skill with which Murray executed his duties as treasurer of the Irish Playwrights' Association (IPA), asking his assistance on two notable occasions in the 1920s. In 1925 she sought his counsel regarding *Cuchulain,* a book by Terence Gray. Written in dramatic form, it quoted liberally from Gregory's book on Cuchulain. Not wishing to endorse Grey's book, thinking it dramatically weak and artistically inferior, Gregory was yet willing to grant quotation permission. Finding herself in a dilemma, she wrote to Murray on 5 April 1925, requesting his advice: "You of course know much better than I what to say. If you prefer my writing, please tell me what I had better say" (BC, NYPL). In 1928, Gregory sought his intercession again. J. J. Hayes, dramatic correspondent to *The New York Times,* was also president of the Irish Playwrights' Association. Financially embarrassed at this time, Hayes neglected to forward playwrights the fees for presentations of their plays by amateur dramatic societies. Murray interceded for Gregory, as well as for playwrights George Shiels, Edward McNulty, and Bernard Duffy, and for the widow of William Boyle. Apprizing Gregory that he had "lent him some money of my own to save his good name," Murray wrote to her on 24 October 1928, asking her forbearance, though McNulty and Shiels had threatened legal action. "I believe he is in a rather desperate plight and to force him into the courts would be of little use" (Gregory Journal, 39:5060, BC, NYPL). This crisis eventually resulted in the dissolution of the IPA; it was subsequently replaced by the Authors' Guild of Ireland, of which Murray became the president.

In 1932, having penned work judged "important, and Irish in character and subject," Murray was invited by W. B. Yeats, G. B. Shaw, and AE to become a founding member of the Irish Academy of Letters, the purpose of which was to promote creative literature in Ireland. A ceremony was held at the Peacock Theatre to announce the formation of the academy, at which Lennox Robinson, according to "Irish Authors: An Academy of Belles Lettres," a newspaper article from 19 September 1932, stated that although a censorship law had existed in Ireland for some years, "it was certainly equally right and proper that there should be some body of authority to crown and commend, perhaps not the same book or author, but some other one" (Ms. 23,514, TCM, NLI). After carefully weighing the issues, Murray accepted membership in the academy, basing his decision on his perception—noted at length in the press—of Ireland's need to encourage the artist and the literary life: "We are essentially a peasant State, and books have little or no part in the peasant's scheme of things."

However, he did not agree with those advocating the abolition of the censorship act, regarding its effects, on the whole, as "wise and temperate," instead proposing the establishment of a council board. In an article from 10 October 1932 in the *Irish Press*, "Mr. T. C. Murray Joins Academy: Reasons Explained in Exclusive Interview—Writer's Rights," he argued "that in simple justice the writer who questions its decree should not be denied the right of appeal—the right, at least, to be heard in his own defense" (Ms. 23,514, TCM, NLI). Murray did not always agree with the decisions of the Censorship Committee; on 30 September 1936, after its ban on Sean O'Faolain's

*Bird Alone* (1936), he wrote of the novel to O'Mahony, "Its lesson is quite a moral one & shouts its message" (Ms. 24,902, folder 3, MOM, NLI). Nevertheless, there was a decidedly puritanical strain in Murray, and throughout his life he was particularly harsh in his evaluation of any work that depicted or even suggested sex. A letter to Holloway written on 27 June 1912, as *Maurice Harte* was premiering in London's Sloan Square, reveals his dislike for the dramatic literature of his contemporary, John Synge: "The 'Irish Players' are Fashions' latest cult. How long though? While they have a woman leaving her husband to go out into the night with a tramp, and a Martin Dhoul [sic] recovering his sight and making love to a young girl, and a Playboy 'killing his da' that is to say while they have the French note to tickle their appetites— things will keep humming all right" (Ms. 13,267, NLI). Although he developed, in later years, a high appreciation for Synge's *Playboy* in its more comic, less realistic, Abbey interpretation, he remained adamant about sexual material in literature. On 12 March 1946, he wrote to Connolly of American novelist Martin Flavin and his prize-winning *Journey in the Dark* (1946): "Rarely have I come on a book so dangerous for young minds. The sex element is introduced with devilish subtlety. . . . I'd have your Martin Flavins of literature flung into the Hudson" (Box 13, folder 17:27–28, TLC, JJBL). Similarly, on 8 December 1949, he wrote to Connolly of Benedict Kiely's *In A Harbour Green* (1949): "Seldom have I read an Irish novel so revolting. The sex element dominates the story and among its group of characters there isn't one whom you would wish to know" (Box 13, folder 17:27–28, TLC, JJBL).

Despite these attitudes, Murray was respected for his literary acumen, and his critical opinion was valued. He was often engaged to preside at literary gatherings and to tender advice to young writers striving to make their way in the literary world. Frank MacManus, one such author, had long desired to meet Murray. The chance meeting occurred near Stephen's Green in May 1932; Murray, perhaps wishing he had given more of his years to writing and less to teaching, urged the fledgling writer, ". . . write and write. Now, in your youth, is the time to get as much as you can done" (qtd. in MacManus 1959, 56). Many emerging playwrights submitted their plays to him for comment, notably Seamus O'Brien, Frank J. Hugh O'Donnell, Paul Vincent Carroll, and, in later years, Michael J. Molloy.

Despite this influence, an estrangement appears to have grown between Murray and the Abbey directors following the London premiere of *Autumn Fire* in 1926. A note of secrecy crept into Murray's dealings with the Abbey as he began to look after his own interests. On 10 April 1927 Murray wrote to O'Donnell about *The Blind Wolf*: "What I write is between ourselves alone— Dublin is a house of whispers. I'm waiting for the *Pipe* to be produced before sending in the new play to the Abbey. Meanwhile I've sent *Spindrift* to Curtis Brown, who though usually very reticent seems sanguine of getting it placed. I would not wish *for anything* [underlining is Murray's] that this should be known here. I know the Abbey people would be wild" (Ms. 21,715, folder 10, FJHO'D, NLI). After the 1928 presentation of *The Blind Wolf,* Murray's fortunes with the Abbey began to fluctuate. Not only did the theater reject his experimental comedy *A Flutter of Wings* (1930), but two of his public actions excited controversy among members of the Abbey Directorate.

In 1929 Murray wrote a satirical poem about Frank O'Connor, ridiculing O'Connor's scathing comments about plays written in Irish.[1] On 26 October 1929, O'Connor harshly reviewed in *The Irish Statesman* a play by Séamus Wilmot, *Casadh an Ratha,* which was performed in Irish by the Gaelic Players (O'Connor, 154–55). In a letter to the editor of *The Irish Statesman,* published on 9 November, Wilmot protested O'Connor's review (Wilmot 1929, 190). O'Connor responded the following week, in the issue of 16 November, under the heading "Correspondence. Author and Reviewer" (Ms. 23,514, TCM, NLI). O'Connor and Wilmot exchanged charges for two more weeks until Murray took action. He responded pseudonymously in the issue of 30 November in a letter addressed "To the Editor of *The Irish Statesman.*" Entitled "Dramatic Criticisms" and signed "Bricriu," Murray's letter stated: "Dear Sir,—Permit an outsider to say a word in the controversy between your critic, Mr. Frank O'Connor, and the young Gaelic dramatist, Mr. Wilmot,

1. Holloway also refers to this Murray piece in his diary: "When Frank O'Connor wrote for *The Irish Statesman,* he continually abused both Gaelic players and plays, and Murray wrote a skit on him and sent it on to A. E. who asked him to elaborate on it, and he did." Holloway notes the cost of this act for Murray: "[Sunday, 13 January 1940] When he [O'Connor] was Director of the Abbey, he wouldn't hear of Murray's name. He became his deadly enemy" (1968, 3:40–41).

whom your critic has so ungently handled" (251). Murray's "word" is a barb in verse:

> On my honour,
> Mister O'Connor,
> though few may know it,
> You are a poet
> (The Rhyme's not true
> But it must do)
> Of quality,
> In minor key —
> Just like the wren—
> "Cheap-cheap". . . . .
> But when
> In solemn state
> You pont'ficate
> On drama, I
> Can only cry: —
> Puck's come again
> And changed a wren —
> Unto a daw —
> "Caw-caw."
> Bricriu (1929, 251)

It is difficult to prove conclusively that it was, indeed, Murray who wrote this piece, as no draft or typescript appears in the T. C. Murray Papers in the National Library of Ireland. However, the evidence points to Murray; on 21 March 1941 he wrote to O'Mahony about O'Connor: "I had the ill-luck to touch him on the raw—through the pages of the *Statesman*—years ago. Week in week out he used to write contemptuously of the productions of An Comar Drámuíocta & I couldn't forbear slinging an arrow at him" (Ms. 24,902, folder 5, MOM, NLI). Murray was given to writing under various pen names, especially if the material was likely to provoke incendiary reaction, as was the

case with *The Serf*.[2] But the most compelling evidence for Murray's author-
ship of this doggerel is the concern the versifier shows for dramatist Wilmot.[3]
This concern, stated clearly in the message that precedes the verses, is indeed
Murray's signature; compassion for young, artistic, oppressed males is the distinguishing characteristic of his plays from *Birthright* in 1910 to *Illumination*
in 1939. Because Dublin was, indeed, "a house of whispers," no doubt O'-
Connor knew the identity of Wilmot's defender. O'Connor's biographer,
James Matthews, cites "rumors of a longstanding feud" between O'Connor
and Murray (1983, 134). When O'Connor became a director of the Abbey in
October 1935, Murray was in for a difficult time. In a letter to O'Mahony
penned on 21 March 1941, Murray confirmed the damage caused by his
1929 attack on O'Connor, writing, "Ever since then he has nursed his resentment & a company producing a Murray play is with him anathema" (Ms.
24,902, folder 5, MOM, NLI).

In 1936 T. C. Murray also ran afoul of W. B. Yeats, who controlled the direction of the Abbey from its foundation until his death in 1939. Murray differed publicly with him over the course the Abbey was to take as a national
theater. In an article published on 24 March 1935 in the *New York Herald
Tribune*, "Abbey Theatre Widens Scope to Continent," Yeats announced a
new policy, whereby the Abbey would "stage some of the best modern productions of the Continent, as well as revivals of the lesser known Irish plays.
We intend to widen our scope" (HTC). To be sure, this was a period of internal stress at the theater. After the death of Augusta Gregory, the Abbey began
to founder. Frank O'Connor said it "was going rapidly to the dogs" (1969,

2. The index to *The Irish Statesman* lists no such piece by Murray, although several poems
are listed under his name (Smith 1966). Murray's most frequently used pen names were "Ariel"
and "Touchstone"; others included "Tomas" (used in the *Irish Independent* article, "The Call of
the Sun: A Sunday in the Park") and "Oisin" (used in another *Independent* piece, "The Heart of
Gaelic Munster") (Ms. 23,511, TCM, NLI).

3. Apparently Wilmot never forgot Murray's gesture, for he attended Murray's funeral. An
unmarked Dublin news cutting covering Murray's 1959 obsequies, "Funeral: Mr. T. C. Murray,"
lists "Dr. H.[Séamus] Wilmot, Abbey Theatre." Wilmot, registrar of the National University, was
appointed in 1958 to succeed Richard Hayes on the board of the Abbey Directorate (Hunt 1979,
186).

174–76). Lennox Robinson, by then suffering from the effects of alcoholism, was unequal to the task of managing the Abbey. The stated reason for the 1935 policy of presenting plays from other nations was that there were no new, suitable Irish plays. Murray was not alone in objecting to this policy. Frank O'Connor and Sean O'Faolain also vigorously objected, asserting that Irish dramatists were treated with rudeness and disrespect and kept waiting for weeks on end for word of their submitted plays (O'Connor 1969, 174–76, 185–87).

In March 1936, Murray, well-aware of what was going on behind the scenes at the Abbey, set forth his convictions as to what a national theater should be in an article, "Whither the National Theatre?" published in *Guth na nGaedheal* (Ms. 21,746:28–29, TCM, NLI). Murray was very open about his action, writing O'Mahony, editor of *Guth na Gaedheal*, on 1 April 1936: "I should not mind your sending *Guth na nGaedal* [sic] to the Abbey. It's good for them to learn what others are thinking! But I don't feel somehow that I should like to have a copy sent to 'Willy' [W. B. Yeats] in view of his present state of health" (Ms. 24,902, folder 3, MOM, NLI). In his essay Murray took issue with Yeats's stated policy, arguing: "In effect the Abbey Theatre is to serve as a medium of expression for the consciousness of peoples other than our own." In doing this, Murray claimed, Yeats would "mar and deform if not utterly destroy" the theater he had created. If airing his views was not hazardous enough, Murray also attacked Yeats's very personality: "He [Yeats] has been always passionate in his beliefs and passionate in their defense. They spring from so deep a conviction that he is usually shocked into anger if a voice out of the multitude is heard in dissent. At times he can be as perverse and wanton as a child, and unhappily, like most perverse children, he is usually given his way" (Ms. 21,746:28–29, TCM, NLI). Indeed, Yeats's policy was already in effect, and the results were not successful.

Murray's essay drew fire in Abbey Theatre offices. In a letter written to O'Mahony on 1 April 1936, Murray said that Abbey Secretary Eric Gorman had written him a letter requesting that "any false impression created by the article" be corrected (Ms. 24,902, folder 3, MOM, NLI). Murray refused to retract his statement, and Holloway claimed that the Abbey Directorate "cancelled all contracts with him [Murray] and have since practically closed down the Abbey Theatre on his work" (1968, 3:65). An examination of the Abbey

Theatre Playbook reveals that Murray's plays were, indeed, performed less frequently after this scuffle, although Murray's censure is difficult to prove conclusively, given the movement away from peasant drama to plays of city life, at which Murray was less successful. Though his one-act play *A Spot in the Sun* (1938) and a last major work, *Illumination* (1939), received Abbey presentations, these plays did not receive the best possible artistic productions. Still, *Maurice Harte* was included in the programming of the Abbey Theatre Festival in summer 1938, and Murray was selected to give a lecture entitled "George Shiels, Brinsley MacNamara, Etc."

Shortly after *Michaelmas Eve* premiered at the Abbey in June 1932, Murray retired from teaching, laying down his "mill stone" the following September 1932, a few years before his sixty-fifth birthday. As Murray explained in 1949 to Larry Morrow, in the latter's article "T. C. (don't call me Dr.) Murray," published in Cork's *Sunday Press* on 6 November of that year, he was ready after seventeen years as headmaster, "to become the captain of my soul" (Box 13, folder 17:27–28, TLC, JJBL). In 1931, the family had moved from Kilmainham to the quieter, more fashionable Ballsbridge section of Dublin. Their red brick townhouse, at 11 Sandymount Avenue in Dublin 4, was within walking distance of the Royal Dublin Society on Merrion Road and the sports stadium on Lansdowne Road. Just two blocks from the Murray home was the Sandymount Station, where trains transported passengers to points up and down Dublin Bay. For Murray and his family, however, the most attractive feature of the location was its proximity to Dublin city center. A ten-minute bus ride brought Murray's children to their work places along Merrion Row and the retired Murray to Merrion Square, St. Stephen's Green, and Kildare Street, where he was a regular patron at the National Library. Now that he was able to write full-time for the first time in his life, he devoted much attention to *Spring Horizon* (1937). Intended as a trilogy about a writer's youth and early adulthood, the novel proved a tedious labor for Murray; despite the novel's good reviews and brisk sales, he chose not to complete work on the sequels. During these retirement years, he also completed *A Stag At Bay* (1934), *A Spot in the Sun* (1938), *Illumination* (1939), and *The Green Branch* (1943).

On 29 June 1926 Murray, confined in Rathduff, had written his friend Frank J. Hugh O'Donnell in London, "I delight in the 'central roar' of the

great city. Give a call when you get back. I'd like to hear of things theatrical &
[sic] if you had any adventures in that way" (Ms. 21,715, folder 10, FJHO'D,
NLI). With the weight of the years, however, Murray's taste for the city's central roar and things theatrical declined. Often described as timid and shy by literary critics, Murray preferred solitude to social gatherings even in the days of
his greatest fame. He was contemplative by nature and seems to have sought
regular periods of quiet. In his later years, he was increasingly regarded as her-
mit-like. J. J. Hayes, theatrical correspondent in Dublin for *The New York
Times,* described Murray in a 1928 article for that paper ("T. C. Murray,
Ireland's Foremost Dramatist: Makes the Tragedies of Young Men the Theme
of His Plays—Is Public School Teacher") as he came upon him one winter,
alone at the end of Dun Laoghaire pier on Dublin Bay. "Somebody was before
me. He was sitting on an old wooden seat, gazing out to sea. Hearing my step,
he turned and I recognized Murray" (Ms. 23,513, 2:29–30, TCM, NLI).

The beginnings of his legendary reclusiveness were linked to the decline
of his wife's health in 1940. Suffering heart problems, she was forced to take
early retirement from her teaching position in the girls' section in the
Inchicore Model School. In a letter written to Holloway on 26 July 1940,
Murray confided that he and Christina were in Carlow. Amid threats of World
War II, he had taken Mrs. Murray for treatment at St. Brigid's, a private hos-
pital run by the Blue Nuns (Ms. 13,267, folder 16, NLI). He manifests a dark-
ened spirit in a letter to Holloway dated only 1943: "I'm not going to the
Abbey tomorrow night. I don't feel somehow just in the right mood for the
function" (Ms. 22,404, folder 13, JH, NLI).

The tender union between Thomas and Christina had a vital effect on
Thomas's writing. In a letter to Terence Connolly written on 26 June 1959,
Murray's daughter Pauline (then Sister Mary Alphonsus, O.S.C.) illustrated
her father's emotional link to his wife and its relation to his work: "It happened once that he and Niall had the house to themselves for about ten days.
We heard beforehand about all that would be accomplished in those days of
quiet. The result was quite different from the expectation. They felt so miser-
able in the empty house that they spent a considerable part of the time playing
table tennis and the only writing done was a long letter to mother each day. If
he ever made a murmur about peace and quiet after that he was promptly reminded of what happened when we were away" (Cat. 112, MJMC, JJBL).

Before his retirement, the demands of schoolmastering slowed the dramatist's pen, but Christina's death in 1944 brought his playwriting career to a halt. On 30 August 1945, Murray wrote to Connolly: "Few people meant so much to each other as she and I and when death came a year ago to sunder a blessed comradeship lasting over forty years my private world seemed to go to pieces" (Box 13, folder 17:27–28, TLC, JJBL). The following year, on 10 December 1946, he wrote to Connolly that playgoing was largely an event of the past. "I have been to the theatre only once or twice since my wife died. Always we went together on Abbey first nights & shared the excitement, but now ——" (Cat. 112, MJMC, JJBL). However, in another letter to Connolly written on 12 March 1946, he did say that he was remaining active, writing essays and book reviews for Dublin newspapers and journals and attending weekly meetings of the Film Censorship Appeal Board, of which he was a member (Box 13, folder 17:27–28, TLC, JJBL). In one book review, he wrote of Sean O'-Casey's *Purple Dust* (1940) for the *Irish Press*, maintaining that its characters bore little resemblance to the Irish people that he knew. The review provoked Sean O'Casey's public ire; O'Casey responded sharply in "O'Casey's Advice to Dramatists: To the Editor," a letter dated 12 January 1941 and published in *The Irish Press* on 17 January (Ms. 23,514, TCM, NLI). In the letter, O'Casey questioned the range of the people Murray knew.

Nevertheless, Murray still commanded respect from young writers. Aspiring playwright Michael J. Molloy submitted his play *The Old Road* to Murray's scrutiny. Upon its production, Murray wrote to Holloway on 5 May 1943: "Young Molloy asked me quite a long time ago to read it critically. He had been, he said, going for the Church but had got a touch of t.b. I felt sympathetic and went through the script carefully & indicated scenes that needed some tightening up (Ms. 13,267, NLI).

In 1948 Murray ventured to the Abbey Theatre to substitute for his friend George Shiels, the invalid dramatist in County Antrim, Northern Ireland, who was never able to attend his own opening nights. In what became something of a ritual, Murray attended the premiere of each Shiels play; later, according to a letter he wrote to O'Mahony on 14 February 1948, he gave Shiels his own response to the production and apprized him of the audience reaction (Ms. 24,902, folder 8, MOM, NLI). In 1949 Murray was awarded an honorary doctorate of literature from the National University of Ireland.

Embarrassed, he first declined this honor, but the entreaties of friends and family eventually led him to accept what, in a letter written to his niece Kitty Madden on 29 March 1949, he referred to as "my (Quack) D Litt." He confided further: "I feel, Kitty, as the conferring day, 7 April draws near as if I were one of those poor wretches in the tumbrils during the French Revolution on the way to the Guillotine" (Curran Family Collection). Murray's keen awareness of his limitations as a dramatist to Connolly triggered the personal storm and stress. "I realized only too acutely," he wrote, "that the range of my work and the reach of my intellect could never justify such a distinction." The prospect of the public ceremony filled him with dread: "The acute strain that it imposed drove me to my doctor who was not a little dismayed at my condition," he wrote to Connolly on 11 May 1949. "There was a recurrent sensation of being just on the edge of a collapse" (Box 13, folder 17:27–28, TLC, JJBL). Despite his apprehensions and with the aid of medication, he enjoyed the degree ceremony immensely; later, in a letter to Kitty Madden dated 9 April 1949, he recounted the details of the ceremony with great relish, taking particular delight in meeting Eamon DeValera, whom he found "ever so agreeable" (Curran Family Collection). Writing Connolly on 8 December 1949, however, he described the periodic melancholy for which he was known: "There are times when the world seems good & I have a sense of well being—& then come days when, as the weather experts put it, 'a ridge of deep depression' weighs on my spirit. I suffer from some obscure nervous malady and the mildest form of excitement leaves me a wreck" (Box 13, folder 17:27–28, TLC, JJBL).

The illness of his only son Niall in 1950 was a source of deep anxiety to this highly sensitive man. A graduate of the Jesuit-run Belvedere College, Niall Murray rose to prominence in Ireland's Department of Agriculture. In 1950 he was diagnosed with cancer. On Christmas Day, both Murray and his daughter Nora visited Niall, hospitalized after surgery. Together, they watched helplessly as Niall struggled for breath. Murray's letter of 2 January 1951 to O'Donnell shows not only the depth of a father's love but also the tragic sensibility that suffused Murray's dramatic work: "Never, I think, in my long life, Frank, did I know such torturing pain as I suffered during those hours of Christmas Day which followed that visit. . . . From my secret heart came the cry again & again 'Say but the word and my son shall be healed' "

(Ms. 21,715, folder 10, FJHO'D, NLI). Leaving a wife and two sons, Niall died at the age of forty-four in February 1951. On the twelfth of that month, Murray poured out his grief to Connolly: "His loss has been a source of such pain of mind that I wonder if so deep a wound will ever be staunched. . . . It seems cruel to see a life so blameless, yet so brimful of promise, cut off so untimely" (Box 13, folder 17:27–28, TLC, JJBL). After Niall's death, Murray became a recluse (Conlin 1991). In a real way, too, he lost his daughter Pauline; in 1952 she became one of a band of seven Poor Clares of Nuns' Island selected to leave Ireland forever to establish a monastery in Sydney, Australia. Images of retreat continually filled Murray's letters. Describing his home as "virtually a hermitage," he wrote, "I have lost contact with most of those interested in creative arts and letters" (Connolly 1960, 369).

Though Murray had ceased to write new plays by the late 1940s and 1950s, his earlier works experienced a surprising level of revival during that period at the amateur level and on radio. In November 1952, in anticipation of his eightieth birthday the following January, Radio Éireann honored Murray with broadcasts of *Autumn Fire* and *The Blind Wolf* on consecutive Sunday evenings. Each broadcast was preceded by a critical appreciation, the first by Daniel Corkery, then emeritus professor of English at University College, Cork; the second by Benedict Kiely, then literary editor of the *Irish Press*. Very grateful to be so honored, Murray reflected on the tribute, writing Connolly on 15 December 1952, "These gestures usually come when the dramatist has made his final exit from the stage. . . . To be frank, my mind's preoccupation is less with time than eternity. There is ever the haunting feeling that at any moment I shall hear a Voice call to me 'Come' " (Box 13, folder 17:27–28, TLC, JJBL). Despite his preoccupation with the voice of eternity, Murray was mightily pleased by the voices of the radio tribute. "I've been snowed under with correspondence and only now has the drift of letters eased," he told O'Mahony in a letter dated 2 December 1952 (Ms. 24,902, folder 10, MOM, NLI). Indeed, he was still alive in the public mind. Even though their 1951 Easter week presentation of *Maurice Harte* had been a commercial failure, the National Theatre Society produced *Autumn Fire* from 16–21 February 1953. The 1952 Radio Éireann broadcast of *Autumn Fire* was repeated in 1954, and Murray continued on, writing O'Mahony on 10 March 1954: "A patch of sunlight falling on the writing pad beckons me out. When I've sealed this I'll gird my loins & shuffle along the Merrion Rd.—and return as weary after an hour as if I had been a sprinter in the Marathon!" (Ms. 24,902, folder 10, MOM, NLI).

Shuffling and hobbling, Murray remained alert to his own theatrical affairs. When *Michaelmas Eve* was broadcast on Radio Éireann in 1956, he displayed sound critical acumen in a letter to O'Mahony dated 7 January 1956. The letter also reveals that Murray was still admired by public commentators and private correspondents: "I felt that Moll Garvey was overplayed & that her poacher father was a long way from the Dan Garvey of Paddy Carolan at the Abbey. On the other hand I felt that the designing mother was just as I conceived her. Oddly several listeners were enthralled by the production. . . . I could write much more, but there is a sheaf of correspondence to be tackled" (Ms. 24,902, folder 10, MOM, NLI). On 6 August 1958, less than one year before his death, Murray wrote to Connolly about a proposed film of *Autumn Fire*. Never wealthy, Murray was gratified, though hesitant, about this turn of events. "Fortune—in its worldly sense—has shed a ray of comfort in the twilight of my years. A film company sought permission to use *Autumn Fire* for film and T.V. showing—mostly in USA—and commissioned Denis Johnston to write the scenario. I tremble to think what liberties will be taken with the play in its translation to the screen" (Box 13, folder 17:27–28, TLC, JJBL). Shortly before his death, in his last Christmas card to O'Donnell in December 1958, Murray announced that the proposed film appeared to be moving closer to realization. "In the way of writing my stock holds firm. I've just sold the rights of *Autumn Fire* to a film company" (Ms. 21,715, folder 10, FJHO'D, NLI).

Sensing his approaching death, he expressed the religious spirit that had distinguished his plays: "Day by day I wait for the call of the curtain on this troubled stage on which I have played so trifling a part, and look with faith and hope to its rise on a world where, with God's grace, I shall know that peace which passeth all understanding" (qtd. in Conlin 1961, 131). His daughters Nora and Eva kept vigil as Murray's health began to fail near the end of February 1959; Murray received holy communion every day for two weeks as his life ebbed away. On 7 March, in his Sandymount Avenue home, Thomas Cornelius Murray died of viral pneumonia at the age of eighty-six. Among the many mourners at the Star of the Sea Church, Sandymount, were

playwright Frank J. Hugh O'Donnell and Abbey actors May Craig and Eileen
Crowe. As a final tribute, Radio Éireann rebroadcast its 1952 recording of
*Autumn Fire,* which featured Michael J. Dolan as Owen Keegan. The Directorate of the Ireland's Theatre, however, failed to make public note of
Murray's passing. Bitterly disappointed, Murray's daughter Eva wrote to Terence Connolly on 13 March 1959: "The Abbey directors in no way acknowledged my father's connection with the theatre." Apparently unaware of the
presence of Séamus Wilmot of the Abbey Directorate, she continued, "Not
one of them attended the funeral and only today we received a message of
sympathy from them. The letter was valueless, as it was only sent when their
complete lack of courtesy was brought to their notice by a friend" (Box 13,
folder 17:27–28, TLC, JJBL).

The freedom of the individual is a theme that runs through Murray's life
and career like a leitmotif. From his boyhood experience with the castle in
Macroom, Murray learned to abhor dominating powers, judging them to be
unnatural. When he judged their actions unjust, he challenged figures of authority in the persons of Father Lawrence Murphy, clerical manager of Rathduff National School, and W. B. Yeats and Frank O 'Connor, directors of the
National Theatre Society. This same theme is evident in his plays. To be sure,
Murray's quest for freedom for the individual was spiritual rather than political, just as Ibsen's had been. Yet Murray wrote at a time of great political up-
heaval and change in his land. While Ireland was struggling for national
independence, Murray, in his plays, championed young protagonists, oppressed by parents and priests. Murray's characters stand, unconsciously perhaps, as symbols of England's oppression of a society, struggling to embrace a
freedom, rightfully its own.

# 2

# Realism, Cork Style

## The Early Plays

"WE KNEW OUR IBSEN," said Lennox Robinson, recalling the beginnings of the dramatic movement in Cork (1942, 119–20). Influenced by the social problem plays of the Norwegian Henrik Ibsen, Robinson engendered a Cork version with his own plays, *The Clancy Name* (1908), *The Cross Roads* (1909), and *Harvest* (1910). When Murray offered *Birthright* and R. J. Ray, *The Casting Out of Martin Whelan,* it was perceived that a school of "Cork Realism" had emerged to present to Dublin audiences Ibsenite social concerns with decidedly Irish subjects and settings. The era of Irish realism had begun in 1903, the year of J. M. Synge's *Riders to the Sea* and Padraic Colum's *Broken Soil.* Synge's realism was more poetic while Colum's was more naturalistic. Brenna Katz Clarke observes that Colum "simply tried to faithfully transcribe the spoken language, while others, like Synge, seemed to create a language all their own" (1982, 152). Two schools of realist writing emerged, then, in the first generation of Irish dramatists, best represented by J. M. Synge of the Protestant Ascendancy and by Padraic Colum of the Catholic working class. In the second generation, this Protestant/Catholic division continued in the works of Robinson and Murray.

The years of 1909–1910 were turning points in the Irish dramatic movement. In 1909, J. M. Synge died in Dublin and T. C. Murray wrote his first play in Cork. In 1910, Colum effectively retreated from the popular stage. *Thomas Muskerry* was his swan song to the Abbey Theatre in that year; in 1914, he emigrated to America. Also in 1910, Annie Horniman, English patron of the Abbey, ceased providing the subsidy for Abbey Theatre operations

when Lennox Robinson, through a series of blunders, chose not to cancel performances on the death of King Edward VII. Horniman's action caused what
was already a trend toward popular drama to become standard practice; in
short, the Abbey lost its wherewithal to be an art theater. In its need to remain
afloat financially, it was increasingly forced to become a popular theater, featuring commercially viable plays. The art theater so desired by Yeats, Martyn,
Moore, Gregory, and Synge was now largely a people's theater. Featuring
scenes of rural life, these "peasant plays" depicted farmers, cottage kitchens,
and turf fires. Robert Welch documents their popularity and their contribution to the Abbey's solvency (1999, 56).

Although Synge had fulfilled Yeats's exhortation to "express a life that has
never found expression" (Yeats 1961, 299), Daniel Corkery claimed that
there was still, in the years after Synge, more to explore. He lamented that features of Irish life like "the fair, the hurling match, the land grabbing, the *priest-
ing,* the mission, the Mass" were not regarded as worthy subject matter for
Irish literature (1931, 15). More important, Corkery argued that too much of
Irish Catholic life remained unexamined, contending that a great Irish literature in English must include three facets of Irish life: the people's devotion to
the land, their religious consciousness, and the drive to nationalism.

Murray was one of the few Irish dramatists, according to Corkery, who
had explored these three facets of Irish life. He in turn subscribed to Corkery's
thesis; in his article "My First Play," published in *The Irish Press* on 20 February 1941, Murray called Corkery's short-story collection, *A Munster Twilight*
(1916), and his only novel, *The Threshold of Quiet* (1917), "something of a literary testament" (Ms. 23,513, 2:128, TCM, NLI). Set in and around Cork
City, his novel shows to a marked degree the resignation also typical of
Murray's tragic characters. In his essay "My Seven Stars of Memory," Murray
disclosed that certain literary documents exerted on his conscious mind "a
new breadth of vision—of old horizons widening" (1939). He cited
Corkery's *Munster Twilight* and Colum's first volume of peasant poetry, *Wild
Earth* (1916). More significantly, he extolled Henry Gissing's *The Private Papers of Henry Ryecroft, The Journal of Eugénie de Guérin* (1865), and Canon
Sheehan's *My New Curate* (1900). These last three books focus with marked
sensitivity on the interior lives of ordinary souls living in the English, French,
and Irish countrysides. For Murray, Gissing's Henry reflected a "sense of

quiet content and well being, of joy in nature, in books, and in the simplicities of life" (59). Of Eugénie, Murray wrote that she was "a devout Catholic, and her luminous spirit leaves on the reader's mind a glow of tender beauty" (60). Of Sheehan's characters, he observed that they "were neither saints nor sinners but normal children of Adam in whom good and evil contend for mastery" (59).

All these works were shaping influences upon Murray's essentially spiritual enterprise: tragic realism dramatizing the daily struggles of Catholic peasants. Murray's source material was the rural life he knew while growing up in Macroom, outside of Cork City. Each of his plays, Murray once said, is a human document, derived directly from the people he had heard and observed. Although Ireland's political turmoil—the struggle for Home Rule, the Easter Rising of 1916, the War of Independence, the establishment of the Irish Free State and the Civil War—does not figure in Murray's body of work, Murray still contributed to the nationalist agenda inasmuch as his peasant studies helped to form an Irish cultural identity distinct from that of England.

Murray's great sympathy for rural life was the notable feature of his best plays. In his novel *Spring Horizon,* the hero Stephen Mangan expresses Murray's compassion for Deasy, a schoolboy who is humiliated in the classroom by both the visiting school inspector—the archdeacon—and by his classmates: "His plight moved Stephen to a deep compassion, through which kept pulsing some inward protest against the cruelty of life" (1937b, 237). Further in this passage, the budding gift of the dramatist is demonstrated in Stephen's ability to empathize with the experience of another person, wondering what it might be like to live in the skin of another. "Imaginatively, as was his wont, he [Stephen] saw himself in the other's place, tortured by the Archdeacon's laughter, the derision of the teacher, the jeers of his companions. In such a crisis he felt he should do something desperate—something crude, or violent, or savage—to release the torment devouring his soul. How—*how* could Deasy stand there by the coal-box so mute and unprotesting?" (237). A wondering question such as this would prompt Murray in adulthood to explore the desperation of rural life in plays like *Birthright, Spring,* and *The Briery Gap.* Murray's protest against the strictures of this life is seen in his characterizations of Maurice Harte, Myles O'Regan, Peter Keville, and Brian Egan. It is presaged in his outrage against the imperial

power, garrisoned in his boyhood Macroom, that prevented him from exploring the woods surrounding the castle. In "Tale of a Town," which he wrote
for *The Irish Press* of 3 June 1940, Murray termed it the "crippling of a boy's
natural freedom of movement" (Ms. 24,891, TCM, NLI). The unnatural
prohibition, Murray argued, fostered in a boy "a sense of wrong and of
smoldering resentment against the tyranny of custom" (Ms. 24,891,
TCM, NLI).

Murray's essential dramatic theory is summarized in "one valuable lesson," addressed to Irish Catholic artists in a lecture, "Catholics and the Theatre," delivered to the Catholic Truth Society (in the presence of the
archbishop of Cashel) at Mansion House, Dublin, on 12 October 1922 (Ms.
24,868, TCM, NLI). In this paper, Murray differed with critic Ernest Boyd's
thesis that the puritanical spirit of Irish Catholicism was inimical to the development of Catholic artists, and that Protestants had carried the Irish dramatic
movement. In response, Murray presented a manifesto for the Irish Catholic
dramatist. Acknowledging the centrality of the peasant in the Irish literary revival, he felt that the work of Yeats, Synge, and Gregory displayed a lack of
close contact with peasant life. Only when they expressed their characters'
Catholicity did they come close to rural reality. In Murray's view, *Riders to the
Sea* truly captured Catholic experience, but most often, Murray advanced,
Synge was "remote from the heart of his subject" (Murray 1933). Padraic
Colum, Murray observed, never needed the notebook that Synge always carried. In his lecture, Murray urged the Catholic dramatist to write of Irish people, not fancifully, but "as he knows them, as he sees them—portraying their
faults no less than their virtues—the meanness as well as the largeness of character—their strength and their tenderness—their intense love and more intense hate" (Ms. 24,868:2, TCM, NLI). He was convinced that if playwrights
created true renderings, then the characters' Catholic identity would "reveal
itself in every circumstance as a flower reveals itself even in the darkness by its
perfume" (2).

Though his portraits of peasant faults and meanness sometimes disqui-
eted the middle-class Abbey Theatre audiences, Murray was convinced that
the language of peasants powerfully revealed their spirit. "I have heard such
rich music of speech," Murray had already enthused in a Cork lecture, "such
fantastically beautiful turns of phrase, such wonderful imagery from country

folk of the older generation, as no one can ever hope to hear from the lips of middle class urban respectability" (1913, 8). He failed to grasp the public protest against Yeats's *The Countess Cathleen* (1892), whose characters seemed to violate Catholic dogma. He related to the Mansion House audience the example of an old peasant woman he had known in County Cork, "one who had the fine gift of colored speech" and who spoke with him during World War I: " 'Isn't it a quare thing entirely, master,' said she, 'that the Almighty wouldn't stop the war and all the prayers and masses that's said all over the world everyday?' " (Ms. 24,868:4, TCM, NLI). The limits of dogma, Murray argued, could not be applied to the speech of such characters *in extremis*. "The dramatist, if he be sincere, cannot ignore such types as this. . . . We must in a word face the truth" (Ms. 24,868:5–6, TCM, NLI).

Though Murray believed that the development of a national drama demanded truth, he faced the truth in only some of his plays. Murray the nationalist playwright came increasingly into conflict with Murray the good Catholic and proved, ironically, the truth of Ernest Boyd's claim that the spirit of Irish Catholicism could deter the development of Catholic artists.

Spiritual conflict is of paramount importance for Murray, and it is no wonder that he was intrigued by the characters trapped in the situations of Racine's plays. Influenced by the philosophy of Thomas Aquinas, the Catholic religion holds that each human person is possessed of intellect and will. The will chooses that which it perceives as good. Conflict between an individual's choice and the pressures imposed by family or community provides Murray with his subject. The flawed human choice—the one that misses the *mark,* coming from the Greek word *harmartia,* derived from archery—is the locus of his examination. Characters that are blinded and constricted by their parochial and domestic needs fascinated Murray.

Murray's dramatic style and structure was limited to that of the 19th-century realistic well-made play. As a schoolboy, he loathed puzzles that others were keen to solve. Having little patience with the existentialist, absurdist, or expressionist schools of playwriting, he once confessed, "definiteness alone allures me" (1898, 229). The Dublin Drama League, founded by Lennox Robinson in 1918, had staged plays by Strindberg and O'Neill, among others, in the Abbey's Peacock Theatre, but their themes and styles of production did not appeal to Murray. Frank J. Hugh O'Donnell solicited Murray's advice on his new play, *Triangle or Circle*. [1] In an undated reply (c. 1926), Murray admitted: "I must first disclaim my right to give a serious criticism of a play of such a *genre* as that to which your latest belongs. I am (to a great extent) a 'bloody realist'—and the school of Pirandello baffles me" (Ms. 21,715, folder 10, FJHO'D, NLI).

The structure of Murray's plays, following the French models of Scribe and Sardou inherited by Ibsen, is carefully crafted: a detailed exposition of characters, themes, and conflict, leading to a finely plotted complication and rising action, giving way to the *scène-à-faire* or necessary confrontation scene in which a character's secret is revealed. The dénouement, or falling action, brings the construction to completion.

Ibsen had exploded the perfect form of the well-made play when, at the end of *A Doll's House* (1879), Nora leaves home, abandoning husband and children. Murray adopted Ibsen's form, as well as his early social concerns. Unlike Ibsen, however, Murray was unable to move beyond this form. A passion for structure marks Murray's work. Widely recognized for this gift, Murray was spoofed in a 1929 cartoon, drawn by Grace Plunkett for the Christmas

1. Frank J. Hugh O'Donnell (1894–1976), born in Tuam, Co. Galway, was an industrialist and a senator (1943–1957), a member of the Council of Irish P.E.N. (*Thom's Directory* 1951, 92), and an author of poems, short stories, and several plays: *The Deluge* (1916), *Michael Dwyer* (1916), *The Dawn Mist* (1919), *The Keeper of the Lights* (1919), *The Drifters* (1920), *Wreckage* (1922), *The Anti-Christ* (1925), *O'Flaherty's Star* (1928), and *The Bar* (1928). He died on 4 November 1976 ("Obituary: Frank J. Hugh O'Donnell" 1976). *The Drifters* and *The Anti-Christ* were presented at the Abbey in 1920 and 1925 respectively (*Thom's Directory* 1951, 92; Hogan and Burnham 1984, 239–40, 322; 1992, 266–70).

O'Donnell became a longtime friend to Murray. In a letter written on 3 January 1956 to Mary O'Donovan, Murray wrote of him: "He had dreams of becoming a playwright, and succeeded in having a play, *The Anti-Christ,* produced by the Abbey, but is now one of the 'high ups' in the industrial world and a senator to boot. While on the crest of the wave Fate dealt him a cruel blow. Only a week after he had been to see me last year he got a stroke which paralyzed his left side. . . . He was recognized as the best looking man in Leinster House and it was heartache to see how ravaged he had become & how difficult he finds it to speak" (Curran Family Collection). Several Frank J. Hugh O'Donnell papers are housed in the National Library of Ireland. A German translation of *The Anti-Christ* by Josef Grabisch is housed in Trinity College Library, Dublin. The other Frank J. Hugh O'Donnell Papers are held in the Irish literature collection of the library of the University of Delaware, Newark, Delaware.

issue of *The Irish Sketch,* depicting the creation of a Christmas pudding; Dublin theatrical celebrities, including Barry Fitzgerald, Walter Starkie and Jimmy O'Dea, circle the huge bowl, tossing ingredients into the mixture. Murray exults, "I'll supply the unity" (Ms. 24,878, TCM, NLI). Indeed, organization was the chief feature upon which he commented when he was asked by young playwrights to appraise their work. On 23 September 1919, he wrote Frank O'Donnell that the sprawling plot of *The Keeper of the Lights* (1919), ranging over "too large a canvas," caused his play to suffer from "an effect of thinness—a kind of lack of body" (Ms. 21,715, folder 10, FJHO'D, NLI). To Holloway, he wrote on 21 March 1930 that Teresa Deevy's play *Reapers* (1930) was "such a woful [sic] tangle of strings for so long that I despaired of ever discovering a pattern" (Ms. 13,267, folder 16, NLI).

Unlike Colum, Murray found his notebook essential in capturing the "colored speech" of his peasant folk. In an essay, "Heard at the Crossroads," published on 29 October 1919 in *The Irish School Weekly* under the pseudonym "Touchstone," Murray demonstrated his fascination with the community mind as it was revealed in the gossip of two farmer's wives discussing the possible identity of their newly appointed schoolmaster. Mrs. Hegarty advances: "Yes, he must be Patsy Shea's son, so? There was one of them up in Dublin. . . . He's a kind o' cousin of my own. My mother's second cousin was a Shea. They were always great at the learning." Mrs. Burke allows: "I wouldn't be surprised at all, for I heard Maurice to say that this young man had great letters entirely. He bested all the rest. They say 'tis an inspector or something very big he's likely to be some day" (Ms. 24,881, TCM, NLI). This excerpt shows Murray studying the "definiteness" of his people, recording their parochial concerns, which valued the "very big" and the "high up," and exploring their interconnectedness. The conversation later discloses the religious locus of their lives: Father Hogan and the bishop who will exercise ultimate power in the appointment. The discussion illustrates the deeply religious nature of seemingly civic concerns. The women's conversation, "heard at the crossroads," would appear two years later in the opening sequence of *Maurice Harte* (Ms. 24,881, TCM, NLI).

With *Birthright* in 1910, Murray became the successor to Colum as the Catholic realist of the Irish dramatic movement. Originally entitled *The Tillers of the Soil,* the play is a tragedy in two acts set in rural Cork. Murray's dramatic construction is economic and tightly controlled, almost to a fault. The plot, with its careful exposition, escalates rapidly. It observes the three unities: one plot, one locale, and a twenty-four hour duration. Murray had long believed that the story of Jacob and Esau, rival brothers in the Hebrew scriptures, contained the elements of classic Greek tragedy. With two brothers, two parents, and one principal action, it presents a compact tale with a theme ready for adaptation to the Irish reality. For years, Irish families had been tenant farmers, subject to Ascendancy landlords and their rent-collecting agents. A series of land wars were characterized by farmers boycotting farms from which other farmers had been unjustly evicted. Various land acts culminated in the Wyndham Land Act of 1903, which enabled farmers to purchase land at last. Their former disenfranchisement had created a "land hunger" in farmers. Once entitled, they were reluctant to relinquish their farms to their sons. Giving over the farm created a thorny nexus of problems. According to peasant custom, once a farmer did so, he and his wife were obliged to move to a small rear room of the farmhouse so that the son might become master and his wife, the new "woman of the house." As a result, a father often delayed surrendering his farm until advanced age required him to do so. But a son could not marry until he was endowed with the economic means afforded by the farm. As a result, a son often did not marry until well into middle age. Furthermore, the small size of these farms meant that they could only support one son's family. If the other sons wished to marry and raise a family, they were forced to emigrate in order to find work; otherwise, they remained single.

Neighbor Dan Hegarty functions in *Birthright* like the messenger of an ancient Greek drama. When he announces that a great hurling match has been played in the town that day and that Hugh Morrissey, the captain of the local team, was its star, the conflict is immediately established. Bat Morrissey, the disapproving father, complains about the match in his first line (Murray 1998, 1.29). The whole town, it seems, has attended. Dan even feels guilty about going on a grocery errand. Hugh's mother, Maura, likens the crowds to "a black flood covering the world" (1.38). Murray sounds the Ibsenite theme of the individual battling against the mainstream of society in order to reach fulfillment, the theme that marks his entire body of work. As in Ibsen's plays, duty to self and community are at odds.

The root problem in this social problem play is the incompatibility of nature to task, a theme explored earlier by Colum in *The Land* (1905). Murray places the two brothers in conflict from the start, contrasting their differing gifts and temperaments. The elder brother Hugh, with a facility for fiddling, versifying, and hurling, manifests no genuine inclination to work his father's land. The younger brother, Shane, duller of intellect and spirit, dutifully tends the farm. But Bat had promised the farm to Hugh from the days of his boyhood. Shane, a genuine farmer, resents his older brother's birthright. Rather than work for his brother, he plans to emigrate to America. Maura Morrissey favors her elder son while the father prizes the true farmer in the younger Shane. While Bat would rather give his farm to Shane, Maura holds Bat to his pledge to his firstborn. The driving force in the drama is Bat Morrissey, who fears his original decision. Bat perceives that not only his farm, but his very identity is being threatened. A hard life allows for no reflective contemplation, no love of beauty, no sport or comradeship. ÓhAodha notes that Murray's characters have "troubles enough of their own" and pay scant notice to "what goes on beyond the stone walls of their little mountainy farms" (1974, 74). This is certainly true of Bat Morrissey, who proclaims in a powerful speech that in order to make his land thrive he "drained the western field that was no better than a bog" and "made the land kind" (Murray 1998, 1.35).

To the theme of the individual against society, Murray adds the naturalistic note of heredity. Bat assails his wife's nature, blaming her for Hugh's personality traits, so unsuited to life *in extremis*: "Your blood is in him. I see it in every twist and turn of his and every wild foolish thing coming from his mouth" (Murray 1998, 1.36).

Although Bat initially contains his misgivings about Shane going off to America, he sees it as a mistake to send away the younger son with the true gift for farming in favor of an elder son possessed of an artistic temperament. In remonstrating with Bat about "the great blindness that's on us all—to be talking that way" (Murray 1998, 1.38), Maura becomes Murray's *raisonneur*, or mouthpiece.

Religion is not the central feature of the plot, but elements of Roman Catholicism function dramatically within it. Father Daly, as the priest and authority figure in the parish, affects the story's outcome even though he never appears in the play. Required to make a sick-call, the priest writes a letter to Hugh, asking him, as captain of the home team, to exercise responsibility in his absence, keeping both teams from overimbibing and brawling during the post-game celebration. Typical of the dramaturgy of the French well-made play, a simple stage prop like a letter affects the turning of the plot. While the priest's letter sets the tragic events in motion, a series of accidents on the farm, for which Bat holds Hugh responsible, accelerate the conflict. In the pivotal moment, Bat, who is semiliterate, orders Shane to cross out his brother's name on the trunk label and to substitute his own. Shane's action shifts the conflict from Bat and Hugh to Shane and Hugh; it proves to be the inexorable event.

Although the land hunger of the father incites the action, the two brothers, quarreling in a fatal fit of rage, bring it to conclusion. Hugh's reversal of fortune and his discovery of his brother's writing on the trunk label leads inevitably to the confrontation between the brothers. In a litany of remembered offenses, Shane recalls Maura taking Hugh to the fair, to the circus, and to the parish priest to serve on the altar. He turns on his mother, bitterly protesting: "That was only one o' the distinctions you made between us when I was a boy, and if God made me rough, he didn't make me rough enough not to feel them and remember them to this hour. 'An when we grew up 'tisn't one nor a dozen distinctions that was made between us, but a hundred and more" (Murray 1998, 2.55). It is the most important speech in the play. It not only engenders pity over the misparenting of the two brothers, but it also reveals Shane, perceived as dull, to be the most aware and articulate family member on the cause of the forthcoming tragedy, for which the parents bear responsibility.

*Birthright* premiered at the Abbey Theatre on 27 October 1910 at the beginning of Lennox Robinson's first year as manager—or artistic director. He directed the play, which featured Sidney J. Morgan as Bat, Eileen O'Doherty as Maura, Fred O'Donovan as Hugh, Arthur Sinclair as Shane, and J. A. O'Rourke as Dan Hegarty. Joseph Holloway's diary records the enthusiastic reception the audience afforded Murray, who was "loudly and unanimously called for" after the final curtain. Yet the graphic realism of Murray's work, so new on the Abbey stage, was far from the sort of play "with an apex of beauty" desired by Yeats and Gregory. Gregory was among those unsettled, presumably finding the stark realism repulsive. "Lady Gregory sat behind Mr. Murray last night," Holloway reported, "but did not know him, and he overheard many remarks about what she called 'the realist school of Cork dramatists,' and spoke slightingly of them." Gone was a romantic treatment of peasant life, common in her own plays. Holloway did not care for the strong language in *Birthright*: "It was studded with oaths. . . . It was nearly damned by damns." The playwright himself was displeased by the costumers' misreading of the characters' attire. According to Holloway, Murray "was not pleased with the dressing of his play; they dress as well as himself on a Sunday in the part of Cork in which his plot was laid" (1967, 144–45).

The favorable estimation of the play by press and audience, however, was important in establishing the Abbey on a popular base. The largely positive press reviews commented on the excellence of Murray's construction, characterization, and dialogue. "There was an enthusiastic demonstration of approval at the close of the piece," reported the critic of *The Irish Times*, "which fully justified the heartiest plaudits" ("A New Play at the Abbey" 1910). Hogan, Burnham, and Poteet stress that "the general opinions were that the play was 'a very good illustration of the excellence of the work that is being done at the Abbey,' 'a noteworthy addition to its repertory,' and 'the strongest play that has been staged by the Abbey people' " (1979, 46).

Although Robinson recalls that *Birthright* "was a perfect piece of art, as perfect as a Chopin prelude" (1951, 90) when Murray submitted it to the Abbey directors, it was produced in an imperfect state. In the 1910 text, no longer extant, an offstage gunshot signaled Shane's murder of his brother Hugh, thereby earning for Cork realism G. Hamilton Gunning's epithet, "the gunshot school of drama" (qtd. in Kavanagh 1946, 100). *The Irish Times* critic offers a record of the play's original ending [2]:

His [Hugh's] father, in a white heat of rage, dispossesses him, and orders him to take up Shane's part, and to clear off to America. Hugh is in no mood to take an order of that sort, and when Shane

2. According to "A Salvaged Letter," which Murray wrote for the 5 May 1941 edition of *The Irish Press*, Murray wrote of burning personal papers—what he termed "the drift of half a lifetime"—in the rear garden of his home (Ms. 2499, TCD). The original *Birthright* manuscript may have been included in this "drift."

interferes, high words and blows ensue between the brothers. In the end Hugh flings out of the house. The mother, in her deep woe, turns on Shane. "I would see you to the gallows to have back my son!" "You mean that?" exclaims Shane with fierce bitterness; "then it shall be so." Snatching up a gun, he rushes out after his brother, and murders him as he is stalking away across the hill. ("New Play at the Abbey" 1910)

The [*Evening*] *Telegraph* critic pinpointed the trouble: "Murray should have made Shane kill his brother when the passion was at its height . . . and not when the passion had partly died down." Categorizing the resulting murder an Aristotelian 'improbable possibility,' he observed that what would have been a properly tragic ending has turned melodramatic instead ("A New Play at the Abbey" 1910). Holloway confided to his journal that Murray asked Robinson to delete the final gunshot, "leaving the ending to the imagination," adding "All the critics say that last shot spoils the play" (1967, 144). Murray revised the play in 1911, eliminating the shooting. Richard Allen Cave, who discusses the original and revised endings in some detail, notes that the revised ending was being performed at the Abbey by 16 February 1911 (Murray 1998, x). In place of the shooting, Murray substituted onstage physical combat between the two brothers, which in 1911 included Shane's attack on Hugh with a hurley. The stage directions for the 1911 text read: *"Shane looks on the prostrate figure. He is dazed and horrified. The hurley falls from his hands and he staggers out into the night"* (1911, 43). Murray's letter to Abbey secretary W. A. Henderson, dated 26 February 1911, shows his pleasure with the revised ending as played at the Gaiety Theater, Manchester: "It was a great satisfaction to find that the ending was not only left unquestioned but regarded simply as inevitable" (BC, NYPL). Murray further revised the text in 1928, eliminating the hurley altogether: *"Gathering himself up, SHANE looks on the prostrate figure. He is dazed and horrified. Pity and terror in his voice, he calls 'Hugh, Hugh'"* (1928b, 2.56). This ending is less melodramatic and more deeply affecting, as the audience sees Shane register more fully and painfully the horror of what he has done to his brother. The ending reverberates with the catastrophic conclusions of Greek tragedy. As he staggers out into the night, unable to endure the reality of his action, Shane calls to mind Oedipus, who cannot bear to look upon the ultimate result of his crime.

As noted by Hogan, Burnham, and Poteet, the structure of *Birthright* already manifests the signal features of most Murray dramas: "a careful, leisurely exposition, through a slow tightening of tension, to a final explosive culmination"(1979, 46). Commonly cited is the dexterity with which Murray shifts the conflict between Bat and Hugh to the two brothers, resulting in a catastrophic climax to the story expressed in physical combat "usually reserved for and indiscriminately used as a tour de force in melodrama" (Canfield 1929, 158). Early Murray scholars also noted Bat's speech about draining "the western field" as an example of Murray's gift for authentic peasant dialogue.

The claustrophobic family situation in *Birthright,* in which a father's lack of vision brings down his entire house, anticipates *Autumn Fire.* Although each character is vividly drawn, none is developed in depth; none grows or changes during the course of the action. Certainly neither Bat nor Maura evinces any awareness of the wrong done to both Hugh and Shane through the parents' early favoring of Hugh. The mistaken judgments of the parents engender great pity for all four characters. Despite its flaws, *Birthright* is compelling in its "grim and surprising ferocity" (Welch 1999, 56). In addition to the issues of autonomy, favoritism, and jealousy within a family, the domestic violence in the text makes the play still timely.

*Birthright* established Murray as a dramatist of international reputation. After its success in Dublin, repeated in London, the play became a central feature of the first Abbey tour of America in 1911. *Birthright* is significant in both Irish and American theater history in that it was selected by Yeats and Gregory to form part of the opening bill for the American premiere of the Irish Players, on 23 September 1911 at the Plymouth Theater in Boston. *Birthright* also appeared during this tour in Providence, Lawrence (MA), New Haven, Wilkes-Barre, Bloomington (IL), and Chicago (Abbey Tour Programmes 1911–1912).[3] Prior to the premiere of Synge's *The Playboy of the*

---

3. In later tours, audiences in Pittsburgh (1912–1913) and in Milwaukee and Dayton (1914) also witnessed *Birthright* (*Abbey Tour Programmes* 1912–1913, 1914). *Birthright* was presented again in New York by the Abbey on 4 February 1913 and 21 October 1932 (Salem 1979, 232).

*Western World,* Murray's *Birthright* was the center of attention. Mícheál ÓhAodha claims that the controversy surrounding *The Playboy* overshadowed *Birthright* during the 1911 tour. "The praise for and opposition to the Murray piece was drowned in the greater tumult about a greater play" (1974, 73). But American critic Cornelius Weygandt judged *Birthright* to be the best new play of the year: "Many who saw *Birthright* in America were moved by it more than by any other play in the repertoire of the company" (1913, 217).

Irish-Americans in Boston were disturbed, however, when Murray overturned their sentimental recollections of Ireland: "Smashing their dream, came T. C. Murray's *Birthright,*" wrote Lennox Robinson. "Here is no cottage with the roses round the door" (1951, 96). In *Our Irish Theatre,* Lady Gregory recalled arriving in Boston to hear from Yeats of the stir created by Murray's *Birthright*: "There had already been some attacks in a Jesuit paper, *America.* But the first I saw was a letter in the *Boston Post* of October 4, the writer of which . . . attacked plays already given, *Birthright* and *Hyacinth Halvey.*" In the text, Dr. J. T. Gallagher proclaimed: "I never saw anything so vulgar, vile, beastly, and unnatural, so calculated to calumniate, degrade, and defame a people and all they hold sacred and dear" (qtd. in Gregory 1913, 178–79). The "Irish Plays" upset so many in Boston that *The Boston Sunday Post* offered a lengthy article on 8 October titled "A Lively Discussion Over the 'Irish Plays': Do They Present A Fair Picture of Life and Conditions in Ireland?" The two brothers are locked in combat while the mother and father look on helplessly. The article includes a full column of excerpts from the text of *Birthright.* It is noteworthy that Gregory's *Hyacinth Halvey* and Synge's *In the Shadow of the Glen* are not so featured, despite the fact that they, too, had premiered by 8 October. An article from 1911 in the *New York Star,* "The Irish Players in a Scene in *Birthright,*" features a large photograph of the fatal fight. J. M. Kerrigan, the actor who played Shane, sent Murray a clipping of this article. At the bottom of the photo he wrote, "This is the cause of all the trouble. [signed] J. M. Kerrigan" (Ms. 23,510:5, TCM, NLI).

When the company opened in New York on 20 November 1911, Lady Gregory recorded in her journal: "One man made rather a disturbance at the fight in *Birthright* saying it was 'not Irish' " (1913, 199). Murray was not sympathetic to the intolerance of Irish-Americans who, to his mind, were viewing Ireland "through a rose mist" (1914). When the Abbey players were incarcerated in Philadelphia in January 1912 after the premiere of *Playboy* there, Murray wrote to Joseph Holloway on 19 January 1912, "You have seen this morning's cable from Philadelphia of course? What splendid comedy! TCM" (Ms. 13,267, NLI). With *Birthright,* Murray challenged both Dion Boucicault's (1820–1890) stage-Irish melodrama and Irish-American sentimentality with respect to Ireland. Several drama critics throughout the tour appreciated Murray's corrective vision, showering praise on *Birthright.* On 12 January 1912, in "Irish Players in Comedy and Tragedy," a reviewer in the *Philadelphia Press* spoke of "the new revelation of the possibilities of the stage in the sordid but elemental horror of *Birthright.*" Amy Leslie concurred in her [Chicago] *Daily News* article, "Four Fine Irish Plays," focusing on "a lesson, a picture of fierce potency and absolutely truthful possibilities" (1912a).

Seeing *Birthright* during the New York engagement proved an epiphanic experience for aspiring playwright Eugene O'Neill, who saw in it the possibilities of truthful playwriting. Barbara and Arthur Gelb observe that O'Neill, "saw through" the "hollowness and glib, philosophical posturing" of Clyde Fitch and Augustus Thomas, American playwrights of the day (1965, 159). "It was seeing the Irish Players," said O'Neill, "that gave me a glimpse of my opportunity. I went to see everything they did" (qtd. in Gelb and Gelb 1965, 110). Louis Sheaffer reports, "One drama that made a deep impression on O'Neill was *Birthright*" (1973, 127). In *Birthright* O'Neill "responded to the play's fidelity to basic human nature" (Shaughnessy 1988, 35). Murray's depiction of the fraternal conflicts occasioned by differing temperaments influenced O'Neill's *Beyond the Horizon* (1920); the raw, elemental power of the familial conflicts of Irish farmers also influenced *Desire Under the Elms*. In creating *Beyond the Horizon* (1920), O'Neill drew upon *Birthright* for rural settings, characters, and themes. Like *Birthright, Beyond the Horizon* has a farm setting, and both plays give prominence to the motifs of land hunger and the mismatch between a person's temperament and a vocational choice. Again the brothers are rivals, and the sensitive, mystical artist is contrasted against the rough, rugged farmer. The theme of personal unfreedom is patent. Although the influence of *Birthright* is apparent, O'Neill never acknowledged his debt to Murray.

Years after its initial success, *Birthright* earned European recognition for Murray. In 1924 it was awarded the bronze medal and a diploma in the literary competition "for men of letters" associated with the 1924 Olympic Games (VIII Olympiade) in Paris (Ms. 23,510, TCM, NLI.) The play was eligible because of its references to hurling. A news report from Dublin's *Weekly Freeman*, "Olympic Honour for Irish Dramatist," published on 9 August 1924, explained that the literary adjudicators included "such distinguished names as M. Jean Richepin, Gabrielle d'Annunzio, Paul Claudel, Marcel Prevost, Blasco Ibanez, and Maurice Maeterlinck" (Ms. 23,510, TCM, NLI). Another article, "Irish Playwright's Honour," published by the *Dublin Evening Mail* on 4 August 1924, drew attention to the international significance of the award: "In the modern drama of Europe, Synge, Yeats, and Lady Gregory have won universal recognition. Mr. Murray has further emphasized and enhanced the literary attainments of the nation" (Ms. 23,510, TCM, NLI). Of *Birthright*'s success in 1911, Hogan, Burnham, and Poteet note, "T. C. Murray . . . was to be for the next quarter of a century perhaps the most solid craftsman of the serious realistic play that the theater has produced" (1979, 45). *Birthright* was a standard in the Abbey repertoire for twenty-two years. After its first production, it received 22 presentations at the Abbey up to 6 August 1932, for a total of 112 performances (*Abbey Theatre Playbook*, n.d., 7).[4]

"I think the workmanship will show a distinct advance on *Birthright*." In this letter of 13 May 1911 to Lady Gregory, announcing his new play with a working title *Priesthood*, Murray reveals himself a playwright more sure, not only of his mentors, but also of his own sense of artistry (Gregory, A 65, B 2018–19, BC, NYPL). He was drafting a two-act tragedy about "the spoiled priest," a term given by the Irish to a candidate for priesthood who does not succeed to ordination. Of its origins Holloway relates: "[Murray] distinctly remembers being told by a man of the sad fate of his son who tried in vain to become a

---

4. A *presentation* is a short run of four to seven performances, which was standard procedure for a new Abbey play at that time. A run of a play was not lengthened until much later, when O'Casey came on the scene. If a play was well received, it might be brought back at a later date for another presentation of four to seven performances. By this standard, then, *Birthright* enjoyed a long run. I use the word *presentation* in lieu of *production*, since today that word usually refers to a new physical production or mounting of a play. This was not the case at the Abbey.

priest. The tragic look in the spoiled priest's parent's face haunted him and set him thinking" (1968, 3:6–7).

After reading the finished work to Christina and Niall, he submitted the typescript, now titled *The Levite,* to Abbey directors Yeats, Gregory, and Robinson. In an undated letter from 1912 to the Abbey Theatre Directorate, Yeats wrote his play reader's report of the script, "Magnificent first act: weak second act: should be performed after revision" (Yeats Papers, Ms. 13,068, folder 27, NLI). On 17 March 1912, Murray told Holloway, "I rewrote the second act since I sent the original ms. and Yeats seems to think it in its present form a much stronger play than *Birthright*" (Ms. 13,267, NLI). Later still, on 17 June 1912, Murray told Holloway about the altered title: "The Abbey people—or at least Robinson—objected to the original title. Maunsel's didn't care for it either, so I adopted that of *Maurice Harte*" (Ms. 13,267, NLI).

Murray was aware that with this play he was breaking new ground in the Irish dramatic movement. On 17 March 1912, he wrote with pride to Holloway, "In one sense it will strike a new note on the Abbey stage in as much as the atmosphere of the play is strikingly Catholic" (Ms. 13,267, NLI). Later, in his letter of 16 July 1912 to Holloway, Murray expressed his desire to please the Irish Catholic audience and, in particular, Irish Catholic clerics: "I think your friend Father [Stephen] Brown will like the play. The whole atmosphere of it is Catholic and Irish in its best sense. In the *American Ecclesiastical Review,* I read an article by Rev. George O'Neill, in which he states that the Abbey plays were either non-Catholic or anti-Catholic. This is a notable exception. Four priests—three of them on the Dublin mission—have read the Ms. and have given it as their opinion that it is elevating and that it introduces for the first time perhaps the true note of Irish Catholic life on the Abbey stage" (qtd. in Holloway 1967, 154).

Before the advent of Murray's plays, William Carleton and George Moore treated Irish Catholic life in their novels and short stories. Carleton's "Going to Maynooth" (1831) depicted the social luster associated with "going for the church," and Moore's *Celibates* (1895), a triptych of stories, detailed the lives of persons using religion to avoid life in the world. Canon Patrick Sheehan's *My New Curate* (1900) and "A Spoiled Priest" (1905) presented the tales of a young priest and a seminarian respectively. Gerald O'Donovan, succeeding Sheehan, wrote two novels treating ecclesiastical material, *Vocations* (1912)

and *Father Ralph* (1913). These are just some of the works of fiction that outlined the effects of the Catholic religion on the Irish peasantry, but before
Murray no play had yet presented a sustained view of the Catholic Church and
its people.

In *Maurice Harte*, the central character suffers a mental breakdown resulting from family pressure, in turn originating in the Irish devotion to
priesthood as a source of both religious honor and social advancement. Here
Murray documents the socioreligious reality of peasant society in which a
priest enhanced his family's "material well-being" (Connell 1968, 124) and
gained "preferment and power" for himself (Brown 1985, 30). It was not un-
common to find "a young giant, whom nature had evidently cut out, mind
and body, for a farmer; but was doomed for the priesthood by family decree"
(Kennedy 1867, 3).

Ellen Harte, Maurice's mother, wants a priest in the family, and she uses
Maurice to gain her desired end; Maurice, however, wants something other
than his family's desire for him. This is the root conflict in the play. Unsuited
to clerical life, Maurice battles against his nature to meet his family's expectations. His being forced into the seminary is the equivalent of an arranged marriage. Maurice's ordination will bring to the family enhanced social status and
financial security. The conflict for Maurice is essentially a spiritual one, as the
Harte family uses religion to secure their desired goal through him. Mrs.
Harte's expectations determine Maurice, placing severe limits on his freedom.
Murray underscores the reality that peasant parents decide the path their children's lives will take.

Mrs. O'Connor, serving both as confidante to Mrs. Harte and as the
voice of the community, sounds the themes of parental dreams, community
pride, and priestly honor in describing the ineffable joy surrounding
Maurice's imminent ordination and first mass: "Almost as plain as you're
standing there, I saw him in my mind, and he coming out the sacristy door,
with the fine vestments on him, and all the little altar boys and they on before
him. . . . That will be a proud day for you, Ellen, and for all of us" (Murray
1998, 1.62). Murray dramatizes the peasants' delight in the status afforded
their religion's priestly station. For the glory of having a son, as Carleton put
it, "with robes upon him," family members, even "brothers and uncles doing
well 'in emigration' " (O'Donoghue 1979, 1:25), shared the expenses of the

nine—or ten-year ecclesiastical training (Connell 1968, 124). Accordingly, the Harte family has endured great sacrifice and gone into financial debt to pay the cost of Maurice's seminary studies. The family's reputation and financial credit—and the older brother Owen's marriage to Bride Burke, with her sizeable dowry—all rest on Maurice's ordination.

Characteristic of his stagecraft, Murray uses both a prop and a story within the story to advance the plot. Aware of the high hopes his mother has for his ordination, Maurice tries to tell her, indirectly, that he is not suited to the priesthood by relating the story of a seminarian told in the novel he is carrying. The novel is the sort of narrative Canon Sheehan presented in his short story, "A Spoiled Priest"; the seminarian learns that he has no vocation. Mrs. Harte's responds to the tale by sympathizing with the boy's parents and wondering what the neighbors will think.

Murray underscores the power of the community to shape family expectations and personal behavior, constructing an Ibsenite conflict in a tightly enclosed, almost Racinian world. The constraint of the seminary rule of life, heavily influenced by the puritanical French Jansenist ethos of sexual repression and self-denial (Brown 1985, 20) heightens the personal constraint against which Maurice is chafing. Maurice keenly feels his freedom circumscribed.

Murray is presenting a critical dilemma. Mrs. Harte, who thinks a priestly vocation rests in an ability with books, fails to recognize the truth of the moment, and Maurice lacks the freedom and courage to act on what he knows to be true. Maurice is painfully aware that he will be unable to persuade his mother to see the hopelessness of his situation. As he fears telling his parents that he must leave the seminary, he turns to his confidant, Father Mangan, the local parish priest. When Maurice protests that his conscience will not allow him to proceed to ordination, the priest assures Maurice that his scruples are "proofs of a true vocation" (Murray 1998, 1.72). In the priest, Murray gives Maurice one more obstacle to confront: the priest is the voice of authority in the community.

Maurice's level of awareness, then, together with his discomfort in the situation at Maynooth, make him bold in addressing Father Mangan: " 'Tisn't to-day nor yesterday I—I realized my own nature. . . . But I buried my wretched secret in my soul" (Murray 1998, 1.72). This is Maurice's most interesting speech in the play, for it discloses much about Maurice's identity—or lack thereof. He says he realized his "own nature," his "secret," some time ago, yet he does not say what this true nature is. He gives no sense of knowing who he is or what he wants. Maurice is a prototype of Murray's male heroes, who reach fullest self-realization in Brian Egan in *Illumination*. These heroes have far to travel on their road to self-discovery, and one can feel only pity for Maurice who, in this speech, shows his lack of self-knowledge, represented by the incompleteness of his statement, "I—I realized my own nature."

Murray focuses on the parents' expectations as determinants, set against Maurice's freedom to act. Father Mangan only intensifies Maurice's constriction by taking the side of his parents. Christina in *Illumination* will play the same role of devil's advocate, trying to dissuade Brian from acting counter to the expectations of his father. Maurice, failing the courage to confront his parents himself, asks Father Mangan to reveal the news to them that he has no vocation and will not return to Maynooth. When she hears the news, Mrs. Harte, responds with fiery force, sweeping away Father Mangan's stock pious palliative. The exalted position of the priest is lowered; priestly "wisdom," given only notional assent by this peasant woman, is dismissed in genuine times of trial. Heartbreakingly honest, she rages against the order of things, refusing to believe the truth and boldly questioning why God would do this to them. For Mrs. Harte, this reversal of fortune truly does have cosmic significance, for the foundation of her family's world is shaken.

Maurice is left with no ally when, telling his mother that he has no vocation, he protests, "God has spoken to me in my soul" (Murray 1998, 1.82–83). Appropriately enough, Mrs. Harte is unable to understand this metaphysical statement, which Maurice himself is unable to explicate. It will fall to Brian Egan in *Illumination* to speak with greater detail and clarity about the spiritual movements of the soul. Dismissing Maurice's protests, Mrs. Harte cuts to the heart of the matter—the social and economic ruin of the family:

> MRS. HARTE: If it went out about him this day isn't it destroyed for ever we'd be? Look! the story wouldn't be east in Macroom when we'd have the bailiffs walking in that door. The whole world knows he's to be priested next June, and only for the great respect they have for us through the means o' that, 'tisn't James M'Carthy alone, but

every other one o' them would come down on us straight for their money. In one week there wouldn't be a cow left by us, nor a horse, nor a lamb, nor anything at all! (Murray 1998, 1.83)

Setting this calamity against talk of "the whole world" underscores yet again the enormous import of the ordination for the family. Mrs. Harte produces the two account books, using them as a tool to regain control of Maurice and his older brother Owen. The latter recognizes the enormity of the debt and is staggered, realizing that his imminent marriage is now in hazard. It is not difficult to feel pity for these characters, for both Maurice and his family have legitimate needs: Maurice needs to be true to his emerging conscience, and his mother needs to keep economic disaster away from the family door. His father and brother join in the forceful assault on Maurice. As Harmon notes, Maurice's role in this assault scene is "reduced to anguished cries" (1977, 154) such as "Don't ask me," "Oh, don't," and "Stop, mother, stop" (Murray 1998, 1.84). No match for the concerted pressure of mother, father, and brother, Maurice capitulates and returns to Maynooth to endure his confinement until his breakdown two weeks short of his ordination. The scene reveals Murray's critique of these religion-bound family members—as well as of their neighbors.

Maurice's final entrance into the cottage is heartrending in its effect on Mrs. Harte and the entire family. As she slowly removes Maurice's belongings from his parcels, *"[t]here is a tragic significance in every movement"* (Murray 1998, 2.98–99). This is Ellen Harte's moment of recognition, expressed not in words but in action. In this moment, it seems, she realizes that she has brought ruin to her family through her "matriarchal strivings to make her son a priest" (ÓhAodha 1958, 190). Witnessing this scene is particularly painful for the audience as they, too, recognize the results of Mrs. Harte's willfulness, replicating the blindness associated with classic heros from Oedipus to Willy Loman.

Ultimately Murray's portrait of the priest is a critical one precisely because he is ineffectual. He arrives near the end of Act Two, bearing the unhappy message of Maurice's illness. When he tries to prevent Mrs. Harte from going out to meet her son in her agitated state, she rebukes him. The priest also attempts to moderate the hopeless responses of Michael and Owen, to no avail.

The curtain falls as *"the priest looks at [Mrs. Harte] with a pained sense of his own helplessness"* (Murray 1998, 2.99). While he tries to offer hope that Maurice's breakdown may be only temporary, the family, pushed to extreme limits, cannot hear this.

Although he is unable to avert the family disaster, Father Mangan is far from Boucicault's stage-Irish priests, such as Father Tom in *The Colleen Bawn*, and Father Dolan in *The Shaughraun*. Murray's Father Mangan is also unlike the grasping, meanspirited priest in Synge's *The Tinker's Wedding* (1908). Rather, Murray has created Mangan out of the clay of peasant reality. Father Mangan's closest dramatic ancestor is Father Mahony in Lennox Robinson's *The Clancy Name* (1908). But even that priest is somewhat simple, easily hoodwinked by Mrs. Clancy into believing that her dead son is a hero. Dramatic ancestor to Mrs. Harte in her wiliness and determination, Mrs. Clancy keeps the priest from knowing that her son is a murderer.

In *Maurice Harte*, then, Murray critiques both the priest and the family. More specifically, he examines their religious ignorance and the socioreligious mores which conspire to make a peasant family oppress their son. It is an example of what ÓhAodha calls Murray's "profound criticism of life in rural Ireland" (1961, 29). It caused Emma Goldman to say, "nowhere does Catholicism demand so many victims as in that unfortunate land" (1914, 271–72). The fate of Maurice Harte amply justifies Thomas Hogan's claim for Murray's characters: "The tragedy of Ireland is that these frustrated sensitive souls do not revolt—the forces marshaled against them cow and repress them and the long years of futility, of partial and public surrender are their fate" (1950, 47). In Murray's plays, Gerald Fitzgibbon notes, "There are almost no victories. Heroes possessing creative or emotional ideals "are broken and destroyed by life" (1975, 63). Thomas Hogan says, "They are always defeated" (1950, 42). Desmond Maxwell observes that Murray's characters have little choice but to "endure within the restrictions." He adds, "From the tension between extreme emotional conflict and their enforced suppression, Murray's plays derive their intense, claustrophobic atmosphere" (1988, 696). Both the Harte home and the Maynooth seminary are tightly enclosed worlds with a stultifying emotional climate. Maurice, his conscience pressed in both arenas, cannot endure the tension. From the extreme conflict of conscience, his health breaks down, and he returns home not priested but shattered.

Fitzgibbon perceptively notes that in Murray's plays, the human spirit is "pushing towards growth, knowledge, achievement, emotional completion" (1975, 65). In *Illumination* Brian Egan makes a self-actualizing choice that integrates the elements of his personality. Maurice, however, possesses little freedom; he is crushed by environmental forces when he attempts to exercise his little freedom to represent his conscience. He is effectively robbed of the limited freedom he mustered.

Through the years, literary figures have held *Maurice Harte* in high esteem. Emma Goldman, in 1914, stated, "[T]he play is of that social importance that knows no limit of race or creed," (271–72). Owens and Radner likewise argue that Murray's treatment of the conflict between family and conscience "has an imaginative resonance which causes the play to transcend its limited social origins" (1990, 169). Yeats said in 1919, "If Mr. Murray gives us more plays like *Maurice Harte,* then we shall deserve perhaps as much attention from history as any contemporary theater" (qtd. in Hogan and Burnham, 1984, 197–98). Una Ellis-Fermor commented, "[T]his play leaves an impression of faithful observation" (1939, 33), while Thomas Hogan asserted, "There are few more perfect plays in the Abbey repertoire than *Maurice Harte*" (1950, 43).

Gregory and Robinson put *Maurice Harte* into rehearsal while the Abbey Players were on tour in London; it was the first play of the Abbey Theatre to premier outside Dublin. In a letter to Joseph Holloway written 16 July 1912, Murray recalled, "I was very disappointed at its non-production in Dublin, and but for Yeats I doubt that it would have been rehearsed on tour" (qtd. in Holloway 1967, 153–54). With Sara Allgood playing the role of Mrs. Harte, *Maurice Harte* premiered at the Royal Court Theater, Sloan Square, on 20 June 1912. In a letter to John Quinn, Gregory reports that after the final curtain, Murray "was called for by the audience and had a tremendous reception" (qtd. in Hogan, Burnham, and Poteet 1979, 191). Murray was the toast of London. Margot Asquith, wife of the prime minister, asked to meet him to offer her congratulations (O'Mahony 1982, 7). Newspaper accounts highlighted Murray's whirlwind two-day visit, trumpeting his leave without pay from his Cork teaching post. On 27 June 1912, Murray wrote to Holloway, "The house overflowed and Society (with a very big S) [filled] the half guinea stalls—not one of which was vacant" (Ms. 13,267, NLI).

The importance attached to the London premieres of Murray's plays can be apprehended in Murray's 1950 appreciation of Sara Allgood regarding the premiere of *Maurice Harte*. In his essay, Murray reconstructs the theatrical context in which *Birthright, Maurice Harte,* and *Sovereign Love* debuted. Regarding the 1912 opening night of *Maurice Harte* in London, Murray recalled in 1950: "The Abbey at this time was in the heyday of its popularity in London," noting, "The Abbey season had indeed become almost a fashionable cult. If you wished to be considered a person of fine taste, you patronized the Royal Court in Sloane Square. Week after week, periodicals of such high literary standards as the *Academy, Nation,* and *Spectator* devoted much space to its productions. Thus on that night of the first production of *Maurice Harte* you had for the most part an audience acutely perceptive of what is, or is not, good art in the theater" (Murray 1950).

Murray copied in his own hand excerpts from the press notices that he deemed "very good" and sent them to Holloway in a letter dated 27 June 1912. *The Star* cited Murray's "freshness of language and feeling," while the *Observer* called Murray "an author who combines force and delicacy in a manner that gives him distinction even among the Abbey Theatre playwrights" (Ms. 13,267, NLI). Though the night was a great triumph for both Allgood and Murray, the reviews were not uniformly excellent. The *Irish Independent* thought the ending too abrupt while the *Morning Post* thought it too painful (qtd. in Hogan, Burnham, and Poteet 1979, 486). Indeed, Murray's postpremiere letter to Holloway, written on 27 June 1912, reveals that he was acutely aware of the deficiencies of the production, rehearsed hurriedly on tour: "The play got a very cordial reception but it was produced in a very imperfect state. With the exception of Sidney Morgan as the priest—a study which will delight Catholic Dublin—there was a lack of subtlety—almost a crudeness in the whole interpretation. More than once it was easy to see Sarah [sic] Allgood prompting Sinclair & Eileen O'Doherty who were simply groping through the entire action!" (Ms. 13,267, NLI).

While still in London, Murray had his eye on the response of the Dublin literary world. In the same letter to Holloway, he asked, "What do your friends of the National Literary Society think of it? I should give much to know the opinion of the Rev. George O'Neill, S. J. You know him, I daresay?" (Ms. 13,267, JH, NLI). Murray was looking for clerical approbation of his subject matter, and one response from the Catholic literary world offered great encouragement. Canon Patrick Sheehan wrote to Murray that he had been following his career since *Birthright*. According to "A Salvaged Letter," which Murray wrote for the 5 May 1941 edition of *The Irish Press,* Sheehan declared his admiration for Murray's work to date and expressed his expectation of a great career ahead (Ms. 2499, TCD). No doubt this encomium from a prominent priest-novelist proved a bulwark against the coming assaults of the priest-manager in Rathduff.

After its four-performance presentation in London, *Maurice Harte* received its first production at the Abbey Theatre itself, encompassing four performances from 12 to 14 September 1912. Although Murray was prevented from attending the Dublin opening of his play because of teaching duties in Cork, he appeared a few nights later. On 16 September 1912, he wrote to Holloway that he deeply appreciated "the applause of the warm-hearted Dublin people who crowded the Abbey on Saturday night. . . . It is a rich memory for a dweller down here in Bogland" (Ms. 13,267, NLI).

*Maurice Harte* proved a great success in America, as well. As a principal feature of the 1912–1913 tour, it enhanced Murray's reputation, established by *Birthright,* in cities such as Chicago, Boston, and New York. The tour commenced in Chicago in holiday season on 30 December 1912. Although O. L. Hall, reporting in the *Chicago Daily,* noted that "It was a rather meager gathering that welcomed the company" (Hall 1912), two other reviews of the same date indicate that *Maurice Harte* created a definite impression. In her review in the *Daily News,* Amy Leslie praised it as "an immense document of feverish truth," citing in particular, "an emotional rhythm like a dirge through its pitiful woe" (Leslie 1912b). Richard Henry Little's review in the *Chicago Examiner* noted the "tense stillness on the part of the audience"(Little 1912). Indeed, the mood of the piece rendered the audience almost incapable of applause at curtain fall. Little added, "Not until the curtain was again drawn aside, revealing the players, did the spellbound audience move, and then its approval was so generous that the actors were obliged to respond to a half-dozen or more encores" (Little 1912).

During the four-week Chicago engagement, the Irish Players were invited to perform a special matinee at the University of Notre Dame on Friday, 10 January 1913. A press release, "Irish Players to Show At Notre Dame School," appearing in the *Chicago News* of 8 January, trumpeted the occasion as "the first time the Irish Players will have appeared in a Roman Catholic institution of learning, here or abroad" (1913). Father John Cavanaugh, the president, selected the afternoon's repertoire, specifically requesting Murray's *Maurice Harte*. Curiously, the Murray play, though announced in a press release, was not performed. Instead of *Maurice Harte, The Rising of the Moon* and *Kathleen-ni-Houlihan* were performed with the scheduled *Workhouse-Ward*. One wonders if a play about a "spoiled priest" was considered, in the end, inappropriate dramatic material to set before the young men at South Bend.

As the tour moved on, *Maurice Harte* was performed in Montreal, Philadelphia, New York, and Boston. The *Montreal Gazette,* in its review of 20 January 1913, called it "a keen and attention-compelling, psychological study" (*"Maurice Harte* A Clever Study"), while the Philadelphia *Public Ledger* of 21 March deemed it "the strongest and most compelling work of the present repertoire" ("A Strong Irish Play," 1913). In his review of 3 April in the *Boston Evening Transcript*, Henry T. Parker proclaimed *"Maurice Harte* remains the finest tragic play of the Irish playwrights since Synge's *Riders to the Sea*" (1913).

Beyond its first production, *Maurice Harte* received through the years 25 presentations at the Abbey Theatre, for a total of 118 performances. One of these, on 12 August 1938, was a performance in Dublin for the city's Abbey Theatre Festival of Irish Drama, held 6–20 August 1938 (*Abbey Theatre Playbook*, 51). Along with most of Murray's other works, *Maurice Harte* also became a standard with Irish amateur dramatic societies. Michael Farrell advocated its adoption by these groups, citing, in particular, the characters, which "offer grand parts to all the performers" (Farrell 1940, 58–64).

Like most of his plays, Murray's one-act comedy about matchmaking, *Sovereign Love* (1913), is what he called "a human document." The situation and characters were derived from life as Murray knew it in rural Cork: "[T]he old matchmaking custom was so prevalent," Murray explained in an interview in *The Leader* of 26 June 1943 ("T.C. Murray: Interviewed by Kathleen O'Brennan") "that one heard of the arrangements between families. A girl had come to town to meet the man chosen by her parents. He renaged [sic], as we say. Higher up the street a man had also arrived to meet the prospective bride, and she failed to turn up. So someone suggested that the two disappointed individuals should make the bargain" (Ms. 23,514:364–65, TCM, NLI).

In this play, a revision of his first effort, *The Wheel of Fortune* (1909), Murray was responding to requests that he write a play different in spirit from *Birthright* and *Maurice Harte*. On 26 April 1913, he commented to Holloway, "I have been rather bored from people saying, 'Why don't you write us a comedy? Life itself is such a gloomy affair we want to forget its oppression in the theater' " (Ms. 13,267, NLI). But there was a dramaturgical reason, as well, for his reworking of *The Wheel of Fortune*. "Some time ago," he explains in the same letter, "I got a number of ex-pupils of mine to do *The Wheel o' Fortune* and I learned such a lot during the rehearsals that I saw possibilities in it, and this was an added motive setting me to work" (Ms. 13,267, NLI). But Murray was concerned how a play slight of length and seemingly light of theme might affect his career; Yeats, after all, had urged all aspiring playwrights to look to *Maurice Harte* as an object lesson on plot construction. When Murray, still a neophyte, sent *Sovereign Love* to the Abbey directors, he was solicitous of Yeats's advice, worrying, as he told Holloway on 26 April 1913, that the one-act comedy might "distract from whatever little reputation I had gained" (Ms. 13,267, NLI). While Murray himself evaluated the play as "commonplace" in theme but "sharp and individual" in characterization, he told Holloway in the same letter that he had received a letter from Robinson saying that " 'Mr. Yeats like [sic] the play very much' " (Ms. 13,267, NLI).

The plot centers on two families, the Kearneys and the O'Donnells, and on Andy Hyde, a wealthy Irishman returned from America to claim a native Irish bride. Farmer Donal Kearney seeks the best possible economic gain in a match for his eldest daughter, Ellen. He finds him in Hyde, but the "Yank" fails to appear as arranged. By a strange coincidence, the O'Donnells experienced the same fate at Barry's public house down the road. As the match intended for young David O'Donnell, son of farmer Charles, has also failed to keep her appointment, Donal Kearney and Charles O'Donnell join their children in a much-needed match.

Ellen is afraid of remaining single and fearful that her neighbors will discover the failure of her intended to appear. Her former emotion presages that of Ellen Keegan in *Autumn Fire* while her fear of her neighbors echoes that of Mrs. Harte in *Maurice Harte*. In all three cases, shame is the root emotion.

But Ellen Kearney in *Sovereign Love* displays an emotion new in a Murray play—romantic, impulsive love:

> ELLEN: He's a splendid young man and I like him in a wonder.
>
> KATY:But I hope he has the two hundred. If he was the King's son himself 'twould be equal with father and he to be short in the reckoning.
>
> ELLEN: Would you believe, Katty, here's that strange feeling come on me, 'tis little I'd heed how much or how little he had and I to have himself only? (Murray 1998, 13)

In this charming but telling exchange, Murray contrasts the attitudes of the older and younger generations, the latter victim to their elders' mercenary streak. Indeed, as the young people discuss love, their parents are determining the couple's future in the corner. In theatrical terms, Cave observes that: "The scene needs careful direction if the double focus of interest is to be sustained: we should not forget the men, indeed their argument should occasionally flare into audible anger, affecting Ellen's attempt to talk herself into believing that she is in love" (Murray 1998, ix).

Just when the two fathers shake hands on the agreement, Andy Hyde enters. When Hyde flashes his bank book, Kearney, *"devouring it with his eyes"* (Murray 1998, 22), reneges on his agreement with O'Donnell, who is enraged by Kearney's duplicity. David and Ellen, the nearly betrothed couple, are crushed in the aftermath of the negotiations. They respond to their desperate plight in half-lines, reminiscent of Maurice Harte's: "For God's sake, David—" and "Ellen, girl, Ellen—" as the "comedy" ends on a bitter note (24).

Far from light comedy, *Sovereign Love* is a dark comedy of character, focusing on the mercenary characteristics of matchmaking. Murray's treatment of this practice was finely observed, honest, and singular. His play is one that few other members of the Irish dramatic movement could have written. Murray is in sympathy with the two young people, twice disappointed in their matches and left in distress at play's end: pawns in their parents' scheming. Ellen Kearney is little more than a piece of property to her father, a commodity to be bartered or sold to the highest bidder. When Ellen protests, her father tells her flatly that she can't afford to be fussy. The young couple, maneuvered by the older generation, anticipates a similar treatment in *The Briery Gap* of the following year. In neither play are the young characters capable of free, undetermined action.

Dramaturgically, *Sovereign Love* is typical of the well-made play with a high degree of coincidence marking the plot; in a play this short, the artifice of the characters' comings and goings is all the more noticeable. Nevertheless, the machinery works well: the dramatic tension created is effective and believable. Once again, a stage prop is central to the climax of the story. But here Hyde's flashing of his bank book is organic, growing out of his character and economic circumstances. Hyde's action functions more as a final flourish clinching a decision Donal Kearney has already made than as a determining factor in his reaching it. Murray was accurate in deeming his characterizations "sharp." No doubt he was aware that his rendering of Donal Kearney's greed, in particular, might rattle his country neighbors, as aspects of *Maurice Harte* had so recently done. In discussing revisions to *Sovereign Love* before its Abbey debut, Murray wrote Holloway in an undated letter: "I must however cut out anything overstrong before its production of which at present nothing is arranged" (Ms. 13,267, NLI).

Living in Rathduff, Murray was also far removed from the operations at the Abbey Theatre. He was not aware that rehearsals for *Sovereign Love* were in progress, and only by reading the *Freeman* did he learn of the play's imminent premiere. Cursing his outsider's fate, he wrote Holloway on 7 September 1913: "But I daresay these things are the natural product of the country parsonage and its attitude of mind to the mere papist" (Ms. 13,267, NLI). As with *Maurice Harte,* Murray was once again unable to attend the Abbey premiere of *Sovereign Love* on 11 September 1913. Frustrated, he relied on Holloway's report of the play's reception. Murray's precious reply of 12 September 1913 reveals his perennial concern: "I am much relieved to find that the little play gave no offense" (Ms. 22,404, folder 13, JH, NLI). Murray's excessive concern about not offending his audience would lead him, in the years to come, to the lamentable practice of self-censorship.

In his diary entry for 11 September 1913, Holloway recorded that *"Sovereign Love* played at the Abbey for the first time tonight, proved a great success" (1967, 159). Although the author of the undated review in the Dublin *Freeman* applauded the "abundance of good dialogue, and shrewdly done character-drawing" ("New Abbey Play" 1913), Jack Point, his counterpart at the *Evening Herald* suggested in his review that Murray's gift lay elsewhere than in comedy, commenting, "the author is more at home in what may for convenience be styled an Irish problem play" (Point, 1913). *Sovereign Love* was performed in London at the Court Theater, paired on the same bill with *Maurice Harte,* a pairing that would become something of a tradition in Abbey programming. On 11 June 1914, *The Stage* reported that the play was "full of wit and humour, and it was received throughout . . . with ripples of laughter" ("Sovereign Love" 1914). Given Murray's excessive worry and the mixed press reviews, it is ironic that his play *Sovereign Love* proved to be a crowd pleaser, enjoying repeated performances at the Abbey.

No doubt the popularity of *Sovereign Love* led to its selection for the Irish Players' very short third tour of America in 1914, the last tour before the outbreak of World War I. Murray's play shared the program with Synge's *The Well of the Saints* as the double bill opening the four-week engagement at the Fine Arts Theater in Chicago. *Sovereign Love* opened with J. M. Kerrigan and Sydney J. Morgan in the matchmaking father roles. On 18 February of that year, Leslie's review in the Chicago *Daily News* described the comedy as "unctuous and immensely amusing" (1914). Ashton Stevens's review of the same date in the *Chicago Examiner* found Murray's characters to be "of mean, low purpose, cheap cunning, physical unbeauty and moral blight" (1914), while James Bennett's review in the Chicago *Record-Herald* discovered the chief virtue of *Sovereign Love* to be "the opportunity it gives us of seeing actors who are masters in the creation of little pictures—veritable etchings they are—in the rustic genre" (1914). After its first four-performance production of 11–13 September 1913, *Sovereign Love* received twenty-four presentations at the Abbey; totaling 140 performances,they made it Murray's most frequently performed work. As late as 1964, *Sovereign Love* was given four presentations of six performances each. The performances of 7–12 September 1964 signaled the last presentation of a Murray play on the main stage of the Abbey Theatre (*Abbey Theatre Playbook* n.d., 81).

Murray's relationship with the priest-manager of his school was deteriorating during this time. The continuing tension may have engendered in Murray an antipathy toward narrow-minded, rural clerics, fueling his next play, *The*

*Briery Gap* (1914), a one-act tragedy. It is one of Murray's most important plays, both for its treatment of the theme of freedom and for its curious history as a theatrical work because of its subject of premarital sex. "On a Sunday morning I attended Mass at a small country chapel," Murray wrote to Ria Mooney on 15 October 1948 (BC, NYPL). There he heard a priest in the pulpit castigate an unmarried, pregnant, young woman of the parish. Though priests denouncing parishioners from the pulpit was commonplace at this time, Murray explained to Mooney: "[T]o my horror [the priest] revealed that the poor father of the girl had come to him begging him not to make public his daughter's shame. The congregation sat frozen. The tension, even as I recall it now, was almost unbearable" (BC, NYPL). Murray pondered, he wrote to Mooney, what effect this sermon would have on a young woman in the congregation—"whose trespass had not yet come to light how desperate would be her reactions—And so *The Briery Gap* leaped into life" (BC, NYPL).

Murray sets the scene at *"the turn of a wild country road,"* hedged by *"bushes and brambly undergrowth"* (Murray 1998, 103). It is a Syngean landscape, reminiscent of *The Tinker's Wedding*. The setting symbolizes both the difficult situation in which Joan and her lover Morgan will find themselves and the divergent turns their lives will take as victims of clerical oppression. Joan has arranged to meet Morgan in the briery gap. The stage direction anticipates the tragic end to the story. It is a *"summer evening after heavy rains. . . . Through the gap one catches a glimpse of a path leading down to the ford of a river"* (103). As the scene opens, Murray establishes the danger of the flood, a symbol of the emotional flood soon to engulf Joan and Morgan. Morgan's explanation for being late—"With the flood in the river there was no sign o' the stepping stones" (103)—prefigures the loss of direction and security both he and Joan will soon experience. Murray introduces the theme of madness, merging it with the theme of deluge, as Morgan further explains his delay: "I couldn't but watch Cracked Terry and he racing the flood singing" (103). When Joan asks Morgan if he has heard of Father Coyne's sermon that morning, she gives her fear and dread cosmic significance, claiming that it is "the talk o' the world by now" (104). Murray also emphasizes the considerable power of the priest to engender terror in the community as Joan tells Morgan,

"There was many a one not able to draw the breath listening to him and he as good as calling down on her the curse o' the Lord God himself" (105).

Joan has good reason to be fearful because of the puritanical nature of Irish Catholicism. It was the office of clerics "to preach a sexual morality of severe restrictiveness, confirming the mores and attitudes of a nation of farmers and shopkeepers" (Brown 1985, 39). Father Coyne is true to type. He shows himself deficient in compassion toward the family and concerned for his own reputation. Morgan, functioning as Murray's *raisonneur,* speaks his disgust at the priest's heartless sermon. "A cruel shame it was. . . . What is it but his trade to be faulting the world?" (Murray 1998, 105).

Fearful of both the priest and the community, Joan expresses her dread in near biblical lamentation: "Wishing I do be sometimes that the hills would tumble down on me or the yellow flood of the river below drag me down with it to the tides of the ocean" (Murray 1998, 106). Murray returns to the theme of madness initiated by Morgan. If Joan were the woman denounced by Father Coyne, she says: "A mad woman running wild over the hills I'd be this minute" (106). Joan's lamentation foreshadows the "mad foolish thing" she will do—not once, but twice—by the play's end.

In this extreme situation, Murray illustrates the differing values that Joan and Morgan hold. When Joan insists that Morgan marry her immediately to spare her disgrace, he hesitates, citing his uncle as a determining factor. With both his parents dead, Morgan, according to Irish custom, must wait upon his uncle to endow him with the economic wherewithal to take a wife. Though he never appears in the play, Morgan's uncle functions as a dynamic character, constituting a major obstacle in the plot and affecting the outcome of the tale. Morgan wishes to delay marriage because he knows that his hope of inheriting land will be lost in the face of his rigid uncle's wrath.

Through his depiction of the uncle, Murray sharpens the central conflict of the play, revealing Joan's and Morgan's differing values. Morgan desires a comfortable married life in secure circumstances, while Joan, caring little about Morgan's dream of owning his uncle's farm, is fixated on her reputation in the parish. The situation as Murray draws it highlights the woman's dependence upon the man in rural Irish society and this society's acquiescence to the power of the clergy, who denounce "all developments in society that might have threatened a rigid conformism in a strictly enforced sexual code" (Brown 1985, 39). Although Joan articulates her dread of "the living world" (Murray 1998, 107), Morgan also fears the forcible power of the community; he surely knows that family disgrace is the issue over which his uncle will disinherit him.

Having broken the socioreligious code of chastity, Joan and Morgan run behind a *"screen of bushes"* (Murray 1998, 109) in the gap when Father Coyne appears. They hide with good reason, for young men and women "company keeping" in rural regions was taboo. Priests in the western counties would habitually walk these rural districts armed with sticks. They would " 'go out by night and anywhere they'd meet a courting couple they'd work the stick on them' " (qtd. in Connell 1968, 138, 113 n. 1). Nevertheless, Joan turns to Father Coyne for help.

When the priest directs Morgan to marry Joan immediately, Morgan demonstrates a remarkable ability to defend his position. Although there is no doubt in the minds of all three characters that it is the office of the priest to take charge of the situation, Morgan protests the priestly directive. Morgan is more self-possessed than Maurice Harte. Unlike Maurice, Morgan knows clearly what he wants, and he is able to state his case assertively, without being intimidated. "If I am 'tisn't the wife of a poor labouring man I'd wish the woman I'd marry to be at all. And 'tisn't a common labourer either I'd wish myself to be all my days" (Murray 1998, 113).

Morgan's desire for a life materially better than that of the elder generation affronts and stymies the priest, who is concerned for his own reputation. He, too, is a determined being, subject to anxieties about what the community will think. Inheritor of the socioreligious norms, it is now his duty to conserve and perpetuate them (Brown 1985, 40). No doubt he is also afraid of what the bishop might think about his watch over his congregation. He tells Morgan unequivocally: "Like it, or like it not, I'll not have another scandal in my parish! I won't" (Murray 1998, 113). Unfree himself, the priest takes responsibility for action out of Morgan's and Joan's power. He tells them that *he* will speak to Morgan's uncle and Joan's parents. Like Maurice, victim of his family's force, Morgan and Joan are reduced to short responses like "God help us!" and "O, Father" (114). Thinking he has done his duty, the priest has effectively disengaged Morgan and Joan from their powers of agency. He robs them of their free will, not resting until he cows Morgan into bending to his own will. Morgan eventually yields to the priest's attacks on his manhood, for he knows the priest's ability to shape community opinion. Ironically, the priest has the power to avert, or at least diminish, the scandal he so fears simply by refraining from preaching the tale from the pulpit, but his blind sense of duty keeps him from this act of charity. A member of the priestly class, he is a seer without vision. A victim, too, he is caught in the web of systemic oppression of the people. Unable to see any other course of action, he precipitates the tragedy to come.

Joan and Morgan cease to function as responsible persons. Morgan, embittered by Joan's appeal to the priest, turns against her for what he believes is her cunning (Murray 1998, 114). Although she remonstrates against his charges of manipulation, Morgan, angry at their loss and hurt by Joan's lack of trust in him, cannot recognize the pressure of the community mind on Joan. Both characters are conscious of their loss of freedom. When Morgan again assails Joan for "destroying us both forever" (115), he adverts to their loss of economic and social freedom—the loss of their farm and reputation. Joan, however, points to Morgan's loss of personal freedom: "Morgan, it isn't yourself that is so hard. It isn't you that is in it at all. It isn't surely" (116). He acknowledges his diminution in person: "It *isn't* myself. 'Fore God, you're right!" (116).

In his awareness, Morgan grows in tragic dignity. Aware of her own loss of dignity, Joan questions, "My life? 'Tis a poor thing now, God help us." When he blames her, " 'Tis as you have made it yourself," she asks, "As I have made it myself?"(Murray 1998, 116). With this question she begins to break from her blindness: she is at least dimly aware that more is at work in this complex situation. Echoing Maurya in *Riders to the Sea,* she calls herself "a straw in the wind" (114). Like Maurya, a victim of nature's power, Joan knows that she, too, is a victim. She has been able to name the social and religious forces weaving the tragic net. Morgan lacks Joan's acute awareness of the socioreligious nexus of forces—priest, family and community—determining their actions. He is unable to see, as she does, that more is at work here than his uncle's wrath.

To Morgan's mind, his only solution is emigration. He will take to the open road, a romantic symbol for personal freedom. Now he will choose it as an escape, leaving Joan behind. Unlike the tramp of Synge's *In the Shadow of the Glen* (1903), who extricates Nora from her lifeless existence by offering her the freedom of the road, Morgan deserts Joan. This marks her reversal of circumstance and her recognition of altered fortune. Joan knows full well that she will be denounced from the pulpit by the priest and that she faces a life of public ridicule as an unmarried and abandoned mother. She walks off—in the original 1914 version—to commit suicide by drowning:

> JOAN: . . . There's only the one way for the like o'me. (*Looking beyond the Gap.*) There's a great flood down there, but twill wash my sin away, maybe. 'Tis the hard penance and I so young . . . but what matter now? (*She blessed herself very slowly.*) The Lord—have mercy—on my poor soul.
>
> (*With sad quiet eyes she passes through the Briery Gap, pausing an instant half expectant, and then slowly disappearing.*) *Curtain* (Murray 1998, 117)

Both Morgan and Joan are deprived by the priest of their human birthright—their powers of agency. When the priest constrains them to make one choice only, they act impulsively. Morgan flees Glenarua, and Joan chooses suicide; both are rash, ill-considered choices. The priest, oppressor though he is, is also a victim of this world. His initial kindness to Joan on his entrance highlights his compulsive fall into the role of rigid lawgiver as the play progresses; and it is this first kindness that saves him from being relegated to the dramatic category of villain.

The influence of the continental playwrights is strong in this play. Notwithstanding the drowning scene in Boucicault's *The Shaughraun* (1879), Murray would have been familiar with the drowning in Zola's play *Thérèse Raquin* (1873), based upon his novel of the same title (1867). Murray's play manifests Russian influence in particular. The subtitle, "a little tragedy," suggests Pushkin's "little tragedies." Like Pushkin, Murray may have been attempting to sketch a tragedy in miniature, as he was to do in 1938 with *A Spot in the Sun.* Corkery had encouraged Irish writers to look to the Russian authors for models, recognizing that the Russian peasant experience was akin to that of the Irish peasantry in its harshness (Fleischmann 1992, 99).

Certainly Joan's suicide by drowning suggests Katerina, throwing herself into the Volga at the end of Ostrovsky's *The Storm* (1899). Murray might have been especially mindful of *The Storm,* as it was presented in Molesworth Hall by Edward Martyn's Theater of Ireland on 20 February 1911.

Although it is powerful, *The Briery Gap* has shortcomings. Joan's lines, While necessary to convey her overwrought state, seem melodramatic. Indeed, when Murray submitted an initial play draft to the Abbey Directorate, Lady Gregory observed that some of the dialogue before Father Coyne's entrance might be monotonous. Likewise, Yeats, in a letter to Murray written in 1914 from Stone Cottage, Colman's Hatch, Sussex, voiced concern that the play's "irredeemably painful" situation was unrelieved by any lighter moments (BC, NYPL). His reservation has been confirmed by a contemporary audience member, who claimed that had the play been full-length, he would not have been able to withstand the intensity of its gloom (Chisholm 1993).

Shortly after completing *The Briery Gap,* Murray read excerpts from the play during a lecture he delivered to the National Literary Society in Dublin on 26 January 1914 (Conlin 1952, 13). He did not disclose that he was the author, but claimed, according to Holloway, that it had been "sent him some time ago by a young man" (qtd. in Conlin 1952, 13). Murray submitted the text to the Abbey directors in late 1913 or early 1914. In an undated letter from 1914, Yeats wrote to Murray from Stone Cottage: "I think it is a powerful and sincere little play written in a vivid speech and we shall of course be glad to play it" (BC, NYPL).

A. Patrick Wilson, manager of the Abbey, wrote to Yeats on 25 January 1915 about Murray's nervousness regarding the play's production: "I had a very shaky letter from Murray when he sent back his signed agreement hoping that the play will not be allowed to go on without you seeing a rehearsal of it, thus getting your decision whether it should be risked before the Dublin public" (qtd. in Hogan, Burnham, and Poteet 1979, 364). Murray also asked that the work be produced pseudonymously because of its theme and—according to O'Mahony in a lecture on T. C. Murray delivered to the Irish Theatre Archive, at Newman House, Dublin on 17 November 1982—"the vexatious difficulties he was experiencing at the hands of his clerical manager" (Ms. 23,976:9, MOM, NLI); his request was denied. Murray informed Mooney in a letter dated 15 October 1948: "The play was never banned—not even unofficially," then adding, "but as I wouldn't agree to have it done under my own name it was shelved. You must remember that this was over thirty years ago when the theme of *The Briery Gap* was taboo in our theater" (BC, NYPL).

With a wife and five children to support, Murray feared the loss of his teaching post. In the same lecture mentioned above, O'Mahony explains: "While Yeats understood the difficulty he was unwilling to allow the production without the backing of the author's real name. He felt that if objection were raised by the public to the play, the Directors could not fight with clean hands if the authorship were hooded" ((Ms. 23,976:9–10, MOM, NLI). Though ÓhAodha contends that Murray "was denied a production when it would have meant most to him" (ÓhAodha 1961, 22), the evidence shows that Murray was responsible for this outcome.

As his new position at Dublin's Model School was free of clerical control, Murray released the play for publication under his own name after he departed Rathduff in 1915. It was published by the Dublin's Talbot Press in 1917. Yet in 1926, motivated by his own religious scruples and his fear of clerical backlash, Murray altered the original suicide ending for the play's second printing. Internationally successful with *Autumn Fire* (1924–1926), Murray was now even more prominent in the literary-theatrical world. Aware, perhaps, of his role as a leading Catholic writer, he may have yielded to his basic conservatism in revising the ending. In the revision, Joan walks off resignedly to face a bleak future.

> JOAN: There's only the one way for the like o' me. There's a great flood down there. (*She moves and pauses, held by a thought.*) But how could I face the Almighty? . . . I—I must only go on and wither with shame. (*With a great sob of self-pity, sinking on a boulder.*) God pity me, 'tis the hard penance and I so young! *Curtain* (Murray 1998, 118).

Although fifteen years later Murray wrote to O'Mahony, in a letter dated 24 March 1941, that Joan is "capable of immense passion" (Ms. 24,902, folder 5, MOM, NLI), he made himself believe that her religious formation would have acted as a brake against her suicide. "I felt that a young girl bred in our Catholic tradition would shrink from facing her God with a sin of such enormity on her soul and decide to suffer like Hawthorne's unhappy woman in *The Scarlet Letter* and thus make atonement for her fall from virtue" (qtd. in Conlin 1961, 30). Judging by this statement, it may have been that Murray was also reflecting the growing conservatism of the nascent Irish Free State. In the years after independence, the Irish Ireland movement was trying to define and solidify the unique qualities in Irish—as distinct from Anglo-Irish—culture (Brown 1985, 68). Whatever the motivations for the revision, Murray acknowledged, "My friends felt that the original was psychologically more convincing" (qtd. in Conlin 1961, 130). Murray's friends were correct; Joan's wildness and impetuosity of character, coupled with references to the flooded river—both so carefully established by Murray—point to the original ending as inevitable and inexorable. Morgan's departure is her reversal of fortune, and her dependence on him seems to preclude traveling to America or Australia alone as a viable option. Altering his original endings would become a common Murray practice as he endeavored to make his plays conform to Catholic dogma and thus please "official" Catholic Dublin. Unlike Synge, who did not care who he offended, Murray appeared restrained by his scruples.

In one of two letters commenting on Murray's initial drafts, Yeats wrote to Murray that the play dramatized "a genuine difficulty of conduct" (1914). In addition to the moral embarrassment of childbirth out of marriage, it presents an unflattering portrait of the country cleric's failure in pastoral compassion. Despite the apparent validity of Frank O'Connor's claim that Murray was "afeared o' the priests" (qtd. in ÓhAodha 1974, 73), Murray was bold in his critique of Father Coyne, and his courage is indisputable, for he knew the play would be widely read once the Talbot Press published it in 1917. Critic Andrew E. Malone offered in 1929: "It ought to have a chance of being seen on the stage, but Ireland has not yet reached the plane whereon moral questions can be discussed openly. *The Briery Gap* will make many weep and many more think" (1965, 191). The "many more" who might have been made to think were, indubitably, these moralizing priests. "I thought myself," wrote Murray in a letter to Ria Mooney on 15 October 1948, "—and still think—the little piece as moral as one of the parables. Its lesson shouts at you" (BC, NYPL). But Ireland was not prepared to hear, much less learn, the lesson in 1914.

*The Briery Gap* did not reach the stage for some years. Directed by J. J. Hayes, it was presented, with two other one-act plays, in a single private performance on 20 May 1928, by the Catholic Writers Guild at the Peacock Theater. In a review published the following day in the *Irish Independent,* the critic said, "The plays were admirably produced" ("Three New Plays" 1928). *The Briery Gap* received its first public production by an amateur dramatic society from Glenties. Directed by Mathew O'Mahony, it was presented in 1941 at a drama festival held in Sligo. It was an acclaimed production. Offering congratulations to O'Mahony on 22 April 1941, Murray wrote: "I need hardly say that reading the wonderful tribute of [Michael] Farrell was quite a thrill. It brought Glenties with a swing right into the limelight for it was reported in both *Indep.* & *Press* [sic]" (Ms. 24,902, folder 5, MOM, NLI).

The success of the Sligo production may have prepared the way for the first public performances of *The Briery Gap* by the Abbey seven years later, when it was presented at the Peacock Theatre by the Abbey Experimental Theatre supervised by Ria Mooney. Directed by Tomás MacAnna, the play received six performances, 25–30 October 1948, on a bill with two other one-act plays (*Abbey Theatre Playbook* n.d., 9). Invited by Ria Mooney to attend the final dress rehearsal of this production, Murray found himself delighted. "Every speech, every gesture, every pause rang true," he wrote the next morning (26 October 1948) to Mooney, tendering special praise to MacAnna "for his inspired direction" (BC, NYPL). Saying little of the play, the *Irish Independent* in "New Abbey Actors at the Peacock" reported on 27 October that, "[c]omposed exclusively of probationers," these plays were performed "with marked success" (1948). The production was not reviewed by *The Irish Times.* Though MacAnna later claimed in an interview that in 1948 he restored the original suicide ending of 1917 (1992), the Abbey Theatre text from 1948, both the printed typescript and its microfilm copy, is mysteriously incomplete, leaving one to wonder if this deletion of the final scene was intentional. The text, held among the Abbey Theatre Papers, appears to be either the director/prompt copy or an actor copy for the part of Father Coyne, as there are several emendations to his lines (Ms. 21 and 42 and microfilm P. 7386–87, AT, NLI).

*The Briery Gap* did not appear again at the Abbey until 1973, the centenary of Murray's birth. Directed by Vincent Dowling, it was presented, yet again, on the Peacock Theatre stage on 26 February and 3 March as part of the Abbey's "Experiment 73" series. Dowling used the play to attack the government's ban on abortion. In "Double Bill at the Peacock," published in *The*

*Irish Times* on 27 February 1973, David Nowlan reported that Dowling created an epilogue to the play that was read over the Peacock Theatre sound system moments after the curtain fell. The tape-recorded message decried, "how we drive unmarried girls to England to have either abortions or illegitimate babies" (Nowlan 1973, 16). The afterpiece pleaded "quite directly for the provision of contraception services and for more sympathetic understanding of the unmarried mother" and suggested "that the community ought to accept more readily the traveling people for the people they are." Nowlan reasserted that the play was really "about how Roman Catholic rural Irish priests did their best to prove that their God was not the God of love." Tomás MacAnna recalls that others, including himself, were critical of Dowling's handling of Murray's material, saying of the epilogue, "The play doesn't need it" (MacAnna 1992).

Murray's irritation with oppressive country priests was sparked by the aftermath of *Maurice Harte*. His anger grew so great that he addressed clerical injustice more fully in his next play. Morgan's defiant remarks to the priest in *The Briery Gap* evolved into Charles Drennan's major protest in *The Serf*. Murray's warts-and-all priestly portrait may well have provided the models for the procession of priests one finds in Paul Vincent Carroll's plays: Father Duffy in *Things That Are Caesar's* (1932), Canon Skerritt in *Shadow and Substance* (1937), and Father Shaughnessy in *The White Steed* (1939). Father Coyne may also have been the ancestor of Sean O'Casey's Father Domineer in *Cock-A-Doodle Dandy* (1949). Priests condemning parishioners from the pulpit are seen most recently in John B. Keane's *The Field* (1965; rev. 1987; filmed 1990) and in the film of *The Playboys* (1992).

*Maurice Harte* and *The Briery Gap* illustrate how priests, families, and communities in rural Ireland frustrated the lives of young country men and women, acting as a deterrent to autonomous action. By the end of *Maurice Harte*, *Sovereign Love*, and *The Briery Gap*, the young people are rendered speechless and powerless before the dominating authority figures. Only Morgan in *The Briery Gap* makes an attempt to confront the priest's power. "It is the psychological restraint imposed on the peasant that damns him to eternal darkness, that destroys his positive self image" (Casey and Rhodes 1977, 10). In *The Serf*, national teacher Charles Drennan rages against the darkness and begins the ascent to *Illumination*.

# 3

# Spring and Autumn

## The Middle Plays

MURRAY'S PREOCCUPATION with the theme of freedom grew stronger in the years following the writing of *Maurice Harte* and *The Briery Gap*. *The Serf* (begun in 1916 but not reaching its final form until 1920), *The Last Hostel* (c. 1921), and *Aftermath* (1922) all illustrate Murray's treatment of this theme. From 1916 to 1922, Ireland was struggling to establish a national identity: the Easter Rising, the War of Independence, the Civil War, and the creation of the Irish Free State were the key political events of this era. During these years, Murray was penning statements on freedom, both civic and personal, in his plays. *Spring* (1918) began this period of Murray's creative work, while *Autumn Fire* (1924) brought his career to its critical peak.

Of the plays written by Murray during his Dublin tenure, *Spring* was the first to reach the stage. Like *The Briery Gap*, it is a "little tragedy" in one act, set in rural Cork. Another Ibsenesque problem play, it presents the plight of an elderly grandfather, Andreesh, about to be turned out of his son Seumas's house by his desperate daughter-in-law, Jude. Although the plot focuses on the grandfather, it illustrates the effects of near penury on three generations of family living under one roof. The theme was suggested to Murray by Joseph Campbell's poem "The Old Age Pensioner." Campbell (1879–1944) likens the retired farmer to King Lear, tempest-tossed and disenfranchised. After having tilled his field for fifty years, the old man is now a burden on his family. No longer productive, he is a drain on their resources. But the new pension is granting him a measure of freedom; as Campbell notes, he is "[a] Lear at last come to his own" (Murray 1926, 45).

Murray sets the scene in the Munster village of Keimaneigh, *"a lonely bog-land district"* (1926, 5), in the spring of 1908. The praise of the kind new parish priest given by Andreesh and his elderly sister Shuvawn contrasts with their discussion of Andreesh's hard life at home. Then, amidst their observation of rebirth and growth in the natural world, Murray introduces a death motif; Andreesh announces, "The thought often comes to me that—that I'll be called away in the Spring" (15). Murray uses the contrasting themes of freedom and slavery, represented by the open fields and the confining workhouse, also known as the poorhouse. Shuvawn states clearly: "The people that do be shut in workhouses and places would give their eyes out to be walking in the fields" (10). The irony is that poor Andreesh is already living in a virtual workhouse.

The primary theme of the play centers on the old man's right to quality of life despite decreased productivity. Like Ibsen before him and Arthur Miller after him, Murray clarifies the social problem as Seumas pleads for social responsibility.

> SEUMAS: (*Conciliatory.*) At best, Jude, sure 'tisn't many years the old man have to live, and if 'tis hard, this struggle to make ends meet, 'tisn't much of an extra burden he is ever.
>
> JUDE: 'Tis a heavy burden anyone is where there's seven young children to be reared and not as much as a brown penny to spare. (*Dashing the tears from her eyes.*) (Murray 1926, 20)

Seumas, Murray's mouthpiece, advances a reasonable and responsible view, ending in the play's thesis, "The old must live too" (Murray 1926, 20). It might be easy to regard Jude as a villain, devoid of any feeling for the old, except for Murray's careful presentation of Jude's plight, articulated first by Andreesh, the target of Jude's diatribe, and then by Jude herself. This presentation allows the audience to understand Jude's assertion that the old man is one more mouth to feed, that he would be better off in the workhouse. She forces Seumas to choose between herself and his father.

Soon afterward, Andreesh returns, carrying a dying lamb crushed by a stone, fallen from a fence hurdle where the sheep had been pasturing. In a touching moment important to the development of both plot and theme, Andreesh and Seumas watch with attention and tenderness as the lamb dies.

> ANDREESH: . . . There's a shivering on her now, poor thing.
> It's the death coming on her, I think. Her eyes are misting too.
> ANDREESH: Yes, you'd know she was near the end.
> SEUMAS: I can feel her stiffening now . . . She's gone.
> ANDREESH: It's well she's out of pain. (Murray 1926, 24)

Every line in this exchange affectingly reveals the native compassion of father and son, establishing them as foils to Jude, whose wrath is unleashed by the lamb's death, for which she blames Andreesh. She demands that the old man go to the workhouse. Sacrificing his own interests, Andreesh intercedes between husband and wife, keenly understanding the conditions that have reduced Jude to meanspirited, premature middle age. Fulfilling the role of the suffering servant and seer, he reawakens Jude's native kindness, which redeems her character:

> ANDREESH: Once you were kind, and 'tis only the black poverty and not yourself at all that is driving me from this roof to-morrow.
> JUDE: (*strangely moved.*) Yes, I *was* kind—I was indeed, though they'll all say I'm a hard and bitter woman now. . . . Once I could cry over a drowned kitten. . . . But the heart within me is withered labouring in the wet an' misery of this perished, God-forsaken place! (Murray 1926, 31)

Two kindly authority figures frame the play, countering Jude's hardness. The child Nora enters with word of the just passed Old Age Pension Act. A messenger of her schoolmaster, she functions as a *deus-ex-machina*, carrying the newspaper that proclaims the historic event. Just as Shuvawn quoted the new priest at the beginning of the play, Nora quotes the schoolmaster at the end: " 'Give this to your grandfather, Nora,' says he, 'and tell him I hope he'll live to enjoy his good fortune' " (Murray 1926, 33). Murray illustrates that two persons of the professional class, exempt from the basic struggle for subsistence, can afford to be kind. But the old man, bursting with joy, suffers a heart attack. In the cruel irony of life, Andreesh never lives to enjoy the hope and independence promised by the pension. As the play draws to a close, each line illustrates the essential and divergent characters of Jude and Seumas.

> JUDE: Not one brown penny of the pension now.
> SEUMAS: WHAT A GREAT STILLNESS ON HIM.
> JUDE: An' the awful cost o' the wake an' the burying. Under Heaven, what will we do!
> SEUMAS: (*Rapt.*) Like a saint he looks. The light o' God to his soul.
> JUDE: Food an' drink for a world o' people. Tobacco an' snuff. Wax candles. Broken we'll be now for ever, Seumas. (Murray 1926, 42)

As Seumas and Jude watch the life go out of Andreesh, they replicate the moment when Seumas and Andreesh watched over the dying lamb. In that scene, Andreesh, who entered carrying the injured lamb, foreshadows his own death. The lamb, a traditional symbol of innocence, comes to symbolize himself. Like Lear, Andreesh is a man more sinned against than sinning. Unless old age is a crime, the old man is not culpable. Although Jude treats him like a criminal, the government's action validates Seumas's claim that the old have rights, too.

The scene is also reminiscent of Ibsen's *Wild Duck* (1884). Murray fashioned Andreesh on the character of Hedwig, the innocent yet scorned daughter, owner of the wounded duck, who dies attempting a sacrificial act, hoping to bring harmony out of domestic discord. Likewise, Jude's reference to "a common tramp woman" having a better life than her own (Murray 1926, 20) recalls Nora in Synge's *In the Shadow of the Glen* and illustrates the marked difference between Synge's and Murray's treatments of peasant life. To be sure, Murray would never allow one of his women characters to leave home, with or without a tramp. In 1929, however, Malone roundly criticized *Spring*'s dramatic structure—particularly the element of coincidence in the plot, with news of the Pension Act arriving just as the old man is about to leave—contending that it highlighted Murray's "chief defect as a dramatist, his tendency to rely upon accidental coincidence for his dramatic effects" (1965, 191). The coincidences in the plot are undeniable; even the lamb's death, which in turn triggers Jude's climactic attack on Andreesh, is precipitated by a barking dog frightening the pasturing sheep. However, ÓhAodha, is right to defend Murray, stressing that in both *Birthright* and *Spring*, "the catastrophe is seen to grow from character," while reminding us that rural life is rife with such accidental happenings (1958, 26). The old man's death, for example, while admittedly both coincidental and melodramatic, is yet plausibly grounded in Andreesh's character. Murray's native observation of these details—not only the events, but also the characters and their language—reveals peasant life. Citing *Spring*'s enduring value, ÓhAodha says rightly that the play has not dated, noting that it "should concern us as deeply today when local authorities deplore the use of mental hospitals as homes for the old" (1974, 76). If anything, *Spring* is newly significant amid current concerns over quality of life, hospice care for the elderly, and the right to die with dignity.

Premiering at the Abbey on 8 January 1918, *Spring* proved a great critical and popular success. *The Irish Times* reviewer focused on the acting skill of May Craig, Fred O'Donovan, and Peter Nolan. The infamously caustic critic "Jacques" in the *Evening Herald* seemed to find the audience more compelling than the play, offering a wonderful sketch of an Abbey audience of the time. Observing that they freely cheered and cried at the turns of the plot, he concluded, "The players got their audience all right, and, as usual, the Abbey audience became actors, too" (Jacques 1918, 3). But upon *Spring*'s quick revival the next month, Con O'Leary in *The Leader* was almost rhapsodic in his appreciation of Murray's character drawing, which, to his delight, revealed a kind heart within the bitter nature of the wife Jude. He allowed, "In the play before us, if it is Jude who at certain moments cries out for our sympathy, that is the artist's triumph" (1918, 636). Although the little tragedy was also well received in its 1925 revival, Murray, who was often vexed by "Jacques," was irked again. On 18 March 1925, Murray wrote to O'Donnell, "[He] called *Spring* 'a Maeterlincian [sic] poem' to be a read 'sitting on the fence in the sunshine' but not acted" (Ms. 21,715, folder 10, NLI). But "Jacques" represented a minority opinion. Even in later years, *Spring* earned favorable critical appraisal. In 1937, when it was presented on the same bill with Teresa Deevy's *Temporal Powers*, a review in the 24 August issue of *The Irish Times* called the Abbey's *Spring*, "one of the most moving in their repertoire" ("Abbey Theatre: Sensitive Acting in Revival"). The review of the same day in the Dublin

*Evening Mail* offered similar appreciation: "Even if Mr. T. C. Murray had never written another play he would always be remembered by theatre-goers for *Spring*. Within the simple framework of its one act is tragedy and theatrical genius" ("Abbey Theatre's Two Plays" 1937).

*Spring* was more popular with the Abbey directors than was *Autumn Fire*. It was featured on the 1934–1935 American tour. With Michael J. Dolan assaying the part of the aged Andreesh, *Spring* was performed in Los Angeles, San Francisco, Seattle, Toronto, Detroit, St. Louis, Cincinnati, Buffalo, Providence, and Hartford, as well as Chicago, New York, Philadelphia, and Boston (American Tour Programmes). Critical comment centered on the play's somber qualities. Everhardt Armstrong in his *Seattle Post Intelligence* review of 12 April termed it "a grim one-act tragedy" (1935) and Len Shaw in the 26 January issue of the *Detroit Free Press*, "a drab, beautifully written little drama" (1935). The *San Francisco Examiner*'s "A.H." (Ada Hanifin) described it in a review on 27 March as "sustained gloom without sunshine" (1935), while Ashton Stevens, *The Chicago American* critic, lamented on 9 February, "The gloom was thicker than the brogues" (1935).

*Spring* became an Abbey standard, programmed regularly there until 1940. After its six-performance first production of 8–12 January 1918, it was given twelve presentations at the Abbey, for a total of eighty-four performances. Its last presentation was 22–27 January 1940, for six performances (*Abbey Theatre Playbook* n.d., 81). *Spring* has an honored place in the Abbey's history. In a photograph of the Abbey Theatre facade included in a history of the Abbey, one can see a billboard poster advertising *Spring* (Skelton 1971, 89). Its publishing history is also meritorious, having been translated into Irish, Welsh, and Japanese, and printed in braille. Moreover, *Spring* still lives in the public mind. It is one of the two plays recalled by the knowledgeable native Irish theater lover at the mention of Murray's name: "T. C. Murray? . . . Ah, yes, *Spring* and *Autumn [Fire]*!" (1992).

Announcing the arrival of a new manuscript, Yeats wrote to Lady Gregory in an undated letter, "I have sent a play of T. C. Murray's under pen-name which he has adopted for protection as he attacks the priests" (qtd. in Hogan and Burnham 1984, 256, 337n.). *The Serf* is T. C. Murray's major dramatic statement on the abuse of power by backwater priests who used their religious office to oppress their people. The play resulted from the harsh treatment Murray received from "that priest in Rathduff" (O'Mahony 1992) after the success of *Maurice Harte*. Hogan and Burnham speculate on Murray's reasons for cloaking his identity: "still a schoolmaster, it was probably politic to have his play produced pseudonymously" (Hogan and Burnham 1984, 256). The fact that, unlike any other Murray play, there are three versions of this work, each with a different title, suggests the struggle that writing this play must have been for the playwright. Murray began writing the text only after leaving Rathduff.

Autographed manuscripts of Act One, written in two copybooks signed "T. C. Murray" and dated "March 1916," show *The Cloud* as the title of the first version of *The Serf* (Ms. 24,860, TCM, NLI). The first draft of Act One, in the first copybook, outlines *The Cloud* as a play in three acts. Its date of March 1916 was a month before the Easter Rising; the undated second draft of this act, in the second copybook, bears Murray's new Dublin address, "136 S.C.R$^d$ [South Circular Road], Kilmainham." In the second draft of this act, Murray alters the act division listed on the "Characters" page; crossing out "Act III: As in Act I" with a red crayon, he transforms *The Cloud* into a two-act play (Ms. 24,860, TCM, NLI).

The undated second version, *The Underdog: A Play in Three Acts*, bears the nom-de-plume "Edward Ogilvie" (Ms. 24,861, folder 1, TCM, NLI). The revised three acts show extensive additions, deletions, and corrections in Murray's own hand. In the first week of July 1916, Murray gave Joseph Holloway a typescript of *The Underdog* to read (Conlin 1952, 15). On 9 July 1916, Murray wrote to Holloway, providing details of the play's composition: "Personally, I think the opening act particularly good, and the last act effective, but that the second act drags. This arises partly from the curious fact that the first act was written long after the other two. This, of course, involved a certain amount of reconstruction, but this was not complete enough to save this middle act from a sense of halting and unnecessary exposition" (qtd. in Conlin 1952, 15).

The third version, dated 1920, is entitled *The Serf: A Play in Two Acts* by "Stephen Morgan," and consists of two complete typescripts. The first contains many revisions in Murray's handwriting, including the autograph, "By Stephen Morgan," written on masking tape and imposed over the previous name; the second, with fewer handwritten changes, appears to be the final version that was staged at the Abbey Theatre (Ms. 24,861, folder 2, TCM, NLI).

The result, then, of three drafts bearing three titles and two pen names, the final play—*The Serf* by Stephen Morgan—boldly trumpets a theme of emancipation. In the exposition, "Persons in the Play," Murray suggests that the problem outlined in the play is writ large: *"The action takes place in Coolglash which may be found anywhere in the map of Ireland"* (Ms. 24,861, folder 2, TCM, NLI). The events transpire in the home of the Charles Drennan and in the parish presbytery. The old parish priest, Father Harold, dislikes the ideas of his curate, the newly ordained Father Owens. As the two clash, the pastor begins proceedings to get the curate transferred. The complication involves the friendship between Father Owens and Charles Drennan, headmaster of the national school, which is managed by Father Harold, as pastor. Charles, an exemplary national teacher (like Murray), has just won formal recognition from the chief inspector of education for his expertly run school (1.31).

Charles agrees to help the parishoners prepare a formal statement supporting Father Owens as he prepares to depart the parish (Ms. 24,861, folder 2, 1.23, TCM, NLI). Margaret, his wife, fears Father Harold's reaction (1.28). The parish priest in Ireland exercised enormous power, extending to every facet of society. In his book *Economics for Irishmen*, P. D. Kenny wrote that: "Useful men, good Catholics, can have their dismissal dictated by the priest, and be driven out of Ireland for nothing more than uttering their opinions on lay matters peculiarly their own" (1906, 153). A Catholic of the time recalled that teachers needed to be especially circumspect, and that customarily they supported the clerical manager "in his arguments with the common people" (qtd. in Connell 1968, 146). In W. P. O'Ryan's novel, *The Plough and the Cross,* a teacher laments, " 'We in the schools who are in the grip of clerical managers, can hardly call our souls our own, or if we try to do so it is with the prospect of dismissal before us' " (1910, 123–24). Father Harold, in fact, views Charles's charity as disloyalty to himself (Ms. 24,861, folder 2, 1.36, TCM, NLI), and he dismisses him from his post (2.38).

Charles Drennan is shown to be a proud man, refusing to accept conciliation from the priest or help from the parishioners, should either party offer it. The extraordinary demonstration of support by the parishioners makes Charles feel that he would be indebted to them, should their plea prove successful: "I'll remember how in days to come my children would have the taunt flung into their faces, 'We kept your father in his job—you can't afford to hold your head so very high maybe!' (*Passionately.*) I'd rather be whipped to a gatepost than live for that!" (Ms. 24,861, folder 2, 2.45–46, TCM, NLI). Beholden to a different master, Charles would still be unfree, with new forces determining his behavior in Coolglash.

Charles's speech is part of Murray's exposé of the national school system. Murray is also revealing the underside of village life. The "Mary Pauline" donkey story and the "brass monkey" story from Murray's Rathduff tenure inform the text of this play as well as that of *Aftermath*, written two years later. Near the end of Act Two comes the obligatory *scène-à-faire*, the necessary confrontation between Charles and Father Harold, sounding the themes of the 1916 Rising with Charles warning Father Harold "that the day of reckoning for you and for all who betray the trust delegated to them by a blind people is at hand" (Ms. 24,861, folder 2, 2.59–60, TCM, NLI). Charles confounds him by his daring.

> FR. HAROLD: How blind I have been! But God has opened my eyes. My little Catholic children—their trusting souls—. . . . To think—good Heavens! that in *my* school—
> CHARLES: (*Quietly.*) Not yours, Sir.
> FR. HAROLD: Yours?
> CHARLES: No, the people's.
> FR. HAROLD: The people's? I am the people.
> CHARLES: The people are they who have built it—who pay for its upkeep—whose children it educates—
> FR. HAROLD: And whose authority is vested in me! But I'm done with you,—and knowing the principles you hold I'll see to it that you shall never again cross the threshold of a National School—not if there were a thousand wanting teachers. . . . Leave my house! (Ms. 24,861, folder 2, 2.60–61, TCM, NLI)

This scene illustrates growth in the central character from the defiance of Morgan in *The Briery Gap*. Morgan's momentary boldness is ultimately ineffective, for he gives the priest ultimate power when he abdicates responsibility, breaking from Joan and fleeing the scene. Charles's spirited argument with Father Harold is an evolution from Morgan's bitter retorts to Father Coyne. Charles manages to make important points. When Father Harold orders Charles to leave his house, the priest is defeated, unable to take the argument any further. Charles possesses the inner freedom to confront the authority vested in the parish priest, an icon of the community and the church. In this case, however, Charles speaks not as an enemy of the people but as their champion.

Father Harold, a martinet, fits almost exactly a caricatured description of "the Maynooth priest," educated at that seminary in the latter half of the nineteenth century. "He was, it was alleged, a demagogue, coming for the most part from the lower ranks of society, more interested in political leadership than in spiritual ministration" (Corish 1985, 162). It is generally held that the education received at Maynooth was "narrow" and could not compare with that received at a university (230).

At the play's end, Father Owens returns as a *deus-ex-machina,* reversing the fortunes of Charles and Father Harold (Ms. 24,861, folder 2, 2.61, TCM, NLI). Owens comes to deliver Charles from his demoralizing predicament with an all-important prop, a letter from the wise bishop, stating that he has appointed Charles to the headmaster's position in the bishop's own school (2.63). Father Harold storms out in melodramatic, villainous defeat. A short dénouement closes the act. Murray echoes the sentiments of national independence as Margaret restates the theme: "Charles at best was only a serf here. Now a new world shines before us" (2.66).

Hogan and Burnham record that once word of the drama's subject matter became public, Joseph Power in the *Evening Telegraph* suggested the possibility of "trouble" along the lines of a notorious Abbey riot (Hogan and Burnham 1984, 257–58). However, two performers interviewed before the premiere by Power believed that nothing in the play's text would cause difficulty. Hogan and Burnham report that Murray took pains to have a conciliatory letter, signed "Stephen Morgan," mailed to Power from England. It was designed, no doubt, to deflect undue attention from himself since—as O'Mahony claimed in a lecture on T. C. Murray given on 17 November 1982—the play's true authorship "was almost an open secret by then" (Ms. 23,976:10, MOM, NLI). In the letter, dated 18 September 1920, Murray, alias "Morgan," wrote in part: "Unless Abbey audiences have lost their characteristic good sense and clear judgment, there will be no 'furor.' There is not a sentence from the opening passage to the last in the play to which offence could be taken on the grounds either of religion or nationality by the most sensitive intelligence" (qtd. in Hogan and Burnham 1984, 257). Despite such sentiments, the fact that Murray wrote the letter shows that he knew that much in the drama could be incendiary.

As early as 9 July 1916, when he sent the script of *The Underdog* to Holloway, Murray wrote of his intention "to get it produced under a pen name. You will see at a glance how many and serious are the reasons which urge me to this course" (qtd. in Conlin 1952, 16). Strained relations between clerics, depicted on the stage, would have been enough to raise Dublin eyebrows, and might even have been viewed by some in Catholic Church circles as scandalous. Added to this was the public awareness that "two incidents of controversy between schoolteachers and local clergy had occurred at Coole and Achill" (Conlin 1952, 16). Conlin continues: "Some in the first night audience felt that the author was most timely with his plot" (16).

Murray stated in his pseudonymous letter to Joseph Power that he had intended in *The Serf* "to put my experience into dramatic form" (qtd. in Hogan and Burnham 1984, 257). This is revelatory, for it seems to confirm that scenes from the play illumine the author's biography, offering possible pictures of the maltreatment to which he was subjected and the great uplift that he and his wife enjoyed after their own deliverance. It is difficult to ascertain the degree to which *The Serf* is autobiographical. Does the play articulate what Murray *might* have said to Father Lawrence Murphy, parish priest of Rathduff National School, without risking the loss of his position over charges of insubordination? The extreme pains that Murray took to disguise his authorship suggest that the conflict, if not the speeches, comes close to what actually transpired.

Holloway had urged Murray in 1916 to offer *The Serf* to the Abbey (Conlin 1952, 16). During the War of Independence four years later, on the evening of Tuesday, 5 October 1920, while George Edwards's operetta *The Maid of the Mountain* played innocuously at the Gaiety, T. C. Murray's controversial play *The Serf* premiered at the Abbey. That same day, Holloway reported that it "met with applause & no opposition." In his journal entry for that day, he noted that the author was called for at the curtain call, "but he appeared not" (Ms. 1857:630, JH, NLI). Holloway returned the following day—Wednesday, 6 October 1920—for a second viewing. He noted, "T. C. Murray was also about & I am told applauded *The Serf* heartily!" (Ms. 1857:636, JH, NLI). Of the play's power to strike home, Holloway observed in the same entry: "Rounds of applause greeted some of the schoolmaster's sallies against the P.P. [parish priest] in the final scene of *The Serf* as if they were melodramatic claptrap sentiments!" (641). The audience reaction offers evidence that Murray was not alone in his experience of autocratic school managers.

Regarding the performance level, Holloway observed that the play appeared "lifeless at times. The final scene well played" (Ms. 1857:641, JH, NLI). He notes with irony that one patron allowed, "Murray could have made a better drama of it" (640). Lennox Robinson, the director, overwhelmed by Abbey administrative duties at this time, may have been responsible for the "lifeless" production level (Robinson 1951, 131). The "final scene" was enacted by Abbey veterans F. J. McCormick as Father Harold, Michael J. Dolan as Charles, Maureen Delaney as Margaret, and Joseph A. Hand as Father Owens. Press reviews, as Hogan and Burnham record, were generally favorable toward the play, taking exception mostly to the ending (1984, 258–59). "T," writing in *Old Ireland* on 30 October 1920, typified critical opinion: "Though he shied at ultimate tragedy, Mr. Morgan, up to the last five minutes, showed a mastering of his art, that many a dramatist of great reputation might envy. He *understands* human beings, particularly Irish villagers, and his dialogue has almost perfect naturalness. . . . It seems small praise to give Mr. Morgan for so much very fine work, but it is all the fault of those five minutes at the end. Why, oh why, did he run away from his tragedy?" The critic for *The Irish Times* observed, "In Father Harold and Charles Drennan, he [Murray] has erected two sturdy characters" (qtd. in Hogan and Burnham 1984, 258).

In truth, each character is drawn too much in the extreme, and the melodramatic strain is strong. Charles is too righteous and Father Harold is irascible to the point of being vicious. He experiences no growth in his character. He evinces no recognition of any wrongdoing. He comes the closest to being a villain of any character Murray created. The *Irish Times* critic attributes this "lack of a softspot in the heart of the Irish priest" to "the author's fixed views" (qtd. in Hogan and Burnham 1984, 259). The priest devoid of a soft spot—unlike Jude in *Spring*—was not merely Murray's notion; it was his experience, expressed dramatically. Indeed, Murray articulates his views, by turns, through Charles and Owens. Father Owens's encomium to the bishop reveals Owens as Murray's *raisonneur* at this point in the drama. The speech recalls the end of Molière's revised *Tartuffe,* in which the messenger enters to announce the glad tidings of the all-good, all-wise, all-gracious king who reverses Orgon's dire situation by turning loss into gain. Something similar occurs in the final scene from *The Serf,* although Father Harold is not directly punished by the bishop as is Tartuffe by the king.

Hogan and Burnham observe: "Despite evidence of Murray's usual craftsmanship, one cannot but feel that his happy ending was more arbitrary than truthful, and that his method of obtaining it smacked too much of a *deus-ex-machina*" (1984, 260). While Murray's own tribulation did indeed come to a happy end, with his deliverance from Rathduff by Dr. Starkie to a headmaster's post in Dublin, the *deus-ex-machina* ending Murray gave *The Serf*—though reflecting true life—nevertheless rings false.

Likewise, the lack of complexity in Murray's characterization of the parish priest, despite its historical accuracy, makes it dramatically unsatisfying. Because Murray experienced clerical oppression directly, he knew how meanspirited a priest could be. He also knew that clerical school managers ought to exercise their office to liberate rather than to oppress. He models this behavior in the bishop. Though the play is not entirely satisfactory, it is nonetheless powerful and, in depicting aberrant priestly behavior, it may bring to mind abusive pedophile priests.

For all the complaints against the melodramatic rescue, insufficient attention has been given to Charles's psychological-emotional growth in the penultimate scene in the play. For, distinct from Murray's dramaturgy, the paramount importance of the play in this study lies in its role in advancing the consciousness in Murray's male heroes. When Father Owens arrives as messenger from the bishop, Charles has already achieved his personal breakthrough in confronting Father Harold. His interior freedom has expanded; he chooses, from a range of possible responses, to state his grievance forthrightly before the titular religious authority of the parish, who shows himself devoid of spiritual substance. With a personal victory won by Charles, Father Owens's message of professional-economic deliverance appears to be more a dénouement to the drama than its climax. It may well be that the drama does not need this scene, but Murray needed to teach "the lesson" in Father Owens' didactic exhortation.

*The Serf* is also significant as a harbinger of *Illumination* (1939), which also treated personal emancipation issues. The Charles Drennan-Father Harold conflict in the former play prefigures the father-son struggle between Charles and Brian Egan in the latter. Melodramatic though they are, the *scène-à-faire* confrontation scenes are similar, and the way in which Charles Egan storms out in defeat is identical to Father Harold's final exit. In both plays, authority figures are dethroned, although by different means.

In his undated letter to Lady Gregory, W. B. Yeats gave a negative evaluation of the play, citing lack of variety in characters and language (Hogan and Burnham 1984, 256, 337n. 32). Lady Gregory herself altered language in Murray's later play *The Blind Wolf* (Ms. 24,847, TCM, NLI). While it is true that the language in *The Serf* is not unique and the characters are unvaried, the play is noteworthy for giving the lie to the charge that Murray did not criticize oppressive forces in Catholicism. Indeed, both *The Briery Gap* (1914) and *The Serf* (1920) show Murray passing through an anticlerical stage. To depict priests, custodians of the country's mores, in an unflattering light was a highly critical action. The reviewer in *The Irish Times* rightly comments, "His [Murray's] bold treatment of the theme is sufficient enough" (qtd. in Hogan and Burnham 1984, 256). Though it lacks subtlety of character, the play reveals a political Murray, writing a thesis drama with a patent *raisonneur*. Its speeches may lack the color of idiomatic peasant language, but they are forceful and passionate. After its first standard production of six Abbey performances, *The Serf* was given three more presentations in 1921 and 1922, just as Ireland was winning its independence. Playing a total of twenty-two performances, the last presentation of *The Serf* was 17–21 October 1922 (*Abbey Theatre Playbook* n.d., 77).

*The Serf* ended one phase of Murray's use of religion in his plays. Perhaps, as O'Mahony suggests, he had succeeded in purging a bitter memory. Murray never acknowledged the play as his own, and later thought that perhaps he should not have written it, a sentiment that led him to revise the endings to some of his plays. Nevertheless, *The Serf* is important as Murray's most extensive treatment of religion as a medium of oppression. Although religion is an undercurrent in most of his plays, Murray would not use religion in thematic material again until 1927 in *The Pipe in the Fields*—and then he would use it in a different way. In *Shadow and Substance* (1937) and *The White Steed* (1939), Paul Vincent Carroll mined the vein that Murray exposed in *The Serf* almost two decades earlier.

*The Last Hostel: A Comedy of the Hour,* a one-act political spoof, is undated (Ms. 24,856, TCM, NLI). In a lecture on Murray to the Irish Theatre Archive at Newman House, Dublin, given on 17 November 1982, Mathew O'Mahony stated that Murray "never released the MS for production" (Ms. 23,976:9, MOM, NLI). The pseudonymous typescript, signed "by Thomas Daniels," shows Murray's clear autograph written on a label, pasted over what is presumably his authentic signature. Murray wrote and crossed out "136 S[outh] C[ircular] Road], Rialto Dr." on the typescript cover; though the text is undated, this address establishes that the play was written in Dublin after 1915. Its date can be traced to December 1921 through January 1922 during the Anglo-Irish treaty controversy by its announcement at the climax of "Home Rule" (Ms. 24,856, 30, TCM, NLI) and the "Dominion of Ireland" (32), lending the play its subtitle, "A Comedy of the Hour."

Depicting farcical situations resulting from British constabulary control over Irish public houses, this comedy is Murray's only play to deal explicitly with the political scene, either before or after the 1916 Easter Rising. This may well explain why Murray, an apolitical dramatist in a highly politicized climate, wrote again under a pen name. Possibly Murray intended to publish the text in a newspaper, as he did his early dramatic satire *Edward VII*. The presence of two endings, one harsher than the other, also lend strength to this theory. Murray's obsessive fear of causing a row may have prevented him from releasing the text in the furor created by the 1922 treaty, which not only failed to deliver the Irish Republic but also divided Ireland into the Free State and a new political entity, Northern Ireland.

The setting is the Star, Ned Lucy's bar in Ballinacarbery, outside Cork City (Ms. 24,856:1, TCM, NLI). As there has been no recent shipment of Beamish from their suppliers, the Lucys have not been able to serve their regular clientele legally. They have been surviving by selling Irish Dominion Whiskey, their illegal home brew (22). On nationalist principle they refuse the offer of Sergeant McAllister, of the Royal Irish Constabulary (RIC), to sell their liquor license to the British government for £300 (12–13). The Lucys would rather sell their entire establishment to neighbor Joe Ronan than to accommodate the British government (19). In Murray's send-up of national heroes, neighbor Tim Slattery, a small farmer and cattle dealer, exults: "Man alive! Think of your besting the whole British Gover'ment. There'll be songs and ballads made for you everywhere." Joe, rising to the moment, proclaims: "I've—I've never faltered yet when there was a blow to be struck for Ireland, and—though I'd like a word with herself—I'm not go'ng to falter now neither!" (20). Spoofing his own brand of tragedy, Murray creates a mock melodrama when McAllister prepares to take a sample of the illicit liquor to headquarters before revoking their license (27–28). Mrs. Lucy cries out in much the same fashion as Mrs. Harte, recognizing the loss of the family hopes attendant upon Maurice's ordination.

> MRS. LUCY: (*Distressed.*) We're ruined, ruined, Ned Lucy, this day!
> NED: You'll be sorry yet, Sergeant McAllister, for what you've done.
> MRS. LUCY: O 'tis terrible—terrible altogether!
> TIM: (*Angrily.*) 'Tis a damn shame! You're no man and you to report it. But the day isn't far off maybe when the like o' you will be swept out of Ireland like the snakes by St. Patrick. (Ms. 24,856:28, TCM, NLI)

Despite his lighthearted tone, Murray nevertheless records the cynical peasant attitude that it was considered virtuous to be "swindling the government" (Ms. 24,856:17, TCM, NLI). Moreover, Tim's speech of the hour—heralding the British "swept out of Ireland like snakes by St. Patrick"—foreshadows imminent great news. At the play's deus ex machina climax, young Doctor Brian O'Connor enters, bearing a telegram (29); as the medical officer of Ballinacarbery, he is a Greek messenger figure, similar to the dashing Father Owens of *The Serf*. Instead of bearing good news from a beneficent bishop, Dr.

O'Connor announces that Parliament in London has granted Ireland "Full Colonial Home Rule, entire control of our own Taxes, Excise, Police" (30), creating "the Dominion of Ireland" (32). Against the peasants' desire for retribution, Murray sets the conciliatory voice of Dr. O'Connor, presumably Murray's spokesperson, urging peace and charting a new vision for Ireland.

> TIM: The day of reckoning is here at last! McAllister. You have new masters now.
>
> DOCTOR: New master or old it's a man's duty to be loyal to those he serves.
>
> SERGT.: Thank you, Doctor. A police officer's duty is often painful but he must obey orders or be sent adrift. We have wives and children to consider. We must live. (Ms. 24,856:31, TCM, NLI)

This comic piece satirizes the behavior of both the Royal Irish Constabulary and the Irish peasantry. The dutiful Sergeant McAllister, in his "wives and children" speech, anticipates in comic form the dutiful police officer in Sebastian Barry's *The Steward of Christendom* (1995). Farmer Tim is coarse, direct, and exacting of McAllister, especially when the peasants get the upper hand; he expresses the disappointment of many in the land concerning the failure of the treaty negotiating team to attain for Ireland the status of an independent republic. The "alternative ending" reveals a harsher, truer disposition.

> TIM: Go to blazes, man! Seize him, men! We're top dog now. (*All but the doctor rush on him and pinion him. They put the spirits to his lips.*)
>
> SERGT.: (*After a struggle.*) Very well—I give in. You're my masters now.
>
> DOCTOR: And you'll find, perhaps, we won't be such bad ones, Sergeant. . . . .All ready now. (*They lift their glasses.*) Here's prosperity to the Dominion of Ireland!
>
> ALL: (*Clinking glasses.*) The Dominion of Ireland for ever! (*Curtain.*)(Ms. 24,856:31a, TCM, NLI)

The language and action of this second ending is more violent, as the peasants take McAllister by force and struggle with him until he, in effect, recants and, complying with their wishes, toasts Ireland, an act which moments prior to Dr. O'Connor's announcement would have been treasonous. The fact that Joe, Ned, and Mrs. Lucy, functioning as a Greek chorus, praise Dr. O'Connor's moderate voice as being worthy of one to represent them in the first Irish government, suggests that Murray wrote *The Last Hostel* as a didactic piece. Recognizing the potential for Irish revenge in this sweet moment of victory, he allows the farmers to symbolize Irish society at large and uses O'Connor to warn against retaliation, pointing a way toward higher moral ground. Nevertheless, Murray's depiction of peasant attitudes, comic or not, may have cut too close to the truth, perhaps explaining why he never released the text. Also, as the deeply divided land was moving closer to civil war, the bitter, daily reality was growing hopelessly out of tune with Murray's hopeful, hortatory lesson.

"Have you any other work on hands?[sic]. I think you should set out on another two act or three act play. You have mastered your tool now and it is a pity not to use it." So wrote Yeats to Murray from Coole Park, Gort, Co. Galway, on 11 November 1914 after accepting *The Briery Gap* for production (BC, NYPL); in a second, undated letter to Murray from Stone Cottage, Colman's Hatch, Sussex, Yeats added, "I prefer you when you are working at greater length, when you are giving yourself more time to develop your crisis" (BC, NYPL).

*Aftermath* (1922) represents Murray's first essay in the three-act form. Recalling themes of *Maurice Harte,* it is a peasant tragedy about a bookish country schoolmaster in love with a city-bred colleague, manipulated by his land-hungry mother into an arranged marriage with a rough but rich farm woman. Myles loves Grace Sheridan, a teacher from Cork City. Mrs. O'Regan disdains Grace Sheridan's city airs and treasures Mary Hogan's healthy dowry, which includes the vast farm Slievenanor. Owned by the O'Regan family for years, Slievenanor was lost through the financial irresponsibility of the late Mr. O'Regan. Mrs. O'Regan and Mary's aunt, Mrs. Hogan, conspire to match their two young people.

But Mary and Myles are very different from each other. Mary has only a rudimentary education, whereas Myles is intellectual and, like Hugh in *Birthright,* gifted in composing verse. Early in their courtship, Myles shows Grace his treasured volume, a book of calfskin-bound poems written in Irish by his grandfather, for whom Myles is named. As he did in *Maurice Harte*, Murray again uses a book as a prop device to advance, in this case, the romantic relationship of the couple. Mrs. O'Regan is deliberately rude to Grace, however, and after the latter leaves with some of Myles's books, she immediately begins to argue her case that it is time for Myles to marry. She asks Myles his age, a question that he will later use against her. Upon his answer—"Twenty-seven next St. Brigid's day"—she expresses her hope for Myles's marriage to a land-holding Ardnagreina girl (Murray 1922, 1.29). However, Myles, realizing that he is not suited to marry a farmer's daughter, states his deliberate intention to marry outside the farming class:

> MRS. O'REGAN:   (*Sharply.*) What's that you say? Aren't you a farmer's son yourself? Didn't your father's father, and all his seed, breed and generation live on the land? The love o' the soil should be as strong in you as it is in me. 'Twould be against nature if it wasn't so!
>
> MYLES:   (*Gravely.*) Marriage to me is too serious to be influenced by such a consideration.
>
> MRS. O'REGAN: Then half the world's after marrying wrong?
>
> MYLES: Maybe. I don't know. It doesn't follow. For one thing I have no intention of following the local tradition. (Murray 1922, 1.30–31)

In this exchange, Myles embodies "the lawless artist trying to escape from lawful authority" observed in Murray's work by Robert Hogan (1967, 28). Fiercely protecting her own turf, like Mrs. Harte before her, Mrs. O'Regan aggressively attempts to discredit Grace Sheridan. In the confrontation that ends the act, Myles accuses his mother of blind pride, while she issues an angry warning that Myles will know misfortune from this day forward.

*Aftermath* offers an excellent example of what ÓhAodha calls Murray's "profound criticism of country life" (1974, 76). Act Two, in particular, provides occasions for this criticism. Agnes Dillon, Grace's older, married sister and confidante, has come from Cork City to help Grace consider Myles's marriage proposal. Alone with Agnes, Grace is revealed to be full of sarcasm for her country neighbors; she criticizes her landlady, Miss Redmond, for her pretensions to gentility, quoting her observations on social stratification:

GRACE: (*Sitting down.*) Let me see. (*Indicating on her fingers.*) There's the gentleman farmer, and the strong farmer, there's your woman of six cows, and your woman of three cows—and then again—

AGNES: But your landlady, where does she come in?

GRACE: O, Miss Redmond has a very exclusive perch. You know her brother's a solicitor in Gortnacarriga—a *solicitor*, my dear. Aren't you impressed?

AGNES: Awfully.

GRACE: That's his photograph on the piano. "My brother, George, the solicitor," is served up as a relish with the table talk at every meal. Happily, however, she's on a visit to him just now. (Murray 1922, 2.42–43)

While Grace and Agnes are discussing this phenomenon, they are interrupted by Mrs. McCarthy, the village scold. Mrs. McCarthy bursts in, raging against Miss Sheridan for preventing her tone deaf daughter Bridgie from singing in the upcoming school concert.

MRS. MC CARTHY: Sick in bed she is now and a blazing fever on her all through the manes o' you, God forgive you. It's bad to be poor, but the poor will have heir revenge in Heaven with the help o' God—so they will! (*Brokenly, passing out.*) My poor little Bridgie.

(*They look at each other in dismay, then recovering break into peals of laughter.*)

AGNES: Well, I never!

GRACE: The country, my dear. A pastoral symphony. (Murray 1922, 2.49)

Although Grace's sarcasm is not far from Murray's own attitude toward life in Rathduff, which he described to Joseph Holloway in a letter written 27 June 1912 as a "bogland," Murray is criticizing the sisters' condescending attitudes to rural peasants as well as the peasants' opinions of city folk (Ms. 13,267, NLI).

In Act Two the power of the parish priest is seen once again as his action

escalates the crisis and affects the outcome. Father Henderson alters the casting of Myles and Grace in the roles of Naisi and Deirdre, the legendary, tragic
Irish lovers, in a school production. Finding this pairing unseemly for colleague teachers, he substitutes Dr. Manning in the part of Naisi and relegates
Myles to the role of the old king. A jealous Myles begs Grace to consider his
marriage proposal again, offering proofs of his love: "Look, Grace, life has a
new meaning for me since you came here. I—I feel as if transfigured. Songs
sing themselves out of my heart as out of a May morning. With you to inspire
me I may do big things some day—a poem—a play maybe—who knows?—
I—I feel like that . . . Grace, you'll—you'll promise?" (Murray 1922, 2.57).
Stimulated by their impassioned love scene the night prior, Dr. Manning also
pledges his love for Grace. When he too asks her to marry him, Grace forces
herself to a decision and, influenced by Mrs. O'Regan's threats, breaks with
Myles, engendering his recrimination against her which brings Act Two to its
climax. The situation, shaped by a meddling priest and a villainous mother, is
steeped in melodrama; Myles's language is sophomoric in its sentiment: "I'll
remember to the last hour how much you cared for me—leading me to
heaven to slam its gates against me—lifting me to the stars to fling me into the
mud like this! . . . Into the mud, Grace" (Murray 1922, 2.77–78).

Act Three opens four years later in the old Hogan farmhouse of Slievenanor. Both Myles and Grace are leading lives of disappointment. Myles, who
married Mary Hogan to spite Grace, is now of uneven temperament. Mrs.
McCarthy comes complaining again, fulfilling the function of a Greek chorus,
taunting Myles with community rumors about his behavior in the classroom:
"Now it's the whole talk o' the parish the mad rages you do be in all times. . . .
The terror is on everyone o' them, poor creatures, and under the dripping
bushes an' the wet ditches down by the river they do be mitching, afeard o'
their lives of you" (Murray 1922, 3.80). Grace's marriage to Dr. Hugh Manning has dulled her once keen literary interests. Myles remembers all the
poems he might have written with Grace as his inspiration; he alludes to
Ibsen's *Hedda Gabler* (1890), now equating the far from gracious Grace to
the murderous Hedda who burned Eilert Lovborg's manuscript. Myles tells
Grace: "You've strangled all my children. . . . The children of my fancy. They
all died unborn" (3.84). Here Murray underscores the reality that both Grace
and Myles are patently mismated to their spouses. Like Hugh Morrissey in

*Birthright,* Myles is unsuited to life on a farm; he is also unappreciative of Mary's skillful sale of the farm's oats at market. In the play's final moments, Myles speaks to his mother, repeating her question to him, posed near the end of Act One.

> MYLES: (*Suddenly.*) How old am I, mother?
>
> MRS. O'REGAN: How old? Sure you know. Thirty on St. Brigid's day.
>
> MYLES: Only so much?
>
> MRS. O'REGAN: Why so?
>
> MYLES: (*With a heavy sigh.*) I feel as old as Time itself. Thanks to my mother.
>
> MRS. O'REGAN: (*Disturbed.*) To me? What's this rambling talk? What did I do?
>
> MYLES: Do? Put out the sun, the stars, blasted everything lovely and precious in life! That's all . . . This a fine aftermath. You should be well satisfied. (Murray 1922, 3.94)

Harboring the poet's romantic drive toward freedom, Myles announces his plans to leave home in search of a happier life. He realizes that his wife Mary has been just as much a victim as he or Grace. Enslaved by fear of what the neighbors will say, Mary begs Myles to stay: " (*Clinging to him.*) What matter, what matter, Myles? I know I'm rough and common with no learning at all— a poor kind of wife maybe for the like of you. But God knows I'm fond of you, Myles. Only promise you'll not go, and look, I'll crawl on my two knees for you. Beat me—kill me—anything but that!" (Murray 1922, 3.98). Their conversation reveals a striking degree of consciousness of their emotional and psychological suffering. Though Mary is uneducated, she comes to recognize the ill-ordered nature of their relationship. This acute awareness engenders great pity for her plight. Murray's depiction of Myles's spiritual-psychological complexity is his greatest achievement in this play. The character is making a painfully difficult choice that he does not fully understand. Yet he knows he must make it at the expense of both wife and mother.

MYLES: There's but one way of escape—you see it yourself? What will it end in otherwise? I—I may return some day—who knows?—but there's a Voice crying to me all hours "Go! Go!" and I dare not disobey. (*Mary is speechless, the shadow of some dimly apprehended horror filling her mind. He lifts the latch, pausing a moment at the sound of his mother's voice.*)

MRS. O'REGAN: Go, and bring misfortune and shame on us all for ever!

(*He passes out. In the momentary pause the latch of the door is heard dropping quietly.*)

MARY: *At the closed door, desolately.*) O, Myles! Myles! (*Curtain.*)
(Murray 1922, 3.98–99)

These final moments create a remarkably bold ending for an Ireland of 1922 despite their melodrama. Though political freedom was in the air, a free personal choice of this magnitude flew in the face of societal convention. The principal characters, except for Mrs. O'Regan and Dr. Manning, grow in a tragic awareness of their situation. Reminiscent of the door slam at the end of Ibsen's *Doll's House,* Myles leaves wife and mother, sounding the latch on the door closing behind him. But the surprising note in the play is the development of the character of Myles O'Regan. Unlike Maurice Harte, Myles honors his conscience. In leaving home, the fragmented Myles is in the process of creating a new self. Speaking curiously of "a Voice," suggesting a metaphysical presence, Myles actually does what he says he intends to do. This voice, a growing whisper in *Aftermath,* will sound more forcefully in Murray's later plays. Myles, the lost poet, will find a surer self as Peter Keville in *The Pipe in the Fields* and as Brian O'Regan, the ideal self in *Illumination.*

Not surprisingly, Murray, once again fearful of giving offense, wrote an alternate ending for this scene for the 1923 revival of *Aftermath.* This fear extended to his relationships with actors as well. Writing to Holloway on 18 January 1923 regarding the changed ending to *Aftermath,* Murray remarked, "I had a note from Perrin this morning [re]newing agreement for *Aftermath.* He spoke of the matter of the alternative ending & said Dolan thought it more effective & I have written giving him permission to try it. I feared that Sara [Allgood] alone was eager for this ending inasmuch as it gave her the last big moment alone on the stage but as Dolan too wishes it there will be no danger of offending one or the other—a thing I should wish to avoid. I am very eager to see the play with the changes in the cast and this alternative curtain (Ms. 13,267, folder 16, NLI). The changed ending, as written in an autographed manuscript in Murray's papers in the National Library of Ireland, gives Mrs. O'Regan the final moment alone on stage, softening the original bitter ending by providing a dénouement (Ms. 21,412; Pos. 7386, TCM, NLI). For one thing, it alleviates the starkness of Myles's departure; even the sound of the latch closing is deleted: "*Myles passes out. The sound of his footsteps on the flag-stones dies into silence.*" After Myles leaves, Mary decides to follow after him.

> MARY: (*Going.*) The Mother O' God will guide me. She will surely. (*She passes into the night. There is a moment's pause.*)
> MRS. O'REGAN: (*Slowly, with immense self pity.*) Almighty God, you're very hard on an old woman. (*Curtain.*) (Ms. 21,412, TCM, NLI)

Mary's appeal to the Mother of God and Mrs. O' Regan's to Almighty God ensures that the play ends on a note of orthodox Catholicity. While Mrs. O'Regan is a close dramatic cousin to Mrs. Harte, she responds in a more restrained manner, even though the implications and consequences of her loss are as great. As in *The Briery Gap*, the revised ending in *Aftermath* is weaker than the original because it seems less truthful. Giving Mrs. O'Regan the final moment of the play lends her further prominence. She is a powerful character, but the final focus belongs properly to Myles because the play is ultimately about his emancipation. Notwithstanding the two endings, the same theme is invoked—of family respect, pride, and honor at the expense of personal freedom.

Directed by Lennox Robinson, *Aftermath* opened at the Abbey three days after the Anglo-Irish Treaty was signed, on 10 January 1922, with Florence Marks as Mrs. O'Regan, P. J. Carolan as Myles, and Eileen Crowe as Grace Sheridan. Christopher Morash marks it as the first Abbey Theatre production presented in a free Ireland (2002, 172). *The Freeman* of 11 January noted "[t]he clamourous calls of the audience" (qtd. in Hogan and Burnham

1992, 70). Holloway, unable to attend the premiere, wrote Murray: "I saw it last night & [sic] it pleased me & the audience from first to last" (1967, 1867:47). Jacques, usually a thorn in Murray's side, also commended the play in the *Evening Herald* (11 January 1922), commenting, "It was all exceedingly interesting. . . . The dialogue was smooth, natural, and witty at times. . . . The various characters were well drawn. . . . In its construction it coils us with each succeeding loop of interest which the author fashions around us like an expert lassoer" (qtd. in Hogan and Burnham 1992, 70). But the London critics were not so impressed. Not surprisingly, St. John Ervine—never a great Murray fan— reviewing the play for *The Observer,* found the three main characters uninteresting and unsympathetic (1923). He regretted, furthermore, Murray's loss of dramatic "force," prominent in his earlier works, noting that in *Aftermath,* "He is more intent on his argument than he is on his people" (qtd. in Hogan and Burnham 1992, 136). Likewise W. J. Lawrence, *The Stage* critic, lamented in his review of 19 January 1922 that Murray, "has ceased to be himself. . . . he is deliberately emasculating his great natural gifts, forgetful of the fact that literary polish is a poor substitute for convincing simplicity and rugged power" (qtd. in Hogan and Burnham 1992, 72). After its first production of 10–14 January 1922, for six performances, *Aftermath* received only three presentations for a total of twenty-three performances. Its last presentation was on 21–26 January 1924 for seven performances (*Abbey Theatre Playbook* n.d., 2).

Late in his life Murray had a melancholy recollection regarding *Aftermath*: "I have long been acutely aware of the wrong turning which I took, as you suggest, when I wrote *Aftermath.* I was deafened from being asked why not write of people other than those of the peasant breed? 'Being young and foolish' (Yeats) I was lured into a realm alien to my spirit—and floundered" (qtd. in ÓhAodha 1961, 24). The comments of the London critics highlight the "wrong turning" Murray notes in his work beginning with *Aftermath,* with its focus on persons from the professional class. Granted that the dialogue of the educated characters is flat, that the character exchanges are highly melodramatic, and that the character of Grace Sheridan is less developed than desirable, Murray and some of his critics have failed to recognize sufficiently the play's merits. Certainly, it ranks with *Maurice Harte* in its criticism of rural life, indeed, exceeds that of the earlier play through a wider gallery of peasant portraits. Even more important is Murray's progressive development of theme in this play. Expanding themes introduced in *The Serf, Aftermath* may be seen as a thematic transition to *Illumination*. Instead of Murray ceasing to be himself, *Aftermath* reveals the author finding himself, creating in Myles a central character moving toward greater personal freedom. Ultimately about personal emancipation, *Aftermath* was not necessarily a wrong turning for Murray, but a point of exploration. Viewed within the continuum of *Maurice Harte* at the beginning of Murray's career and *Illumination* at the end, *Aftermath* dramatizes familiar themes of self-discovery and self-determination.

Having written a new play, Murray invited his circle of friends for a first reading at Gortbeg: "I'm reading *Autumn Fire* to a few friends next Sunday evening at 7 o'clock," he wrote to Frank O'Donnell on 10 February 1924. "I'd like to have your views on it before sending it for production. I think it is fairly good stuff particularly in the third act. The other two amble along quietly enough but there is sufficient in them to carry the argument through logically, and they have gleams of quiet comedy not infrequently" (Ms. 21,715, folder 10, NLI). *Autumn Fire,* a peasant play in three acts, remains the drama for which Murray is most remembered (Murray 1998, 119–77). A tragedy with a Phaedra motif, *Autumn Fire* dramatizes a September-May romance between the older Owen Keegan and the lovely young Nance Desmond and the ensuing complications between them and Owens' grown children, Michael and Ellen.

Nance Desmond returns from the city to establish herself as a dressmaker among her native country folk of Tobarnabrosna. Act One, set in the farmhouse of prosperous dairy farmer Owen Keegan, quickly establishes a conflict between pretty, fun-loving Nance, aged twenty-two, and Owen's homely unmarried daughter Ellen, aged twenty-seven, who looks older than her years. Ellen, much like her mother before her, is ruled by a strong work ethic, which has enabled her to run her father's kitchen, henhouse, and dairy superbly. The different governing life principles of the two women cause their conversation to escalate into a row. A series of powerful, revelatory speeches, in which Ellen discloses a deep hurt, culminate in a pitious protest against her bitter fortune: "Look, because I'm plain no man ever thought to look at me. I've cried scalding tears in my heart seeing you and your like and men drawn to you as a fly in the sun. Summer nights I pass ye in the shadows o' the hedges and ye look at me going by as if myself was some poor perished creature out of a world not yours. 'An old dried-up stick,' an old hag of a beggar-woman called me this very day, and now—now you come hot on her heels to mock me—tearing the very heart out o' me!' " (Murray 1998, 1.125). The combination of Ellen's pain and her diligent husbandry—with which she masks this pain before the village—will lead her to fiercely protect her rights, as well as those of her brother Michael.

Taken by Nance's beauty, Owen attempts to impress her with stories of his recent participation in hurling contests with the men of the village half his age. He boasts of his skill and vitality: "Who's old? A man is as young as he feels—I heard a great scholar once to say that. Show me another man, east or west, that plunges into the river in October and runs round the field naked to the sky in the dews o' the morning. I tell you this, Ellen, I feel as young this minute as—as Nance Desmond herself here. I do, so help me, God!" (Murray 1998, 1.128).

As Michael is also instantly captivated by Nance, the two Keegan men quickly become rivals for her attention just as Nance and Ellen become rivals for Owen's attention. The plot is structured around these two rivalries. Both women have legitimate rights to protect and great needs to satisfy. With a widowed mother in her care, Nance is taken by Owen's successful farm and his comfortable standard of living. Should Owen wed Nance, however, Ellen will lose her place in the running of her father's household. But there is an another unspoken rivalry between the two women. While Nance easily holds a man's gaze, Ellen must endure the whispers of the neighbors over a man she lost, a man who fled with her money—if not her virtue. Jealousy, humiliation, and pride are tangled in the domestic mix.

Act Two features the revelation of Owen's decision to marry Nance over Ellen's protests. Act Three reveals Owen's stubborn refusal to listen to sound advice. Against Ellen's reminder of what happened to his own father, Owen suffers a stroke from the strain of riding a young horse to the fair. Failing to heed warnings and to respect heredity, Owen becomes an invalid. Because the doctor has advised him to put his affairs in order, Owen sends for his older brother Morgan to discuss the drawing up of his will. Morgan serves dramatically as both confidant and oracle, taking exception to Owen's plan to leave the farm to Nance when Ellen and Michael have made it what it is. Morgan also questions Owen's wisdom in sending Nance and Michael together to town on errands. In neither case does Owen heed Morgan's caution; instead, he drives his brother away. What has seemed inevitable to Morgan has already come to pass. Michael and Nance, living under the same roof, have grown passionately attracted to each other.

Yet again the climax of the plot is effected by an unseen priest, who tells Nance in the confessional that she must make Michael leave home. After Nance begs him to leave, Michael agrees, but asks for a parting kiss. Michael kisses Nance *"with passionate tenderness."* Then, in one of Murray's carefully contrived coincidents, Owen, who has struggled downstairs, sees Michael and Nance, son and wife, just as they share this parting kiss. It is a melodramatic moment, which, if not played with great care, can provoke laughter from the audience (MacAnna, 1992). When Owen confronts the pair, Michael struggles to explain their dilemma, but, as usual, Owen will not hear.

> MICHAEL: Don't misjudge us, Father. Pity, not blame, you'd have if you could only understand. We did no wrong—I—I mean —
>
> OWEN: It was the wickedest wrong that ever a whelp of a son did the father that begot him. And look, boy, look! if I had only the strength this minute I'd— (*He staggers feebly.*) But I'm crippled, God help me, and my son and my wife only mock me in my misery.
>
> MICHAEL: No, no, father. It isn't true. God knows if we could help it. What were we but straws dragged into a whirl and wrestling against it?
>
> NANCE: 'Tis true, Owen—'tis indeed. As God is in heaven —
>
> OWEN: Aye, a fine holy saint you are!—your mouth full o' prayers and your heart full o' wickedness. (Murray 1998, 3.174)

Michael and Nance, protesting their fate, recognize the inevitability of what transpired in a situation not entirely of their own making. Owen, however, blinded by bitter jealousy and wounded pride, refuses to see his own responsibility for the events unfolding before his eyes. Persistent to the end, refusing to hear, Owen drives Michael from home and turns on Nance, accusing her of cunning as Morgan does to Joan at the end of *The Briery Gap*. Quietly she accepts his anger: "Say all the bitter things you like against me. I'll—I'll listen and no word o' complaint you'll hear from my lips. To live is to suffer, and I'm satisfied" (Murray 1998, 3.176).

Moved by Nance's resignation, Owen comes close to a recognition of responsibility for his own predicament: " (*Very quietly, after a long pause.*) No, Nance, I'll not blame you. . . . There's only myself to blame. Myself. I see it now—I see it. . . . 'Fool,' they all said, 'he'll rue the day.' I laughed at that. . . . 'A couple o' years and she'll be dancing a jig with some fine young fellow on the grass of his grave.' I laughed at that too. 'Liars, every one o' them,' I said. 'Mad jealous they are because she's so high above their own bits o' women.' And now . . . God, 'twas a pity . . . a pity . . . Lave me to myself" (Murray 1998, 3.176).

Though he seems to accept responsibility for what has transpired, Owen's final "seeing" does not seem to lead to any character growth; there is no discernible learning or ennobling of character. And it is ironic, though realistic, that he would drive from his view the two persons who are only partly culpable. Bereft of lamplight, moonlight, and starlight, he sits in the darkness alone, praying his rosary beads, failing in the end to see his own complicity in the situation, reverting, quite pathetically, to blaming the others: "They've broken me . . . —son—wife—daughter. (*He pauses, looking intently on the cross.*) I've no one now but the Son o' God. (*As the curtain falls he is heard mumbling prayers while the beads pass slowly between his fingers.*)" (Murray 1998, 3.177).

*Autumn Fire* is perhaps T. C. Murray's most Aristotelian tragedy in the sense that Owen Keegan brings his house down through his own errors in judgment. While MacAnna suggests that Nance is not entirely innocent of the outcome (1992)—very possibly seeking a comfortable old age for her mother and, after Owen's demise, a farm for herself—Owen is the primary instrument in the ruin of four lives. Unlike Maurice Harte, Myles O'Regan, or any other Murray character, Owen's fall is not precipitated from a force outside him; rather it comes from within. From his youth, we are told, Owen was noted for a mad streak; he is blinded by a flawed willfulness that Ellen and Morgan have warned against. In the end, all four principal characters are alienated from each other. Four lives that were full and prospering in the beginning are dissipated.

Among scholars Malone is not alone in his estimation of *Autumn Fire* as a play "of quiet despair. . . . an exceedingly good play, one of the best plays of its time in any country" (1965, 192–93). Robert Hogan complains that Murray's profusion of short speeches prevents the play from catching fire emotionally, suggesting that Murray has substituted his celebrated structure in place of emotion. But this is not entirely fair, for he fails to note Ellen's powerful self-revelatory laments and Owen's lyrical yet boastful proclamations of manful vigor near the opening of the play (Hogan and Burnhan 1992,205–6; Hogan 1996, 160–61).

*Autumn Fire* portrays themes previously treated by Sophocles, Euripides, and Racine. However, it also bears a similarity to Eugene O'Neill's play of the same year, *Desire Under the Elms,* which followed *Autumn Fire* onto the stage. Murray, commenting on the two plays, noted: "As regards the theme, I suppose they are somewhat similar, but the treatment and the viewpoint are entirely different. I know the Irish peasant pretty thoroughly and his religion means a great deal to him" ("Cork Playwright in London" 1926). It also meant a great deal to Murray, and a more frank presentation of the sexual attraction between Michael and Nance would have run counter to the socioreligious ethos of the day, to which Murray adhered. ÓhAodha observes the similarity to Moberg's *Fulfillment* (1943) (1961, 27). Hogan and Burnham cite Sidney Howard's *They Knew What They Wanted* and note that Eugene McCabe treated the same theme for the Abbey in *The King of the Castle* (1964) (1992, 204–5). Friel did likewise in *Living Quarters* (1977). Christopher Murray discusses the differing treatments of the sexual material in the plays of T. C. Murray, O'Neill, and McCabe, noting Murray's restraint as a product of the time (1997, 171–72). Sean O'Casey spoofed the rosary bead ending in his own play, *Cock-A-Doodle Dandy* (1949).

Although *Autumn Fire* is T. C. Murray's most celebrated work, its days in preproduction did not suggest its future success. The directors of the Abbey did not seem particularly fond of the play. Lennox Robinson judged it slightly "verbose" (Conlin 1952, 17; Hogan and Burnham 1992, 184), while Lady Gregory found the play "rather heavy and machine made, but good enough to put on" (qtd. in Hogan and Burnham 1992, 202). Then, during dress rehearsals, Michael J. Dolan, the play's director and leading man, asked Murray to refrain from attending rehearsals. Murray was both hurt and annoyed, claiming that Dolan, whom he thought was miscast in the lead role, "shut me out" (Hogan and Burnham 1992, 202). *Autumn Fire* opened at the Abbey on 8 September 1924 with Dolan playing the role of Owen Keegan. Sara Allgood played Owen's daughter Ellen. Eileen Crowe played Nance, and Arthur Shields, Owen's son Michael.

Joseph Holloway was captivated by *Autumn Fire*. "Since I first saw Irving in the Dream Scene in *The Bells* I haven't been so thrilled by a scene as by Michael J. Dolan's playing of 'Owen Keegan' in the final act of T. C. Murray's great play *Autumn Fire* at the Abbey to-night. . . . The stillness of the audience almost could be felt" (qtd. in Hogan and Burnham 1992, 203–4).

Holloway also noted that Murray was not terribly pleased with the night's events. "Sara Allgood's forgetfulness put his nerves on edge, and he moved restlessly in his seat when words failed her, and the prompter was heard" (qtd. in Hogan and Burnham 1992, 204). Murray remained dissatisfied, writing to friend O'Donnell on 10 September 1924, two days after the premiere: "Now that 'the tumult and the shouting' of a first night has passed I feel that the play didn't get a fair chance. [Michael J.] Dolan was magnificent particularly in the third act. It was a supremely good piece of work. Miss [Eileen] Crowe was quite excellent in the first two acts but less so in Act III. But [Sara] Allgood was all bad all through! She spoiled the movement of the play whenever she appeared & [sic] it is something of a miracle considering the way in which she tore the text to rags that the others were able to save the situation" (qtd. in Hogan and Burnham 1992, 204). Later in the run Murray was still unsatisfied with the production given *Autumn Fire* by the Abbey. Again he wrote O'-Donnell, in a letter dated only "Tuesday Evg." 1924, "Friend Dolan gives me the hump in the last scene—he looks so repulsive. My script has it '*there is a rough dignity in the broken figure.*' There is no dignity in the Abbey Keegan. But to criticise that great man Dolan is to be anathema. Did you notice the awful interior of the Desmonds' Cottage? As you know, the modern labourer's cottage is usually quite pretty. Ah, well! ——" (Ms. 21,715, folder 10, NLI).

Despite Murray's unhappiness about the Abbey's treatment of the play, *Autumn Fire* was warmly received by both public and press. Susan L. Mitchell's review was representative. She wrote in the *Irish Statesman* of 13 September 1924 that it "is a remarkable piece of work, and will, I think, deepen its effect on audiences as time goes on." Jacques of the *Irish Indepen-*

*dent* dissented. On 9 September 1924, he wrote, "One serious fault is a lack of humour" (Hogan and Burnham 1992, 202–3). This comment may have reflected the shift in theatrical tastes from peasant drama to the urban drama of Sean O'Casey, whose Dublin tenement plays, skillfully blending large measures of comedy into tragedy, were becoming very popular with audiences.

Murray was dissatisfied with the failure of the Abbey to program *Autumn Fire* frequently enough. After the year in which the Abbey held sole rights to the play, Murray released it to the De Leon Brothers, theatrical producers in London. According to a Dublin lecture on Murray given by O'Mahony on 17 November, he also secured an agent, Curtis Brown, in England (Ms. 23,976:12, MOM, NLI). The first result was an Australian production of *Autumn Fire* which premiered at the Palace in Melbourne on 3 March 1926.

*Autumn Fire* was a great popular success for Murray in London, where it opened at the Q Theatre, operated by the De Leons, on 22 March 1926. It trumpeted a cast of recruited Irish actors, including Kathleen Drago and Una O'Connor, performers once associated with the Abbey. Hugely successful, the Q production transferred to the West End, opening at the Little Theatre, off the Strand, on 13 April 1926. The next day, 14 April, Murray, who was present for the opening, sent his friend Frank J. Hugh O'Donnell a theatrical postcard advertising *Autumn Fire*. The message, though brief, told all: "Play got a splendid reception though the playing was uneven. Very good press (save for *D[aily] Sketch*) & evening papers wonderful. Hu[bert] Griffith in *Standard* is wildly enthusiastic" (Ms. 21,715, folder 10, NLI).

Given the London acclaim, it is not surprising that the management of the Abbey began to see *Autumn Fire* through new eyes. For the first time in its history, however, it had to pay a performance fee to a licenser for a play that had originated in its own theater. Naturally, public notice rose to a higher level when *Autumn Fire* came home to Dublin in May 1926 with the original all-star Abbey cast largely intact. The company included Michael J. Dolan, Eileen Crowe, Arthur Shields, Maureen Delaney, May Craig, F. J. McCormick, Shelah Richards, and P. J. Carolan. On 18 May the critic of the *Dublin Evening Mail* reported, "Renewed interest was apparent at the Abbey Theatre last night in the reproduction of Mr. T. C. Murray's *Autumn Fire*" (*"Autumn Fire"* 1926). On the same date, the critic of the *Irish Independent* commented, "It seems to have advanced considerably in popularity since its first production here" ( *"Autumn Fire* at the Abbey" 1926).

Irish-American actor-producer John L. Shine brought *Autumn Fire* to America in a production, directed by George Vivian, that featured Irish actors. Shine, himself, played Owen Keegan. The American premiere took place at the Providence Opera House on 18 October 1926. L. E. M., the reviewer for *The Providence Evening Bulletin,* warned, "Times have changed since *Birthright* established an enviable recognition for its author on Yankee soil and not for the better, so far as the reception of plays of purely artistic merit is concerned." He suggested that the somber mood of *Autumn Fire* was "at variance with the flamboyant and frivolous style in the American theatre of our time" (L. E. M. 1926). This was, after all, "the Jazz Age."

*Autumn Fire* opened at the Klaw Theatre, New York, on 26 October 1926. *Variety*'s critic, "Wintermute," cautioned, "It is art, without any dollar signs visible. . . . It cannot be relied upon to summon the Sein Feiner from the Bronx and from Brooklyn. There is no jigging in it. But the cultured all will love it; it is a product of genius. There is much wit and humor with its sadness" (1926). In "Hibernian Domestic Affair," the reviewer for *The Wall Street Journal,* warned "that the play might fail to draw a large audience of Irish Americans in New York City due to high ticket prices" (Metcalfe 1926). *Autumn Fire* was not a popular "draw," and the production closed after a run of seventy-one performances (Salem 1979, 232). Though the production trumpeted "Irish actors," the performers were not the skilled Irish Players of the Abbey Theatre (Byrne 1929, 120). Nevertheless, judging by a letter from Theodore Johnson of the Walter H. Baker Company of Boston, MA, *Autumn Fire* was noticed in American "little theater" circles. In the letter, dated 24 October 1929, Johnson solicited Murray as a client, arguing, "It is my earnest conviction that your play, *Autumn Fires* [sic], might have a greater number of unlicensed amateur productions if it were known that the printed text was available." Warning against pirated use of the text, he added, "Such practice might easily be stopped if it were known that our office were acting as the author's agent" (Ms. 23,510, TCM, NLI). Baker's Plays became the licensor for amateur productions of Murray's plays in America.

The Abbey Theatre did not offer *Autumn Fire* in America until the 1931–1932 tour when it was seen at the Hollis Street Theatre in Boston at tour's end in April 1932 (American Tour Programmes, 1931–1932). Lennox Robinson, under whose "personal direction" the tour was conducted, may not have programmed the drama in preceding cities because the Abbey repertoire, both at home and abroad, was now marked by comedy. Though O'-Casey's *Juno and the Paycock* was widely programmed and St. John Ervine's *John Ferguson* was introduced, George Shiels's *Professor Tim* and Robinson's *The Far Off Hills* and *The White-Headed Boy* were the crowd pleasers on this tour. American audiences demanded to see the latest Abbey Theatre comedies. In a feature story, "Dublin's Abbey Theatre Rediscovers America," Jack Quigley explained that "The company was particularly anxious to play *Autumn Fire* . . . but when a college or a local committee pays the piper it has the right to call the tune" (1932).

Boston, however, was a city always appreciative of Murray's work. Robinson was told by one Bostonian that *Autumn Fire* was "the crowning event" of the tour (Holloway 1968, 2:10). The Boston press notices were, indeed, glowing. "A gem of the playhouse," said the *Boston Evening American*. The *Boston Herald* cited the "consummate workmanship." And "The play was a work of art," concluded the *Boston Traveller*. A much pleased Murray transcribed, in his perfect penmanship, extended excerpts from these lengthy reviews into one of his albums of press cuttings (Ms. 23,510, TCM, NLI).

Perhaps a result of its success in Boston, *Autumn Fire* was programmed again on the tour of 1932–1933 that opened in Hartford in October 1932. A 1932 press release in *The New York Times*, "The Abbey Players to Open Here Oct. 18," had announced that the Abbey management would present Murray's three-act play, *Michaelmas Eve*, performed with great success at the Abbey in June 1932. It did not, however, appear on any program throughout this tour. Paul Vincent Carroll's *Things That Are Caesar's* and Yeats's *King Oedipus*, along with *Autumn Fire*, supplemented the comedies in the repertory. Again the reviews for *Autumn Fire* were laudatory. The critic of the Philadelphia *Public Ledger* pronounced that *"Autumn Fire* is easily the superior of any of the more serious playhouse productions offered here this year" (Waters 1932), but the reviewer for the *Chicago Journal of Commerce* makes clear that the playgoing public, beset by an economic depression, was not in the mood for serious entertainment (*"Autumn Fire"* 1933). The critics in Chicago, New York, and Toronto underscored the grim nature of the play, yet

Henry T. Parker, critic for *The Boston Evening Transcript*, again gave *Autumn Fire* a rave review (1933).

In 1924 Murray received a silver medal for *Autumn Fire* in the revived Annoch Tailteann Games. He was quite pleased with the printed text of the play, published by Allen and Unwyn, his most steady publisher. Responding perhaps to Robinson's reservations concerning verbosity, Murray wrote Holloway on 13 July 1925, "I felt that in its final form the play was as clean & [sic] tight as it could be made" (Ms. 13,267, folder 16, NLI). The most reprinted of all Murray's plays, it was first published in 1925 and reprinted in 1927, 1952, and 1964. In 1949 *Autumn Fire* became the first play of the Irish theatre ever to be seen on American television. On 8 December of that year, Murray wrote to Terence Connolly: "I had a moment of good fortune during the last few months. *Autumn Fire* was televised in New York . . . & [sic] were it not for Uncle Sam's grabbing a big slice of the fee as Income Tax, & the Agent's following suit, I should have had a pocketful of your precious dollars" (Box 13, folder 17:27–28, TLC, JJBL). It was, moreover, optioned as a proposed film by a Hollywood studio in 1958. According to another letter from Murray to Connolly written on 6 August 1958, the screenplay was to have been written by Denis Johnston (Box 13, folder 17:27–28, TLC, JJBL). Indeed, in the 1950s, Murray continued to be amazed, writing on 22 February 1956 to his sister Mary Murray O'Donovan: "that fire of Autumn which I kindled so long ago is still burning" (Curran Family Collection). The Abbey Theatre produced *Autumn Fire* in February 1953 at the Queens Theatre for six performances. The immensity of the auditorium may have proven inhospitable to the subtleties of the text, and at least one review suggests that the actors may have been underrehearsed, as well. This was the Abbey's final presentation in English of a full-length Murray play. After its first production of 8–13 September 1924 for seven performances, *Autumn Fire* received fifteen presentations at the Abbey for a total of ninety-six performances (*Abbey Theatre Playbook* n.d., 6). The revival of *Autumn Fire* in Irish from 22–30 November 1973 was critically acclaimed. Reviewer Desmond Rushe of the *Irish Independent* lambasted the Abbey management: "It is not to the credit of our National Theatre that it should have so disgracefully neglected the centenary of T. C. Murray's birth" (1973, 24). Critic Dominic O'Riordain echoed these sentiments in *The Irish Times*: "It is a pity that in this centenary year of T. C.

Murray, such a great and original dramatist, should be shown such little honour" (1973, 10). Both Rushe and O'Riordain praised *Loam Luisne Fomhair*, translated by Michael O'Siochfhradha and directed by Tomás MacAnna. Noting "how well it has stood the test of time," Rushe observed that *Autumn Fire* "has a powerful theatrical impact. It has moments as riveting as any in more recent plays, and despite the changed attitudes of modern life, it is an engrossing human drama" (1973, 24). O'Riordain praised the "extraordinary passion and lyricism" of Murray's writing, remarking that the play "lives powerfully on stage" (1973, 10).

In recent years *Autumn Fire* has attracted new attention. In 1992 and 2000, the Abbey retained a one-year option on the professional performance rights to *Autumn Fire* (Fahy 2001). At the amateur level, in March 1992 the Skibbereen Theatre Society revived *Autumn Fire* in the West Cork Drama Festival, and in May 1993 the Dublin Shakespeare Society revived *Autumn Fire* for twelve performances in their thirty-five seat theater off Gardiner Street. In March 1999 the Sionnach Theatre Company presented *Autumn Fire* at the New Theatre in Temple Bar, Dublin; reviewer Linda Kenny observed in *The Examiner* that the seventy-seat theater was "packed with a largely young audience," and judged that the play "still resonates with realism, fine characters, and biting dialogue." Her appreciation for Murray's "finely drawn characters, firmly rooted in the clipped musical dialogue of West Cork" demonstrates that *Autumn Fire* is still eminently stageworthy (1999).

It is generally held that most of Murray's work after *Autumn Fire* was a recovering of familiar ground. For this reason, ÓhAodha marks 1924 as the turning point of Murray's career (1958, 186). Certainly, *Autumn Fire* marks the turning point in Murray's audience popularity and commercial viability at the Abbey Theatre. But it is too facile to say that his later plays were mostly retrograde for in them he explored new settings and probed themes of freedom and religion more deeply.

# 4

# The Continental Touch
## The Experimental Plays

WRITING TO SEAMUS O'SULLIVAN, editor of *The Dublin Magazine*, on 12 December 1926, Murray said that he regarded his new play, then titled *A Flute in the Fields*, as "a breaking away from the note of strong realism" that typified his previous work (Ms. 4633/726a, TCD). After *Autumn Fire*, Murray began an experimental period that encompassed his next three plays. The first of these, *The Pipe in the Fields* (1927), is a one-act play dramatizing the artistic awakening of young Peter Keville through the inspirational effect of a flute's music. In the dedication to the published edition of the play, Murray claims he wrote it in response to his nephew's plea that he write a play " 'with a very happy ending' " (Murray 1998, 179). While he was working on the play, Murray promised O'Sullivan the text for publication. *The Dublin Magazine* published *The Pipe in the Fields* in its issue of April-June 1927, prior to its stage debut at the Abbey.

*The Pipe in the Fields* centers on the nature of religious experience. In the opening dialogue, Murray establishes a visionary son, Peter Keville, in conflict with his pragmatic mother, who sees no value in Peter's wonderment at the moon. Peter wishes she could see the world "with my eyes." She responds incredulously: "That's foolish. Who could see anything with another's eyes?" (Murray 1998, 181).

Mrs. Keville's question brings into sharper focus Murray's tragic vision. The first principle of this vision is the inability of one individual to recognize and to accept another's way of seeing; the second principle is that person's unwillingness to accept the legitimacy of the other's claim, which in turn leads to

106

the latter's oppression and diminution of personhood. This dynamic is operative in *Maurice Harte*, *The Briery Gap*, and *Autumn Fire*. Mrs. Harte cannot accept Maurice's claims of conscience; Joan, Morgan, and Father Coyne cannot accept each other's motivations. Owen Keegan cannot see his son Michael's natural inclination toward Nance Desmond, nor recognize the legitimacy of the warnings of his daughter and his brother. In *The Serf,* Father Harold's inability to yield to a new order, decreed by the bishop, is pathetic rather than tragic because the priest is devoid of any redeeming quality that might be lost in a fall from station. In *The Pipe in the Fields,* Murray posits his tragic principle and transmutes it through the play's "happy ending."

Peter becomes visionary after buying a flute from an itinerant musician. When Peter plays the pipe alone in the field at night, he sees visions and hears voices in his music-making. Reality is transformed for him; the existing order of things has changed. He soon moves beyond the bounds of behavior expected by community and family. The noticeable change in him disturbs his parents, who fear he is enchanted.

Once again, the plot turns on the importance of a prop, in this case a musical instrument. In *The Pipe in the Fields,* the prop is an organic element of the story, central to its theme of artistic awakening. The field likewise functions symbolically as a lawless region, devoid of society's strictures. Mrs. Keville sees the field as a frightful place precisely because, once there, Peter moves beyond the community's restraints. Peter, however, sees it as a place of opportunity where "alone out there in the fields, music comes to me lovely an' shining" (Murray 1998, 183). Peter has a need to express himself, a need that opens him to receive a gift in this nighttime wilderness. The pipe in the fields, a religious symbol, offers Peter something which both frees him from community constraints and offers him "new life" in the gift of art. For Peter the change is life-giving; for his mother it is dismaying. Mrs. Keville, in her lack of understanding, cries against Peter's "wild fancy—rambling talk" (183), recalling the similar shortsightedness of Mrs. Harte in *Maurice Harte* and Mrs. O'Regan in *Aftermath.* For Peter the flute is like the treasure in the field or the pearl of great price, but for his mother it is a gift too dear, "costing not less than everything" (Matt. 13:44–45).

Part of the cost of the gift is the risk to the Keville's reputation, which means "everything" to Nora Keville. Mrs. Carolan, a neighbor who has heard the music, thinks it is enchanted (Murray 1998, 185). She represents the view of the community to which Mrs. Keville also subscribes, but Nora feigns ignorance of the event in order to protect her son. In doing so, she is not unlike Mrs. Clancy at the end of Robinson's *The Clancy Name,* keeping her dead son's identity as a murderer a secret from the community. The discussion of spirits points the play toward the subject of religious experience. Neighbor Carolan wonders if the music is of good or evil origin. "You'd never know, Nora. One to believe the old stories, there's nothing the Devil can't do to fool even the wise" (185). In this exchange Murray articulates something more than peasant superstition. He posits the principles of light and darkness as underpinnings of the spiritual order. He establishes the need for someone trained to interpret them to discern the source of the spirits. Discernment of spirits is an ancient spiritual practice found in both the Hebrew and Christian scriptures.

As he did in *Maurice Harte* and *The Briery Gap,* Murray uses internal narrative to supply further expository material. But in *The Pipe in the Fields,* Murray does not rely on a prop to occasion the storytelling, as he used Maurice's novel in *Maurice Harte,* and he does not place the expository narrative at the beginning of the drama, as he did in *The Briery Gap.* In this play, rather, he places the narrative midway through the plot, where it appears as a natural outgrowth of the priest's arrival, deepening interest in Peter's plight. Mrs. Keville recounts for Father Moore the story of how Peter came to purchase the fife five weeks earlier from "a tramp going the way" (Murray 1998, 188). Taking pity on the tired wayfarer, Martin invited him to dine with the family. Having no other way to repay the Keville's generosity, the tramp asks to play his pipe for them. Peter buys the flute, giving the tramp all the money he has: " 'I'm in sore need,' says he—I remember the words—'and only for that I wouldn't give it for as full a measure o' gold as you're offering silver.' 'My soul has gone into that instrument, boy,' says he, 'but the hunger has beaten me dead, and you can have it' " (188–89).

The situation and dialogue recall Synge's *In the Shadow of the Glen* (1903), illustrating why some commentators considered Murray a successor to Synge. The tramp with his pipe is the agent of Peter's self-discovery and inner freedom, just as the tramp in Synge's play offers another Nora, more willing and accepting, the romance of the road, a symbol of personal freedom.

The similarities end here, however, for the characterizations of Peter and the tramp are quintessential Murray. More in keeping with Murray's enterprise, the situation and dialogue also allude to themes of the Christian scriptures. Mrs. Keville's compulsion to work rather than to listen at the feet of the piper recalls the scriptural account of Martha and Mary (Luke 10:38–41). Murray invests spiritual significance in "the stranger," who functions like an angel-messenger: he performs divine service and departs. Murray also alludes to the parables of the treasure in the field and the pearl of great price, noted earlier. Murray's characterization of Peter recalls the man who sold all that he had to obtain the treasure in the field. Clearly, the pipe is Peter's treasure, and it leads him out to the field where he makes music. The stranger offers not the freedom of the road, but, through the pipe, the possibility of art, Peter's path to freedom.

In this play, the character of the priest takes a new turn. Murray presents him as the eagerly sought figure of wisdom in the community. Father Moore is distinctly different from Synge's grasping, mercenary priest in *The Tinker's Wedding* and is also more enlightened than any of Murray's prior priests. Having an eye for beauty himself, he recognizes Peter's aesthetic bent. Refusing to pre-judge Peter's seemingly aberrant behavior, he withholds assent to Mrs. Keville's claim that Peter's "mind's astray" (Murray 1998, 189). Instead he asserts that Peter differs from other boys in possessing an artistic eye: "He could slip a few flowers into a vase, for instance, in a way a nun might envy. . . . At Christmas he'd give little touches to the Crib that often made me look at him dumb with surprise" (189). This passage substantiates Ellis-Fermor's claim of artistic, sensitive minds in Murray's plays (1939, 192–93). As the scene continues, we also learn that Peter exhibits behavior associated with a mystical or contemplative mind. Earlier Nora told Martin that Peter had been "staring at common things as if they were miracles. Lost in a trance like" (187). This, in itself, is a definition of contemplation. William Barry and William Connolly explain that contemplation begins "when a person stops being totally preoccupied with his own concerns and lets another person, event, or object take his attention" (1982, 48). Peter possesses this capacity. Martin recalls that Peter would linger "in the middle of the fresh furrow to listen to a bit of a lark singing," and Nora remembers him "stretched on his back for hours in the ferns looking into the sky as if it was an enchanted book" (Murray 1998, 189).

Such behavior is often associated with the artist or the saint. The effect of contemplation is to lift one into a state of transcendence: "that is, of forgetfulness of self and of everyone and everything else except the contemplated object" (Barry and Connolly 1982, 49). This is clearly Peter's experience, but his parents misunderstand it. Father Moore, in his role of spiritual teacher, explains the need for discernment in the situation before taking action of any kind: "Human minds aren't human bodies, Mrs. Keville—they're finer woven. Very dull men can learn everything of the body in a few years: with the mind it's different—the wisest know very little—they're merely groping" (Murray 1998, 190). Unlike Father Mangan in *Maurice Harte*, Father Moore shows himself wise and skillful in assuaging the parents' fears, explaining that Peter's gift for music may have been latent within him: "Things long hidden in the mind, as well as in the earth, sometimes break suddenly into flower" (190).

Murray is attempting to provide a realistic basis for Peter's spiritual awakening. Thus Father Moore articulates an established theological principle found in Thomas Aquinas: *gratia supernaturam edificat*, that is, grace builds on nature. Grace, as theologians define it, is God's presence and action in the human person. Richard McBrien explains, "Grace is essentially God's self-communication to us men and women and, secondarily, the effects of that self-communication" (1981, 158). The spiritual presence works through Peter's human nature so as to transform it. The social formation that Peter received as a youth served as an environmental barrier, alienating Peter from his true artistic nature. Peter finally confides to the priest that he had always experienced "I don't know what—a dark cloud like—in my mind. When I breathed into that fife and the lovely notes came out, I felt the shadow lifting, and a light—like a clean wind—rushing into my soul" (Murray 1998, 192). Peter alludes to the Pentecost narratives in the Christian scriptures when he cites the "clean wind—rushing into my soul" (192). Peter plays the pipe for the priest to help him to see as he does. The stage direction states that Peter plays *"an evocation of the spirit of Spring. It moves at first in a slow dance, but gradually rises to a swifter, wilder movement"* (193). Thus, for the first time in a Murray play, another principal character comes to see what the central character sees. After some confusion and misgiving, Father Moore accepts Peter's visions (195). Although Mrs. Keville remains unperceiving, Mr. Keville, too, begins to grow in understanding of Peter's consciousness. By the play's end, the priest ratifies Peter's playing of the pipe and persuades both parents of its holiness as Peter goes out into the field to play a tune:

> MARTIN: He's very happy in himself, Father? Happier than us, I think?
>
> FATHER MOORE: Aye, Martin, our feet are only on the earth.
>
> MRS. KEVILLE: And Peter's, Father?
>
> father moore. Peter's, Mrs. Keville? . . . His feet are on the stars.
> (*Curtain.*) (Murray 1998, 199)

*The Pipe in the Fields* is a definite advance upon Murray's prior work. First of all, Murray succeeds in moving Peter beyond oppression to freedom. The ignorance of his parents and the wider community functions as an obstacle, repressing Peter's artistic nature and preventing him from emerging into the fullness of his personhood. Then, however, the priest makes a pastoral intervention, discerning the spirits and validating the authenticity of Peter's quasi-religious experience. Father Moore, regarded as the seer of the community, legitimizes Peter's gift saying, "It makes the night holy" (Murray 1998, 199). Father Moore is different from Father Mangan in *Maurice Harte* and Father Coyne in *The Serf*. In this play, the priest is allied with forces of growth within Peter. In his attempt to interpret Peter's experience and in his ultimate blessing of it, he stands as *raisonneur*.

*The Pipe in the Fields* also advances Murray's exploration of religious experience. Una Ellis-Fermor regards *Maurice Harte* as the beginning of Murray's treatment of "the imaginative or the mystical, highly sensitive minds" (1939, 192–93) which, she asserts, comes to characterize his work after *Birthright*. This is not entirely accurate. Although Maurice is a highly sensitive and intelligent fellow, he displays no imaginative or mystical capacity. Nor does Myles O'Regan, though he is also sensitive and intelligent. Rather, it is Peter Keville of *The Pipe in the Fields* who first displays a mystical capacity which will culminate in Brian Egan in *Illumination*. While *Illumination* develops these themes most fully, *The Pipe in the Fields* moves beyond *Aftermath* in developing the theme of self-discovery. More importantly, in *The Pipe in the Fields* Murray moves beyond the behavioral practices and customs associated with the Roman Catholic religion to explore interior religious experience, which will form the central subject of *Illumination*.

Ellis-Fermor claims further that the imaginative, mystical mind is not made "the center of study" in other Irish plays, except in Padraic Colum's *The Fiddler's House* (1919) and Rutherford Mayne's *The Turn of the Road* (1906). Through Peter Keville, however, Murray explores the mystical mind further than these other two playwrights. Colum and Mayne depict musicians who cannot resist the romantic call of the road, but only Murray delves into the mystical consciousness of his musician. William James describes mystical experiences as "states of insight into depths of truth unplumbed by the discursive intellect. They are illuminations, revelations, full of significance and importance." The mystic, James says, "feels as if his own will were in abeyance, and indeed sometimes as if he were grasped and held by a superior power" (1971, 300). This description definitely fits Peter Keville.

Concerning the issue of religion and oppression in Murray's plays, the characterization of the priest is as significant as that of Peter. Father Moore, quite simply, is not cut from the cloth of a Maynooth educated priest. He is more than what one would expect from a country cleric. He has far more understanding of human nature and the human spirit, yearning to breathe free. He shows more awareness of God's action in the human person, luring the spirit to recognize its true human nature.

This wise, kind priest, sympathetic to art and contemplation, is really T. C. Murray's alter ego. He is Murray's meditation on what a priest might be. He is also like Murray himself, befriending, as was his wont, young artists in a country whose climate, inimical to artistic self-expression, would lead to the passage of the Censorship Act of 1929. In *The Pipe in the Fields*, the priest is necessary, ultimately, to validate and legitimize Peter's experience; in *Illumination*, no such authority figure will need prevail.

In Peter Keville, Murray has drawn his self-portrait. In a *New York Times* article, J. J. Hayes stated emphatically that Peter "is Murray himself, the boy in him who refuses to grow up and delights in the things that delight a boy" (1927). Murray was very much a romantic renegade, breaking from the common crowd of boys in Macroom and the mercantile concerns of his parents to pursue his own artistic inclinations. As Peter went into the fields, Murray turned in his early adult years to writing poetry, submitting it with success to the *Cork Examiner*; in his mature years, he ventured into remote areas of Dublin that offered him artistic nurture and sanctuary from the press of civic life: "He who would find him should seek him in the second-hand book-shops, with which Dublin abounds, or among the book barrows which take their stand along certain quays or side-streets" (Hayes 1928b). Even in the city, Murray sought the equivalent of wilderness or desert places to nurture his artistic-spiritual world. Unlike Peter, however, he assented to many of the constraints of Ireland's conservative culture, including the Censorship Act of 1929, and, though he suffered from them, to the continuing influence of priests in Irish society.

The *Pipe in the Fields* opened at the Abbey Theatre on 3 October 1927. Directed by Lennox Robinson, the play featured P. J. Carolan as Martin Keville, Eileen Crowe as his wife Nora, F. J. McCormick as Peter, and Michael J. Dolan as Father Moore. The author, popular and famous, drew crowds to the theater. "The Abbey Theatre box offices were besieged last night for seats," reviewer "M" reported (1927). J. J. Hayes concurred. "Long before 8 o'clock [sic]," he said, "every seat in the house had its occupant and the more than capacity audience sat in hushed expectancy several minutes before the curtain went up" (1927). Holloway noted: "The play gripped in no uncertain way and gave most people thrills and moved them deeply" (1968, 1:28).

The press reviews of the time were generally favorable. *The Dublin Evening Mail* announced on 4 October: *"The Pipe in the Fields . . .* was a revelation of the author's art in conveying a message of hope, happiness and cheer. . . . Mr. Murray . . . adopts unconventional methods to express his conception, and achieves his aim with conspicuous success" (*"The Pipe in the Fields"* 1927). On 8 October, critic C. P. Curran of *The Irish Statesman* described the play as like "the quiet intense unfolding of a flower. . . . The text is lit with poetry" (1927). Nevertheless, some critics felt that Murray was only partially successful in his use of expressionistic elements to capture an essentially intangible, spiritual experience. Critic "M" commented: "It is easy to see what the author aims at but it cannot be said that he hits the mark" (1927).

The *Pipe in the Fields* played for seven performances, closing on 8 October. It received five more presentations at the Abbey, for a total of forty-two performances. It was last performed at the Abbey on 19 August 1933 (*Abbey Theatre Playbook* n.d., 65). Reactions continued to be generally favorable. In

1929, literary critic Andrew Malone wrote, "It cannot be said that this play is altogether successful. But it is delightful either to see or to read, and it reveals the author in a new mood" (1965, 193).

The problem with the play lies in its dramaturgical structure: Murray is not true to the world of observable reality. On the other hand, his play is about metaphysical reality, and he is true to that world in the accuracy of his description of spiritual movements within a person. Murray has really written a parable—a short narrative illustrating a spiritual truth. Notwithstanding his claim that the play breaks with his usual strong note of realism, *The Pipe in the Fields* does not go far enough in this regard. The problem lies in Murray's still largely realistic style, which makes it difficult for an audience to suspend disbelief. One wonders, for example, if the "dance of spring" would play effectively in the realistic framework Murray constructs. An expressionistic treatment of the theme may have served Murray better. One can recognize expressionistic flourishes, both in the dance sequence and in Murray's omission of a specific age for Peter. The play, in fact, might work more effectively in a presentational staging than in a representational proscenium stage. On an arena or black box stage, for example, the absence of a completely detailed farmhouse setting might enhance the symbolist or expressionistic element in the play. A table and chairs, for example, might merely suggest the farmhouse. As with medieval miracle and morality plays, such a spare staging might highlight the parabolic dimension, making it easier for an audience to recognize and accept.

Even with its shortcomings, *The Pipe in the Fields* is a luminous achievement. Murray effectively dramatizes the proper work of the artist to realize himself in the face of the uncomprehending larger community. He also dramatizes his doctrine of the true teacher, as presented in his radio talks on the nature of education. Despite his initial misgivings, the priest—in his role of chief teacher of the community—comes to see Peter's work as artist as holy. Murray sets forth his position that the making of art, and the nature of all learning, is religious in the sense of liberating the spirit.

With the rise of O'Casey's tenement studies, there began in the mid-1920s a movement away from the Irish peasant plays that had come to form the core of the Abbey repertoire. In her journal entry for 24 May 1926, Lady Gregory noted that one day Yeats had asked her what she was writing. " 'A play,' " she replied, " 'but I mustn't mention it to you because it is a peasant play. It is on the Index.' For he had been saying, 'Dublin won't stand any more peasant work' " (Gregory 1947, 264). One reason for the eclipse of peasant plays was the movement of the rural population into the cities. This gave rise to notorious slum conditions in the northern section of Dublin and explains, in part, the popularity of O'Casey's urban studies.

There were other reasons, as well, for this shift in taste. Regarding this change, a critical ÓhAodha notes that an errant idea took hold among ambitious playwrights that led to a crop of interesting yet not entirely successful works. This "erroneous idea" turned Murray from what ÓhAodha calls his "singleness of purpose," writing his plays of Irish peasant life. ÓhAodha explains: "The notion was abroad that in the future there could be no place in the theatre for plays without a measure of international significance and that the dramatist should write about . . . cosmopolitan aspects of city life or urban life or, in short, about any kind of life rather than that which the playwright knew best" (ÓhAodha 1961, 23). The push for plays with international significance stemmed from Lennox Robinson's desire to present the best of continental dramas through the Dublin Theatre League (1919–1928) which he had founded at the Peacock Theatre, the experimental stage for the Abbey. Eventually this led to the founding of the Dublin Gate Theatre by Mícheál Macliammoir and Hilton Edwards in 1928. Robinson's own plays, like *Ever the Twain* (1929) and *Church Street* (1934), manifest his serious study of European drama. Like Murray, Robinson was largely unsuccessful in his attempt to move beyond Irish life.

Murray's play with an "international" flavor was *The Blind Wolf* (1928), a tragedy in three acts inspired by a family murder in Hungary. Murray had read an account of the incident in a Cork newspaper at the turn of the century. In "An Abbey Theatre Play," an *Irish Press* column on *The Blind Wolf* from 10 March 1950, he recalled the impression the dramatic situation made on him: "Here was a story out of life that seemed to me to have something of that pity and terror which are the elements of Greek tragedy. The story sank deep into my mind. For many years it seemed to clamour so insistently for dramatic expression that I was driven, for my peace, to set it down" (Ms. 23,513, 2:122, TCM, NLI). Unbeknownst to Murray, a similar story had already been treated dramatically by George Lillo in *Fatal Curiosity* (1736); it would be treated later again by Albert Camus in *The Misunderstanding* (1944) (ÓhAodha 1961, 27). Originally titled *Spindrift* and later *The Karavoes, The Blind Wolf* is the story of Franz Karavoe, a son who had emigrated to America in an effort to help his impoverished parents, wife, and child. His family has not heard from him in years because he had been reduced to beggary in America. At last successful, he has returned home to provide for his family, only to discover from an innkeeper that they are destitute. He intends now to turn his family's sorrow into joy. Sounding much like the prodigal father in the Christian scriptures, he exclaims to the neighborly innkeeper that there must be feasting and music. He plans to surprise his family by disguising himself as a lost, wealthy traveler asking a night's lodging; he will reveal his true identity to them in the morning.

All the Murray signature dramaturgical practices are present: the bitter, black dramatic irony; the careful exposition, involving a narrative; the contrast of characters—the generous fiddler Gregory and baker Fleischmann with the niggardly innkeeper Tompa; the biblical theme—this time the prodigal son, who, returning not destitute but fabulously wealthy, prepares his own party at great price. As usual, Murray satisfies the need for plausibility; to prepare for and to render believable his family's tragic mistake in Act Two, the innkeeper's wife warns Franz that his family might not believe him because his beard and expensive wardrobe have changed his appearance so completely. What is unusual for a Murray piece is the strong note of merriment and joy introduced by Franz. This, of course, serves to heighten the dramatic irony in Act Two.

As Act Two opens, Peter Karavoe, hopeless and bitter, is preparing hemlock for himself and his wife Marina as the only solution to curb their ceaseless hunger. Daughter-in-law Elizabeth appears with a chicken she has stolen, against her better judgment, from a fat, wealthy woman. One of the most interesting moments of the play occurs at this point; Murray introduces a discussion of the rights of the poor, framing it within the natural law theology of Thomas Aquinas. Of Elizabeth's scruples about her act, Peter says, "The hungry can snatch whatever they will. It's the law of life" (Murray 1928a, 2.26). Peter's claim of wanton license, of course, prepares the way for reckless behavior to come.

"The Stranger" presently knocks at the door seeking refuge. Unrecognized by parents, wife, or child, he sits at the fire, and *"leisurely draws from his pocket some gold coins. They catch the light of the fire"* (Murray 1928a, 2.30). As the Stranger intends, Peter and Marina see the coins and grow excited. They also keenly feel the gulf that separates them from the wealth of this wayfarer, who seemingly travels the road as a whim. To them, the Stranger is "the rich man" in the parable of "Lazarus and the Rich Man" (Luke 16:19–26), who spent his days eating in luxury. Peter's bitterness and hunger make him, by turns, assertive of all rights and no rights for the poor.

In a speech filled with irony, the Stranger explains that he understands Peter's bitterness: "Once I was given to thinking like you and cursed perhaps as bitterly. But what's the use? Life's all wrong and we can't mend it. Be wise and make the best of things. Morning comes however long the night. (*Drawing a flagon and a parcel of sandwiches from his bag.*) Come, share this wine with me, old Grandfather, and 'twill cool the distemper in your blood" (Murray 1928a, 2.31). Peter readily accepts the guest's bread and wine, but fails to grasp the exhortation to hope. Peter and Marina, excited by the wine and fixated on the gold, see in the Stranger not their long-lost son, but their new-found fortune. Peter conceives the plan to kill the Stranger with an axe. And a cock crows. Peter commits the murder as Act Two ends.

Murray tries to recreate the Elizabethan world view in this play. The atmosphere leading up to the murder is filled with dark suspense and references to haunting sounds, contrasted with stillness, reminiscent of *Hamlet* or *Macbeth*. After the murder, Nature reacts to the crime. The family goat comes untethered during the night. Daughter Ilma recovers the animal, but it flees as it nears the house (Murray 1928a, 3.47).

Murray presents the religious dimension of his characters as Peter discusses the intentionality of evil. His speech, which gives the play its title, is interesting for the ethical-moral code it reveals: "The famished wolf—does He blame him for satisfying his hunger? Does He call him off? Does He blind him with a shaft of His lightning? Why should He? He made him so. He made our bodies with the same needs. If we are driven mad, must we not do as he does? If God is just, as men say He is, He cannot blame us. I have thought it out, Marina. I know" (Murray 1928a, 3.41). Murray is covering naturalistic ground similar to that which he explored in *Spring* ten years earlier. Murray posits, as Zola might, that dire poverty will reduce human persons to the level of unfeeling, wanton predators. In this play he treats the religious consciousness of Peter, left unexplored in the character of the wife Jude in the former play. Peter claims that he is no longer a human being. Driven mad by long-lasting hunger, he ceases to exercise rational judgment and action. Lacking freedom, his want determines his actions.

A motif of blindness threads through the text. Earlier Peter had accused Elizabeth of being blind to the liberty that the poor possess to take advantage of the rich. He sounds the blindness motif again in the above speech, high-lighting his deprivation, in the Thomistic sense, of an *ought good*, that is, a good that ought to be present in human persons. Peter's speech is striking for he insists that he has "thought it out." This conscious awareness renders him a tragic, rather than a merely pathetic figure. The perversion—or deprivation—of the thinking faculty leads him to faulty decision making. Ironically, he says, "You're mind's clouding, Marina." He tries to make her see that their "tasting death before it came" justified their action (Murray 1928a, 3.45). Another example of blindness is articulated by Elizabeth. The Stranger, she says, "shared his bread and wine with us at this table. Every word from his lips breathed only good will" (3.46). Murray makes the uninvited guest a symbol of the risen Christ from the Emmaus account in the Christian scriptures (Luke 24:13–23). Unlike the disciples, however, the Karavoes fail to see the God-sent presence in the breaking of the bread.

In the most bitter of dramatic ironies presented in any Murray play, Sandor the innkeeper reveals the Stranger's identity at the appointed hour the next morning. Peter Karavoe finally recognizes the enormity of what he has done. Finding no escape from their tragic error, Peter and Marina drink the hemlock prepared in the beginning of Act One.

> PETER: O woeful hour! God's hand is heavy upon us. The bruise of His finger is deep on our souls.
> MARINA: (*In anguished horror.*) My son!
> PETER: No pity on earth or in Heaven. (*He draws from a pocket the flask of hemlock. He takes a draught.*) Sleep—sleep and forget, Peter Karavoe. (*He hands the flask to Marina who takes it like one in a dream.*) Drink, drink, good wife. (*She drains the vessel.*)

PETER: So—— (*With a sense of bewilderment and pain.*) Why—
why were we born, Marina?
(*Curtain.*)(Murray 1928a, 3.54–55.)

Highly melodramatic, especially in its ending, the play is not a true melodrama as some critics facilely labeled it. Nor is it a "thriller" as some reviewers
termed it in its later, highly successful radio broadcasts. Though the characters
are the least developed of any in a Murray play, with the character of Peter, especially, being dangerously close to one dimensional, Murray strives to present Peter as a sympathetic figure, providing a rationale for his actions. He is a
blind man, but he is not a villain. In Murray's estimation, years of misery and
want have driven him to his deed. Murray was not as successful in drawing
Peter as in creating Jude in *Spring,* but he does provide enough character motivation to keep *The Blind Wolf* from descending to simple melodrama.
Robert Hogan says the play lacks "richness of texture" (1967, 28) and agrees
with ÓhAodha that the play might be more distinctive had Murray set the
tragedy in his native Munster (1961, 27). The final scene, for example, might
be more compelling and authentic had Murray used the colorful peasant
speech of rural Cork, allowing Peter and Marina to approach the eloquence of
Ellen Harte when she fully recognizes Maurice's illness and her family's ruin.

On 27 June 1927, even before sending the play to the Abbey directors,
Murray gave his own assessment of the work in his invitation to Frank O'-
Donnell to join the traditional Sunday night play-reading circle at Murray's
home: "It is not a very merry entertainment for an age of jazz but I feel it is
good theatrical stuff of its kind and gives scope to big acting to several characters" (Ms. 21,715, folder 10, NLI). Murray proved prescient, for many of the
reviews would confirm his estimation of the play. In early 1928, before its
Abbey Theatre production, Murray incorporated into the final draft suggestions for revisions made by Augusta Gregory (Ms. 24,847, TCM, NLI).
These included occasional changes of language and the suggestion to reintro-
duce the musician at the end of Act Three, a notion for which the playwright
was grateful, thanking Gregory most deferentially in his letter of 21 November 1928 for "helping so much by your suggestions. I feel that it will be a distinct gain to bring back the musician. He will now be an organic part of the

drama" (Gregory Journal, 39: 5122, BC, NYPL). Murray also provided a revised ending to Act One (Ms. 24,847, TCM, NLI).

Directed by Arthur Shields, with Michael J. Dolan in the role of Peter Karavoe, the premiere of *The Blind Wolf* on 30 April 1928 was quite successful. The critical reviews from the following day, 1 May 1928, convey the sense of expectation generated among the public. One press notice, "The Abbey Theatre," appearing in Dublin's *Evening Mail* on 1 May, reported that the theater "was taxed to its utmost capacity" for the first night performance (1928). Holloway observed that all the important critics and "everybody that was anybody in the dramatic-arty way was present" (1968, 1:33–34). In *"The Blind Wolf*: Mr. Murray's New Play at Abbey Theatre," the critic for *The Irish Times* noted the play's gripping quality: "For two hours and a half the audience, that filled every foot of space in the house, forgot everything but the stage. . . . At the final curtain the outbreak of enthusiasm was remarkable" (1928). J. W. G. in the *Irish Independent* proclaimed that Murray "gets his big effects" and observed that the play "was splendidly produced by Mr. Arthur Shields" (1928). In a later review, from 27 May 1928, J. J. Hayes shrewdly noted in the *The New York Times* that the play's subject "is one that might easily lead a less sensitive playwright into the realms of melodrama of the unrestrained kind" (1928c). Almost prophetically, Hayes averred: "The play may not have a permanent place on the stage, although it should find its way into little theaters for various reasons" (1928c). Hayes was accurate on both points. Although the play was a critical success, its popularity on the Abbey stage was not long-lived. After its seven-performance first production, from 30 April to 5 May 1928, it received only one more presentation at the Abbey, from 28 January to 2 February 1929, for a total of fourteen performances (*Abbey Theatre Playbook* n.d., 10). In his piece for the 23 June 1928 issue of *The New York Times*, J. J. Hayes reported rumors of a Broadway production, but the production never materialized. Charles Hopkins was the rumored New York producer (1928a).

In a letter to O'Mahony written 3 December 1934, Murray described *The Blind Wolf* as "terribly gloomy," its somber quality too sharp a contrast to the jazz age (Ms. 24,902, folder 1, MOM, NLI). This view is a key to understanding its performance history. Sean O'Casey's brand of tragicomedy, as found in *Juno and the Paycock* and *The Plough and the Stars*, was now tremendously popular. On 27 April Holloway wrote, *"Juno and the Paycock* is packing the Abbey each night this week" (1968, 1:33). On 3 May he wrote, "This week at the Abbey O'Casey's play, *The Plough and the Stars,* is attracting crowded houses of curiosity seekers" (1968, 1:34). O'Casey's work was re-shaping audience taste, shifting it away from unalloyed tragedy. Even O'-Casey's own new play, *The Silver Tassie* (1928)—very different from his *Juno* and his *Plough*—would fall victim to the audience expectations he himself had created.

But J. J. Hayes foresaw the success of *The Blind Wolf* in amateur circles; it was rediscovered by dramatic societies in the 1950s through a Radio Éireann broadcast. When Larry Morrow at Radio Éireann first expressed interest in *The Blind Wolf,* Murray warned him, as he related to O'Mahony on 15 February 1949, that "its production would bring maledictions on his head, that the play was one of almost unrelieved gloom, and that the majority of listeners craved for laughter, laughter all the way" (Ms. 24,902, folder 9, MOM, NLI). Much to Murray's surprise, *The Blind Wolf* proved a great success when it was produced one Sunday evening in 1949. Adapted for radio by P. P. Maguire, the broadcast triggered new interest in the play. Murray confided his delight to Mathew O' Mahony in the same letter, writing: "Since Sunday night I've got a sheaf of correspondence from people who were intensely moved by the play which has been mouldering in the Abbey archives for more than twenty years. Most surprising was one from [Thomas King] Moylan who is given usu-ally to very sober & measured criticism & who while contrasting its drama-turgy with that of those five prize radio plays describes it as 'magnificent.' Tonight, too the *Herald* radio critic puts it on the plane of the great tragedies—but that of course is the veriest nonsense" (Ms. 24,902, folder 9, MOM, NLI). A month later, on 12 March 1949, Murray wrote to O'Ma-hony: "Requests for *The Blind Wolf* have come in from six drama societies since the broadcast" (Ms. 24,902, folder 9, MOM, NLI). Near the end of the year he was pleased to note that interest in the play was still running high, writing to O'Mahony on 14 November: "There were so many applications for the play that [Thomas King] Moylan got several copies typed. It is curious that both *Michaelmas Eve* & this play, so long neglected have been attracting so many amateur dramatic societies during the past year" (Ms. 24,902, folder 9, MOM, NLI). Despite this popularity, *The Blind Wolf* was never published.

• • •

On 27 June 1927, upon completing the draft of *The Blind Wolf*, Murray wrote to O'Donnell, "After this no more tragic playwriting—so this is my swan-song!" (Ms. 21,715, folder 10, NLI). Murray himself viewed *A Flutter of Wings* (1930) as an experiment, "conceived," as he explained in a letter to Lady Gregory on 24 September 1929, "in a spirit of satirical comedy" (Removed from Gregory Journal, 41: n5646. BC, NYPL). ÓhAodha describes *A Flutter of Wings* as a play "which attempts to contrast the freedom of the city with the narrowness of the country town" (1974, 75). It concerns the struggle of rebellious Tess Luttrell to break free of her father's domination and choose her own vocational course. Thematically, the play looks back to *Maurice Harte*, but in setting and social class, as well as theme, it looks forward to *Illumination*. The new features include a so-called comic treatment of the material, a female character in rebellion, and a comfortable, middle class family in an Irish country-town setting, all of which are a sharp break from Murray's tragic peasant milieu.

Set in the home of John and Anne Luttrell, the play expresses a mood different from those in Murray's previous plays but similar to the atmosphere created by his own children during their Rathduff childhood. Presumably, the teasing and arguing of the three Luttrell children are based on the behavior of Murray's children, given Pauline Murray's description of their antics and her father's need to broker peace among them. Here too, the children are generally obedient to their father's will. But Tess, the youngest—seemingly in her late teens—is rebellious. Markedly different from her diligent, studious brother and sister, George and Helen, Tess has deliberately failed her examinations in order to avoid becoming a teacher, a career her father has chosen for her. The principal theme of *Maurice Harte*, the unchosen vocation, emerges at once. John, a clerk of Rossallen Union, is a martinet, similar to Father Harold in *The Serf*, Father Coyne in *The Briery Gap*, and Charles Egan in *Illumination* in their abuse of authority. John Luttrell has chosen the careers of doctor, dentist, and priest for his sons. The most interesting conversation in Act One, between Tess and Helen about their father, looks back to the earlier plays and forward to *Illumination*. Helen asserts that their father is "doing what he considers best for all of us" while Tess insists "I'm not made for it—

that's all that matters—though it doesn't enter into his scheme of things" (Murray [1930], 1.6).

*A Flutter of Wings* is a thesis play. Murray is recovering his own experience, recounted in *Spring Horizon,* of not wanting to be a teacher and of being forced into becoming one by his parents. When John Luttrell and his daughter Tess have their expected standoff, Tess leaves home, precipitating a major confrontation between John and his wife Anne. It is impressive assertiveness coming from a wife in the Ireland of 1930: "For thirty years I've given in to you—blindly, unquestioningly. I had no will but yours—my one wish was to please you—to serve—to make life as easy as I could for you. I asked you for little, and got little, but I was satisfied. Never yet have you heard me murmur—not even once in all those years—but this—this is too much" (Murray [1930], 1.29).

Murray, usually a master of construction, wrought his play in a rather awkward fashion. Act Two, for example, leaves the Luttrell family behind in Rossallen as Tess moves to Dublin; it opens just before noon on the next day in the home of Brian Dalton, Tess's uncle, who is recovering from heart trouble. Of all the characters, he alone is likeable throughout, and he has a great liking for his niece Tess. After she explains her row with her father, Brian assures her she may stay in his home, and, moreover, offers her a job in his law firm.

In Act Three, nine months later, Murray pursues the subject of unprofessional behavior. Shortly after the curtain rises, Tess reveals that Frank Harmon, a junior colleague in the firm, has made a drunken, amorous pass at her, upsetting her terribly. Nevertheless, Harmon comes to Dalton's residence both to declare his love to Tess and to apologize to her: "Against my better instinct I had drunk overmuch. A friend—I had done him a service—he insisted. I'm not used to strong drink. It set me burning—in every vein. I'm torn with remorse for having hurt you." She rebuffs him: "What's that to me? You've killed something precious in me—something that will never live again. Common decency should have held you from crossing this threshold. Go, please. Never let me see you again" (Murray [1930], 3.82). The dialogue is stilted. Tess anticipates Christina in *Illumination;* in this play, too, the ingenue's dialogue is stiff; the tone, strident. Both characters have male protectors as well: Tess has her uncle; Christina has her father. Despite Harmon's protestations and apologies, Dalton dismisses him summarily from the firm. A bitter Harmon leaves, promising revenge on Dalton, and the mild-mannered Harold Holland wins Tess' regard—if not her eventual hand—in the end.

Although Murray was ahead of his time in treating sexual harassment, the play's ending is unconvincing in the swiftness, both of Dalton's dismissal of Harmon and of Tess's attraction to Holland, so soon after her encounter with Harmon that "killed something precious . . . that will never live again." Tess Luttrell appears inconsistent throughout the play. She proceeds too easily from rebelliousness in Act One to demur reticence in Acts Two and Three. Also unconvincing is Murray's reintroduction of the Luttrells in Act Three; when they appear in Dublin, John Luttrell is converted from tyrant to benevolent family man, simply because he has retired from the Rossallen Union. Anne Luttrell's explanation that John's job was poisoning him supports Murray's thesis that vocational happiness is essential to a happy life, but this thesis is left unexplored and undeveloped in this play.

The Abbey Directorate rejected the play. Once news of the rejection became public, Murray was inundated with messages of support from his friends, all of which proved consoling. He confided to Joseph Holloway: "The years have cooled my blood, and I feel glad that I can take a reverse like this quite philosophically. I look at the matter in this way. I've been working for the Abbey for twenty years and have never had a play turned down till now" (Holloway 1968, 1:64–65). He shared with Holloway the reason for the rejection: "Yeats said I hadn't caught the time of life I set out to describe—and possibly he is right. . . . though I have to smile at Yeats's counsel of perfection to write another *Maurice Harte*! Were I to say to him, My dear Yeats, write another *Kathleen ni Houlihan*, I wonder what he would think of my intelligence?" (1:65–66).

The Abbey rejection of *A Flutter of Wings* proved a *cause célèbre*. *The New York Times*, in its obituary of Murray, "Thomas Murray, Playwright, Dies," called it "a theatrical sensation" (1959). The Abbey's management, in fact, took a critical drubbing in the press. In an article published in the *New York Evening Post* on 24 October 1930, P. J. Hooper proposed one expanation: "So firmly established is his [Murray's] reputation that Dublin theatre goers find it hard to believe him capable of submitting a play unworthy of an Abbey production, and the question is again raised whether the Abbey directors are not applying unduly high standards to the work of particular authors." A caption concerning *A Flutter of Wings* from an unnamed 1930 Dublin newspaper, found in a collection of press cuttings among T. C. Murray's papers, read: *"King Lear* is being produced this week by the Abbey Theatre. There is no truth however in the rumour that they have rejected a play called *Macbeth* by the same author" (Ms. 23,513, TCM, NLI). In November 1930, the *Dublin Opinion* published a cartoon beneath which ran the title "A Corner of the Abbey Churchyard." The illustration by C. E. K depicts two tombstones in front of the Abbey Theatre, beside the main entrance. On one tombstone the epitaph reads: "Here lies *The Silver Tassie.* Beloved Child of Sean O'Casey. Died 1928." The second tombstone bears the epitaph: "Here lies *A Flutter of Wings.* Beloved Child of T. C. Murray. Died 1930" (Ms. 23,513, 2:26, TCM, NLI). Another 1930 cartoon illustrates a young playwright telephoning the *Daily Express.* He speaks into the telephone: "Is this the *Daily Express?* Yes? Well, I have four or five plays here that have been rejected by the Abbey" (Ms. 23,513, 2:26, TCM, NLI). From 13 to 23 October, the play was serialized in the Dublin edition of *The Daily Express.*

The play was quickly snatched up by Hilton Edwards at the Gate Theatre, Dublin. A heartened Murray explained to Holloway his decision to give his play to the Gate: "I saw Hilton Edwards producing a scene from *Methuselah,* and I feel that he was born to make live Shaw's very abstruse meanings. It was an intellectual treat of the first class to watch him drilling his players" (Holloway 1968, 1:68). Edwards staged *A Flutter of Wings* at the Gate on 10 November 1930. The production, cast with non-Abbey Theatre actors, featured Betty Chancellor as Tess and William Dennis as Brian Dalton. Anticipation was keen and expectations high among the opening night audience, most of whom had read the play in *The Daily Express.* The *Express* critic, in his 12 November review, judged that the play "has come with complete success, through its severe (and theatrically unique) test," noting the audience ovation accorded Murray at curtain fall ("Play Which the Abbey Rejected" 1930). After its scheduled run at the Gate, *A Flutter of Wings* received no further performances. The Abbey did experience lingering fallout from its directors' rejection of *A Flutter of Wings.* Holloway reported in the new year: "The Abbey has been hard hit over the Murray rejection. Rightly or wrongly, the Abbey patrons think that Murray was villainously treated by Robinson, Yeats, and

Company. And their giving the Abbey the go-by was the most telling way they could show their disapproval" (1968, 1:71).

*Intellectuals: A Little Comedy* is an undated, unpublished play of T. C. Murray's experimental period (Ms. 24,855, TCM, NLI). Comprised of just six manuscript pages, it is really a playlet. More finished than a working draft, there are no corrections or revisions of any kind. No information is extant concerning the provenance of the piece. Internal evidence suggests an authorship date between 1932, the year of the founding of the Irish Academy of Arts and Letters and 1935, the year of AE's death. The piece is a spoof on Yeats, AE, and Lennox Robinson, the moving forces behind the Academy, who are mentioned at the end of the piece.

In "Confessional," a 1933 essay in the magazine *Inisfail*, Murray recounts one memorable meeting with Yeats, AE, and Robinson. He relates a scene of Yeats holding court: "I had once, and once only, the happy experience of intimate contact with the poet. It was in Lennox Robinson's flat—many flights up in one of those Georgian houses in Clare Street. Robinson brewed coffee—admirably too—provided food and wine, and we talked, or, to be more precise, Yeats discoursed." Murray then offers what may have been his rationale in penning his "little comedy": "I am still haunted by the memory of all that wizardry of speech which came from his [Yeats's] lips. In his great moods, Yeats must surely be the most enchanting company in the world. Words flow from him with some of the beauty of stars trembling into the firmament. Even when he gives voice to theories which have obviously no logical basis, the lyrical beauty of his speech charms into silence the challenge on your lips." At the end of the essay, Murray confesses: "I came away grieving that every syllable of it was to go unrecorded—lost irretrievably like that golden goblet of the King of Thule" (Ms. 23,513, TCM, NLI). Murray's *Intellectuals: A Little Comedy* may well be the playwright assuaging his poetic grief, giving permanent record to the lyrical wizardry he witnessed the one day he was brought within the inner circle. Murray comments satirically on Robinson and Russell, satellites of Yeats. He makes thinly veiled references to Russell's journal, *The Irish Statesman* (1923–1930), and to the Irish Academy of Letters (1932).

The scene is set in *"one of those Georgian houses. . . . Zeats, the distinguished poet; walking up and down gazing abstractedly into where there is nothing. Lobinson the distinguished playwright, is seated at a table entering into a notebook the immortal sayings of the master. Wurzelle, brown bearded, broad-shouldered, somewhat preoccupied comes in. He too is a distinguished poet"* (Ms. 24,855:1, TCM, NLI). Murray continually changes the name of the Russell character from "Wurzelle" to "Bruzelle" (Ms. 24,855:1, TCM, NLI). As the scene begins, the trio discuss Bruzelle's disturbingly understandable new poem.

> ZEATS:  (*Pausing.*) The poem that is intelligible is not a poem. Great poetry is mysticism. It is moonlight dimly perceived—a sense of beauty only half-revealed half-apprehended.
>
> LOBINSON: Excellent that. (*Entering into notebook.*) "Great poetry is Moonshine dimly perceived —
>
> ZEATS:  No, No—moonlight—moonlight, Lobinson—not moonshine.
>
> LOBINSON: Sorry. (*Zeats again moves dreamily up and down.*)
>
> BRUZELLE: My theory of poetry is precisely that of Zeats. The reader must be moved to exclaim—"It's damn clever—but what is it all about?" (Ms. 24,855:2, TCM, NLI)

Later, the piece suggests editorial differences over the space allotment given each artist in Wurzelle's *Modern Politician* [*Irish Statesman*]. Lobinson contends with Wurzelle/Bruzelle who claims that the literary community is laughing about their self-promotions and "this crowning mummery at the Academy" (Ms. 24,855:5–6, TCM, NLI). Murray may be referring here to the opening of the Irish Academy of Letters, at which it was perceived by many that Yeats rambled on interminably. Holloway records the spectacle at length in his diary (1968, 2:17–18). The little comedy ends in true wizardly fashion as Zeats prepares to exit.

> (*He moves towards the open door besides which a broom is leaned.*)
>
> LOBINSON: (*Alarmed, to Wurzelle.*) Where is he going?
>
> ZEATS:  (*Plucking the strings of an imaginary zither.*) I will arise now and go to Innisfree. (*He vanishes on a broomstick.*)

LOBINSON: (*Chanting prophetically.*) "He shall be remembered forever."

BRUZELLE: "The people shall praise him for ever."

(*Curtain.*) (Ms. 24,855:6, TCM, NLI)

*Intellectuals* is an obvious piece that shows Murray in a playful yet satirical mood. Murray never considered himself an intellectual and sometimes spoke of "intellectuals" in his letters as a breed apart. As a way of dealing with his own inadequacies, he dealt with intellectuals, as many do, by making fun of them. It was this keen sense of his own shortcomings that led him to the brink of a nervous collapse in 1949, when he learned that he was to be conferred with an honorary doctorate of literature from the National University of Ireland.

In the interval during which Murray was working on *Spring Horizon,* he became, O'Mahony avers, so taken with an idea for a play that he ceased writing the former—which he was finding intensely difficult anyway—to begin and complete work on the latter. Yet another one-act tragedy, *A Stag At Bay* (1934), is one of the few plays of the Irish dramatic movement to deal with labor unrest and strike action. In theme, mood and tone it is strongly reminiscent of Ibsen's *An Enemy of the People* (1882).

The scene is set in the row house of Roger McKenna *"in a large industrial town in the north of England"* (Murray 1934, 75). Roger is in conflict with his co-workers, who threaten him with violence because he is not joining in their strike actions. His wife, Bessie, sounding the Ibsenite theme of the individual against the community, states Murray's thesis: "You're only one against the crowd. Some of them are desperate" (76). Until recently, Roger was a leader, the man his fellows sent to face the directors of the plant when they had a grievance. Now, because he refuses to join the striking men, Roger will be the stag pursued, caught in a situation created by his own conscience-driven choices. These choices rest on a secret from his past—the fate of his sister Maura, who drowned herself after a rape attempt in South Wales, the family having emigrated from Dublin. The attacker was Jeff Williams, who now works at Roger's mill; he is, according to Roger, "the man for whose sake the men have struck work. Six hundred of them" (80).

The story provides Roger's motivation and offers pale recollections of the drowning motif and theme of moral misbehavior in *The Briery Gap*. Roger refuses to make his sister's story public and win his co-workers' sympathy; he also refuses to forgive Jeff Williams. George Evans and Sam Owens come from the works to persuade him to join their cause. But neither Owens's threats, nor Evans's reasoning can shake Roger's stand. Roger rigidly persists: "I'm ready to accept the consequences. Nothing can shake my resolve. Some day perhaps you'll understand that once in a fellow's life his loyalty to a cause may—may clash with his honour" (Murray 1934, 89). This proves to be the inexorable event. Shortly after Evans and Owens depart, a crowd advances, shouting " 'Blackleg,' 'Renegade'. . . . *A stone crashes through the window. The sound of falling glass is followed by a cheer*" (93). Roger goes out to meet the crowd and is struck dead by a stone to his temple. Two policemen bring his body inside his house, and lay it down, recalling the ending of *Riders to the Sea*.

Although it was never presented at the Abbey, *A Stag at Bay* was aired on Radio Éireann. On 5 October 1937 Murray wrote to O'Mahony of this production: "The little play . . . got over marvelously well. I was dubious about the venture and was frankly astonished at the production by Dorothy Day. She had in the cast three of the Gate players & they were perfect each in his own part" (Ms. 24,902, folder 4, MOM, NLI). Nevertheless, the play is unsuccessful. First of all, it is undistinguished in its use of language, failing to provide any of the "colored speech" for which Murray was noted in his early plays. Second, it fails in development of character. Murray painstakingly provides Roger's motivations, but despite his honorable code of conduct, he is not a sympathetic figure; his rigidity in being unable to forgive his sister's assailant in any way makes him insufferable. Murray's inability to explore him in greater depth leaves Roger a largely unlikeable character. His attitudes over sexual matters are Victorian. The character of Bessie, furthermore, is entirely undeveloped. Her calling Roger's name at curtain fall is a good example of ÓhAodha's claim that Murray's latter plays fail from lack of insight. Murray's inability to probe and universalize Bessie's loss, as Synge does with Maurya at the end of *Riders to the Sea*, is notable for the contrasting treatments of similar losses. These failures in dramatic exploration render the play essentially a melodrama.

• • •

At the end of January 1938, Murray completed *A Spot in the Sun,* another one-act tragedy, set in a sitting room in middle-class Dublin. Denis Harman, a young banker, embezzles bank funds to finance the vanity publication of his wife's novel. Rose Harman is unaware that her manuscript has been rejected by the English publisher Hornibrook's. Murray examines individual differences, both weaknesses and gifts. He contrasts the couple's characters, exploring the artistic temperament about which Denis and his parents have little understanding or sympathy. Rose was raised to love books whereas Denis was taught to value financial status. One is left to wonder why these two characters married if they differ so markedly in their outlooks and why they have not had a discussion about their core values before this point. So important, in fact, is her novel to Rose that she tells Denis: "It's a living part of myself. If it's turned down my little world goes all to pieces. Nothing will ever be the same again" (Murray 1938, 19). This extreme position is her blind "spot" before the "sun." Denis, realizing this, succumbs to his own blindness, his inability to see a woman unhappy.

Mrs. Harman tells Denis that it is his duty as Rose's husband to make her face the reality of the situation: "Deception is a bad foundation for marriage. Between man and wife there should be above all things the most absolute trust" (Murray 1938, 27). Rose returns with the important prop, the faux letter that both accepts the manuscript and perpetuates her illusions. Two messengers enter to arrest Denis, and Mrs. Harman reveals Denis's secret plan to keep Rose happy. She exposes his character weakness, *his* "spot" in the "sun": "I can see him risk even his good name to save a woman some grievous disappointment" (34). Though she has known of her son's folly and irresponsibility in dealing with his wife and his career, Mrs. Harman unfairly places the blame for her son's predicament on Rose. Before heading to the bank to attempt to clear her son's name, she tells Rose with bitterness and sarcasm: "You have matter now for a real story—not an imagined one. And remembering what my son is suffering, you might call it—*Heartache*" (36).

It is difficult to call this play a true tragedy because neither Denis nor Rose truly recognizes the mistakes they have made. Although they are stripped of their illusions, they experience little character growth. There is no expression of insight, and Rose, in particular, remains at the level of Ibsen's childlike Nora in the first act of *A Doll's House*. Mrs. Harman, in the function reserved to the priests and seers of Greek tragedy, explains the dilemma of the moment to Rose, and the matter is left there as the curtain falls. One reviewer in "New One-Act Play by T. C. Murray" (Ms. 23,510, TCM, NLI) found implausible Mrs. Harman's lecturing Rose "on the evils of novel writing" after Harman is led away: "They would surely have both been straining every nerve to pacify the bank and have the charge withdrawn"; other reviewers pointed to an opportunity for further character exploration when they suggested that the miniature drama might have been expanded to three acts (Ms. 23,510, TCM, NLI).

Murray submitted *A Spot in the Sun* to the Abbey, and, to his surprise, it was accepted two days later. Holloway claimed in his diary that Murray wrote it upon the request of Seamus O'Sullivan for a one-act play for *The Dublin Magazine* and that afterwards, Murray's wife suggested that he send it to the Abbey. Frank O'Connor, now a member of the Directorate, had been soliciting new plays by established Abbey writers to atone for their alleged discourteous treatment under Lennox Robinson's then slack tenure. O'Connor realized that the Abbey was in need of new plays. O' Connor remembered: "Though Robinson had blown cold on our two best plays—Carroll's *Shadow and Substance* and Teresa Deevy's *Katie Roche*—we produced new plays and recovered lost ground. I had gone the rounds begging for plays and had a few promises, one from Sean O'Faolain and another from Brinsley Macnamara" (1969, 189). James Matthews, O'Connor's biographer, confirms this search and suggests a liaison with Murray in the fall of 1937: "[O'Connor] talked another Corkman, T. C. Murray, into writing one [a play] despite rumors of a long-standing feud between them" (1983, 134). The play to which Matthews refers is *A Spot in the Sun*. Rather than suggesting a rapprochement with Murray, it shows O'Connor and Hunt searching for new dramatic material. According to Holloway in his diary entry of 11 February 1938, Hugh Hunt even asked Murray "if he had any particular players in mind for the parts, and he said, 'Cyril Cusack, Shelah Richards, and Christine Hayden.' It was put into rehearsal at once, and Hunt invited Murray down to rehearsal" (1968, 3:6). O'Connor and Hunt may have felt their quick action to be in the best interests of the Abbey, but this was not the case for the dramatist.

Directed by Hunt, the play opened on 14 February 1938 with the actors still unready after only a single week's rehearsal. The leading man in the shaky production was a young Cyril Cusack. Holloway had found the text satisfactory, but he deemed the production less so, "robbed of much of its dramatic effectiveness by being too casually taken and underplayed." He faulted Cusack, in particular: "[He] was the worst offender in his casual way of delivery—breaking up the continuity of his lines to make them appear mere everyday empty chatter" (1968, 3:7). The reviewers plainly thought the production theatrically ineffective. They faulted the small dramatic canvas Murray employed and the underrehearsed actors. In his review of 15 February, the critic for *The Irish Times* observed: "The 'spot in the sun,' as the play implied, was the virtue which in extremity may be vicious. . . . Unfortunately, all that Mr. Murray could offer in a single act was the prelude to it" ("The Abbey Theatre: New Play by Mr. T. C. Murray" 1938). D. S. in the *Irish Independent* remarked that audience members thought the subject was more suited to a full-length play: "In three minutes I counted seven people say words to that effect to him [Murray] in the foyer" (1938).

Murray shared his own dissatisfaction in a letter written to Matthew O'Mahony on 15 February 1938: "You have probably seen the notices by this. The play was frankly only a dubious success but I feel and most of the audience felt that it was ruined through [Cyril] Cusack who was maddeningly inept. Never once did he get within the skin of the character & he was quite inaudible even to those blessed with acute hearing. A spot in the sun implied just a single weakness in a decent man's character. The sun that Cusack created was as full of spots as if he had spiritual measles! I saw the dress rehearsal on Sunday & told him bluntly that it was my creed that every word in a script should be heard by everyone of normal hearing in the audience. He agreed in his nice way but last night he was if anything more inaudible, and presented not the Denis Harman I had in mind but a weakling" (Ms. 24,902, folder 4, MOM, NLI). Then he offered evidence of the hurried state of production, which had left the actors ill-prepared to serve the play: "The others were better but they were all in a high state of tension. Would you believe that I sent in the play only on 1st Febry [*sic*]? I thought it wo[uld] take many weeks before a decision would be made. I was rung up by Hunt *two days* later to say it had been accepted & that it wo[uld] be put on quite soon. They had a week's rehearsal and the prompter's voice was (like that of the swallow in Solomon) 'loud in the land' " (Ms. 24,902, folder 4, MOM, NLI). After the six performance first production of 14–19 February 1938, the Abbey gave no other presentations of *A Spot in the Sun* (*Abbey Theatre Playbook* n.d., 6). Regarding the play's upcoming publication in *The Dublin Magazine* in March 1938, Murray wrote to O'Mahony in the same letter: "I think you will then find it pleasant reading and carefully built up, & I feel that it will survive its somewhat inauspicious birth. Anyway I'm glad to have it off my chest" (Ms. 24,902, folder 4, MOM, NLI).

# 5

# A Final Illumination

## *The Later Plays*

"YEATS THINKS IT the best play Murray has written since *Maurice Harte,* but he thinks it likely to prove a more popular one," wrote Holloway in his diary after Yeats accepted *Michaelmas Eve* for production at the Abbey (1968, 2:11). Once again the plot of this three-act peasant play centers on an arranged marriage and engenders the raw passions of jealousy, hate, and deception. A single woman in her late thirties, Mary Keating, is owner of a prosperous farm, Droumduv. Mary was jilted years earlier by Terry Donegan, who seemed to love her. But Terry's family, desperate for money to pay their mortgage, pressured him to marry Peg Conlon, who came from a family of means. Much like Ellen Keegan in *Autumn Fire,* Mary was humiliated, having been romanced by Terry before the parish. Its members still recall the event, especially now that Peg has died and Terry, an emigrant to America, is newly returned to seek Mary's hand and farm. He seeks Mary's forgiveness, explaining his endurance within the restrictions of the loveless match with Peg. Mary, who has knowingly encouraged Terry's repeated visits, rebuffs his offer of marriage to repay him for the heartbreak and shame he caused her.

Mary has two faithful servants, the lovely Moll Garvey, her tinker servant girl, and the handsome Hugh Kearns, her farm worker. At the beginning of the play, Moll and Hugh share a great sexual attraction. Hugh has dallied with Moll's affections; she tells Hugh she's "mad crazy" for him (Murray 1932, 1.12). Murray is careful to establish Moll's fiery nature, which issues from an equally fiery family, rebellious in the face of the law and community convention. Sahal notes Murray's attention to heredity in developing Moll's character, since it provides the motivations for her subsequent actions (1971, 43). Her jealous nature is of central import. She is fiercely jealous of Hugh's attentions to any other woman, and he is at times discomfited by this. A difference in their natures is revealed when the free-spirited Moll proposes marriage and emigration to America. Hugh, much like Morgan in *The Briery Gap*, prefers life on the land in Ireland to the uncertainty of life in American cities, a life for which he has little preparation or marketable skill. Notwithstanding their common social class, age, and sexual vitality, all of which make it appear that they are meant for each other, Hugh declines Moll's proposition.

Feeling rejected, Moll vows revenge. Part of Hugh's caution stems from his mother, who fears her son's physical attraction to Moll because of her notorious family; rather, she urges Hugh to seek to become master of Mary Keating's farm. Hugh is astonished by the suggestion, not only because he is Mary's servant but also because he is so much younger than she. Yet, to Hugh's further amazement, Mary offers marriage to Hugh after she spurns Terry Donegan. Encouraged by his mother, Hugh marries Mary, rather than Moll. As in *Autumn Fire,* the younger marries the older, and the more natural union of the two young people is prevented. In marrying Mary, Hugh frustrates Moll, who continues to reside in Mary's house, serving both her mistress and her former lover, now her master. Moll is tormented in this claustrophobic situation, telling Hugh: " 'Tis the hours I do be lying down in my bed in the room beyond with the candle quenched, an' the dead quiet, and I hearing your voices through the boarding between us. Wild an' jealous I do be that time and I thinking to my self that 'tis I should be making pleasant talk with you—an' she in my place bitter, an' cold, an' lonely. And I could cry out and strangle you that time for the pain I do be suffering" (Murray 1932, 3.74–75).

Despite her apparent hatred for him, Moll still loves Hugh intensely. In a moment reminiscent of Michael and Nance at the end of *Autumn Fire,* Hugh kisses Moll at her invitation. Feeling himself tempted, Hugh spurns Moll, calling her a Jezebel. In retaliation, Moll attempts to kill Hugh, putting rat poison in his tea. After failing in her nerve, she falsely accuses Hugh of infidelity to Mary. Hugh confronts Moll, in Mary's presence, forcing Moll to swear upon a crucifix, "the image of Christ crucified," that she is not lying. She begins to swear, but backs away from perjuring herself:

HUGH: "By this image of Christ."

MOLL: By. . . . (*Pause—her eyes held—suddenly by these of the image.*)

HUGH: (*Repeating.*) "This image of Christ crucified." (*Moll's eyes are riveted to the figure of the dead Christ. A tremor passes over her. She lays down the crucifix as if lost in a dream.*)

MOLL: Let—let—me—home. (*Hugh withdraws the bolt and throws the door wide open. Moll is about to pass through when Mary, moved by a sudden impulse, goes to her.*)

MARY: Stop. (*Moll turns slowly.*)

MARY: (*With intense feeling.*) It—it wasn't true?

MOLL: True? . . . No . . . In a passion o' jealousy—God forgive me my sin!—I made up the story. (*She goes away brokenly—a figure of tragic defeat.*)

(*Hugh and Mary watch her go. There is a moment's pause.*)

MARY: (*Half to herself.*) Mother o' God, what an evening!

HUGH: (*Nodding.*) Aye. (*Curtain.*) (Murray 1932, 3.87)

In this original ending Moll recants, going off into the night, a broken woman. The scene highlights the blot on Murray's dramatic record, his flinching from complete dramatic honesty. Brinsley MacNamara, a hearty Murray supporter, draws attention to this tendency in *Michaelmas Eve*: "It would seem, as in the present case, that sometimes, after splendid preparation, he burkes the issue and denies the benefit of the *katharsis* [sic] to his endings" (1933, 62–63). The review of the premiere in *The Irish Times*, "The Abbey Theatre: Brilliant Production of *Michaelmas Eve*," approves of Murray's self-imposed "Irish" limits in treating the tense dramatic situation created when two women, one a subordinate, the other a superior, love the same man: "Hugh Kearns in other lands would probably have taken both women, but in Ireland there are inhibitions which forbid that, and Mr. Murray was certainly true to his people when he left the problem unsolved at the final curtain" (1932).

This approbation of Murray's dramatic choices underscores the restrictions that Murray accepted because he did not want to offend Irish Catholic audiences. In an interview with the author, Tomás MacAnna called the original ending "not truthful." Referring to the moment when Moll holds back from poisoning Hugh, MacAnna said that a tinker girl like Moll would not refrain from committing dire deeds if provoked. He also cited a "very puritanical" Murray, noting his diffidence with sexual material in the face of what he calls the "tremendous surge of earth flow" in Murray's West Cork where the people are "of the soil." Murray's plays, MacAnna asserted, "have the beat of sex right through them," and a director today would need to emphasize this reality (1992). It is amusing that Murray, writing with customary decorum at age eighty-one, acknowledged with some freedom the sexual undercurrents both in himself and in his plays. On 31 March 1954, he wrote to O'Mahony about a photo of the actress who played Moll Garvey that year: "He must needs be made of granite who wouldn't fall for Moll Garvey! You may tell her so" (Ms. 24,902, folder 10, MOM, NLI). Robert Hogan suggests that Murray should have "punished" Hugh rather than Moll, judging that the "major fault is Hugh's and so should the tragic suffering be" (1967, 28). Moll suffers tremendous pain, as Joan does in *The Briery Gap* and as Christina does in *Illumination,* but Mary and Hugh, as well as Terry, also suffer greatly in the tragic net.

Murray wrote two "alternative" and one "revised" ending to this play (Ms. 24,858, folder 3). In one of the alternative endings, in the Production Copy, Moll indeed swears upon the crucifix, and does not back down (Murray 1937a). The tragic effect is heightened.

> HUGH: Liar! Perjured liar.
> MOLL: Liar you! (*To Mary.*) It's the truth—and he knows it in his heart.
> MARY: (*Stricken.*) O God, don't say that.
> HUGH: (*Pained.*) Mary —
> MARY: (*Desolately.*) Under Heaven, what did I ever do to deserve this?
> HUGH: Look, as God's my judge 'tis false, Mary.
> MOLL: The truth's bitter.
> MARY: How could you? How could you?
> HUGH: (*Earnestly.*) Mary, listen to me? (*He puts his hand on her arm.*) Listen?

MARY: (*With revulsion.*) Don't touch me! I trusted you—I loved you. Without scruple I gave you all I had to give. And look at me— look at me now—a mock and a show to all the living world.

HUGH: O, no, no, no, Mary.

MARY: Never in this life, Hugh Kearns, do I want to see you again. Never! Never! Never! (*She turns from him and, crumpling into a seat, breaks into passionate sobbing. He looks at her, dumb and helpless. Moll moves to the door and quietly releases the bolt. With a pitiless smile she looks upon their torment and then passes out. The sound of her derisive laughter can be heard, almost drowning Mary's desolate sobbing. Curtain.* (Murray 1937a, 63–64).

Writing to Mathew O'Mahony on 25 January 1954, Murray admitted: "The second ending is of course more in tune with Moll Garvey's make-up. She is 'the woman scorned,' and is of the rebellious Garvey blood, and wo[uld] have very little hesitation in her tempestuous mood in swearing that black is white. But then such an ending may possibly offend the Catholic sensibility" (Ms. 24,902, folder 10, MOM, NLI). For this reason, Murray continued to prefer the original ending as he thought it more aligned to the spirit of Catholicism and less likely to give offense. Murray appears unduly restrained by his scruples. Robert Hogan has observed that sometimes the artist in Murray triumphed over the unswerving Catholic. *Michaelmas Eve* provides such an example. The alternate endings illustrate that Moll is capable of passion-provoked crime, as MacAnna argues above. Having committed perjury, she bears culpability for her action. In the end, all four of their lives, including Terry Donegan's, are undone. And all four are responsible for the choices they have made.

With the alternate endings, *Michaelmas Eve* becomes one of Murray's best plays. The characterizations are insightfully drawn; the language is rich; the action is swift; the emotions are deep and elemental. The theme of rejection is multilayered, with the rejection of Mary by Terry reinforced and mirrored by that of Terry by Mary and then of Moll by Hugh. As in *Autumn Fire,* the situation, with the three key characters living under the same roof, is Racinian in its claustrophobic intensity. Though the plot is marked by undeniable melodrama and the treatment by sexual reticence, *Michaelmas Eve* would play very well today with the restoration of one of the alternate endings. The unfolding action would then be truthful, as well as compelling to observe. Its presentation of a middle-aged woman's need for love and its atmosphere of violence, both physical and emotional, anticipates Martin McDonagh's peasant drama, *The Beauty Queen of Leenane* (1996).

*Michaelmas Eve* was well received in its Abbey premiere. Holloway recorded that "The critics after Act 2 were all very high in praise of the play and delighted that Murray had come back to his own. Malone, Sears, Brosnan, Frank Hugh O'Donnell, Mr. Connolly, Mrs. Meldon all sang the praises of the play" (1968, 2:10). In his review "The Abbey Theatre: Brilliant Production of *Michaelmas Eve*," the critic of *The Irish Times* joined in singing these praises: "In *Michaelmas Eve* he shows that he can get into the hearts and behind the thoughts of scorned and soured women also. There are two discerning and remarkably sympathetic studies of such women in *Michaelmas Eve*." He praised the cast, who "acted as if inspired," singling out Eileen Crowe. He observed that she had "never done anything so magnificent," calling her Moll Garvey "one of the greatest pieces of acting ever seen in the Abbey Theatre" (1932). A review in *The Observer* of 3 July 1932 likewise praised both the play and the acting but faulted Murray's characterization of Moll Garvey: "Now Hugh Kearns fetched the crucifix in a mood which partook very much of the superstitious. But a Moll Garvey does not succumb to this mood. . . . Holding it, or not holding it, should have been all one to her" (Donaghy 1932). In a lecture on Murray delivered in Dublin on 17 November 1982, Mathew O'Mahony attested to the popular appeal of the play: "It played to packed houses throughout the whole of that week of the Eucharistic Congress" (Ms. 23,976:16, MOM, NLI). Murray confirmed, writing O'Donnell on 1 July 1932 that, " 'House Full' has been displayed every night, and the house for tonight & Saturday has already sold out" (Ms. 21,715, folder 10, NLI).

As with *The Blind Wolf*, however, there was a notable decline in the number of performances of a Murray play. This is striking because of the strong popular and critical reception of *Michaelmas Eve*. Yet after the first production, of seven performances running from 27 June to 2 July 1932, it received only one more Abbey presentation from 31 July to 5 August 1933, for a total of fourteen performances (*Abbey Theatre Playbook* n.d., 53). When O'Mahony wrote to Murray, complaining of the Abbey's neglect of the play, Murray revealed his feelings toward Ernest Blythe, then managing director of the Abbey, in a letter written 27 January 1954: "Not that I don't feel that Blythe—or more justly 'Blight!'—has been scurvy in his neglect of the play. That it has some compelling quality is evident from its winning the much coveted trophy at Douglas, and snatching the blue ribbon at many drama festivals in Ireland" (Ms. 24,902, folder 10, MOM, NLI).

Originally titled *Toppling Towers*, the play finally known as *Illumination* (1939) began to grow in Murray's mind in the late 1930s. According to Holloway, its genesis was a trip by Murray and his solicitor to Roscrea to investigate an unlicensed production of *Autumn Fire* (1968, 3:6). Holloway wrote in February 1938 that Murray learned in Roscrea of a solicitor's son who spurned the idea of becoming a solicitor and "went on for the church which was somewhat of a shock to his father. On hearing this, Murray got an idea for a play" (1968, 3:6–7).

As in *A Flutter of Wings* and *A Spot in the Sun*, Murray continued his treatment of a middle—and upper-middle-class environment in *Illumination*, his last play to be produced by the Abbey Theatre. Though it is not a masterpiece, *Illumination* is an important Murray work. The play explores further the religious dimension of human experience first investigated by Murray in *The Pipe in the Fields*. It also is the culmination of a gradual progression in Murray's male characters from oppression to freedom. For these reasons, *Illumination* illustrates the final phase of Murray's philosophic growth.

Murray worked on *Illumination* for at least a year and a half. He revealed a great deal about its composition to Terence Connolly. On 6 June 1939, Murray wrote to Connolly: "I have just submitted to the Abbey a play entitled *Illumination*. I had been working overlong on it—a bad sign—and when I wrote the final 'curtain' I felt that I had been just the mountain in labor." Characteristically self-deprecating, Murray continues: "It isn't a very good play but I think it is of sufficient interest to warrant its production" (Box 13, folder 17:27–28, TLC, JJBL). Connolly is the same priest who created an incident at the Abbey Theatre Festival in 1938 when he pointedly asked about the meaning of Yeats's play *Purgatory*. It was during this conference at the Gresham Hotel in Dublin that Murray and Connolly first met. Murray eventually sent Connolly a typescript of *Illumination* in 1946, seven years after its production. This typescript is now held by Boston College. It is signed "T. C. Murray, 11 Sandymount Avenue, Ballsbridge, Dublin," and contains corrections and additions written by the author for the Guild Players in Enniskillen (University Archives, Irish Collection, JJBL).

In an accompanying letter written on 12 March 1946, Murray included his recollection of the production with his own critical appraisal of play and performance: "The interior struggle of the young man, torn between conflicting loyalties, is left a good deal to the imagination. Our modern audiences shy at the spiritual travail which young Brian Egan suffers, and the playwright is the slave of his audience, and must keep the purely dramatic element in the foreground of his work" (Box 13, folder 17:27–28, TLC, JJBL). Murray later sent Connolly revisions of the text with instructions in his own hand as to the proper points of insertion into the existing typescript. These more substantive revisions supercede the rehearsal "corrections" that Cave notes are to be found in the Abbey Theatre opening night prompt copy (Murray 1998, 221), from which *Selected Plays: T. C. Murray,* edited by Cave, is drawn (Murray 1998, 222–69). Therefore, the Boston College edition of the text will be used in this discussion, although the *Selected Plays* citations will also be provided for easy reference.

Murray sets the action in Ardcullen, a fictional Irish provincial town, in the comfortable home of Charles Egan, a long-established country town solicitor. Brian Egan, recently admitted to his father's firm at age twenty-two, is unhappy in his job. In the heart of the opening scene, he discloses to his mother, Helen Egan, the conflict of conscience created by his professional duty to represent any prospective client willing to pay, no matter how morally questionable the cause. Murray establishes Brian's sensitive nature, contrasting him with his quarrelsome, pragmatic father, who is unaware of his son's discontent. Murray uses Mrs. Egan as the confidante for the two male characters, keeping the two men apart until the climax in Act Two. Brian and his mother are kindred spirits. Brian is introspective, an intellectual. His intense reading of theological works also suggests a religious cast of mind.

Charles thinks that Brian's moodiness might be a sign that his son has fallen in love. He tells his wife Helen that he would like to see Brian marry Christina Moore, daughter of their friend Dr. Richard Moore, a respected physician. Charles is furious because Helen refuses to foster this union. Charles's irritability recalls John Luttrell in *A Flutter of Wings* and suggests that Luttrell was an early sketch for Egan.

Mrs. Egan's position is important in light of Murray's dramatic work to this point. Apart from the gentle Maura in *Birthright,* Murray had previously depicted the mother in his plays as manipulative, seeking to arrange the desirable match. Here the mother renounces this option, *her* birthright. When Murray emphasizes Mrs. Egan's ungrasping nature, he breaks the mold in which he had cast mothers Harte, O'Regan, and Kearns.

The Boston College text contains an additional scene between mother and son in which Brian's motivation is clarified. The arrival of more theology books prompts Brian to share with his mother a hint of the "secret" behind his reading: "Look, mother. I chanced to come on something in my reading and I can't rest till I follow it through. I've struck gold, as it were—or if not, something strangely like it. I may be self-deluded. I don't know. So far it's only a gleam on the surface. To get down to the heart of things I've to delve deeper and still deeper. Books are my implements—my pickaxe and spade" (University Archives, Irish Collection, 1.1.20, JJBL). Brian's discovery of the theological books at an auction represents the turning point in his life. He says, "It's all so absorbing that I grudge every moment given to other things" (1.1.20–21). He shows, for example, no desire to pursue a vacant solicitor's post in Dublin. He manifests, rather, the absorbing quality of religious experience, the desire to go beyond the self, to become lost in the Other, commonly known as God. Since an absorption in the other is also characteristic of being in love, Charles has reason to suspect that Brian has fallen in love. In a news feature published prior to the premiere of the play, "T. C. Murray Puts the Modern Irishman in a Play," Murray said: "I have taken as a theme a spiritual crisis. . . . a conflict between philosophies; that of the worldly man as dealt with by Omar Khayyám and that of one who tries to make his life harmonize with the teachings of Thomas à Kempis" (1939). A devotional classic, *The Imitation of Christ* by à Kempis (1380–1471) stressed the conflict between secular and spiritual values and exercised great influence in the history of Christian spirituality.

Brian's childhood friend, Christina Moore, further complicates the plot as a love interest. She recapitulates the motif of Brian's single-minded absorption in a project, telling Mr. Egan that when they played as children, Brian would "fly into a rage because I was forever wishing to change over from one game to another. He'd have us go on and on—putting all of ourselves into it. And I think he's still like that" (University Archives, Irish Collection, 1.2.42, JJBL; Murray 1998, 1.2.243). Murray has been preparing for the first of two extended conversations around which the play is structured. Lacking the language to tell Christina that he is being continually drawn into a more deeply spiritual life, he can only convey the experience indirectly, describing the effect God's action has on him. Brian tells her he has discovered, "my own frightful ignorance" (1.2.46; Murray 1998, 1.2.245).

In introducing the motifs of blindness versus vision, illusion versus reality, darkness versus light, Murray contrasts Christina's understanding of knowledge, acquired through the rational faculty, with Brian's growing awareness of metaphysical realities. Brian speaks of the clarity produced by deepening religious experience that leads to conversion. The Boston College text includes a new line for Brian in which he states: "One's vision becomes clearer" (University Archives, Irish Collection, 1.2.48, JJBL). Murray paints an accurate picture of the gradual coming to clarity associated with religious conversion when Brian says: "What sudden notion prompted me to open a page I don't know. But I read on and on. I had to. Never did words mean so much to me. It seemed somehow, as if I had been all my life looking at things with blurred vision. Now I was seeing them in their true light" (1.2.46–48; Murray 1998, 1.2.245–246). This tendency toward absorption in the Other is common in the artistic or sensitive minds previously noted by Ellis-Fermor. Certainly Brian possesses a sensitive mind, and he is cousin to Maurice Harte, Myles O'Regan, and Peter Keville. Yet Brian himself realizes the otherworldliness of it all. Brian immediately recognizes the differing values between Christina and himself. He acknowledges, too, that by the standards of the world, which Christina holds, he would be viewed as a fool.

At this point Murray interpolates a revised scene of three pages, lettered "a," "b," "c." In this scene, Murray brings Mrs. Egan back on stage, explaining—in a letter to Connolly from 10 December 1946—"I have made two changes in the play—both in the second scene of the first act. . . . I felt that that second scene needed something—I knew not what—to strengthen its interest. Then there came what seemed to myself a flash of inspiration. At the final curtain you may remember that the mother reveals to her son something of her inner life—the cankering memory of having failed to answer what seemed to her a direct call to the cloister. By a foreshadowing of this in the second scene I thought it would create a deeper interest in her" (Cat. 112, MJMC, JJBL). Murray inserted more new material, bringing Charles back on stage for a final moment between Helen and Charles "to give a more emphatic curtain" (Cat. 112, MJMC, JJBL).

In the added scene, Mrs. Egan discloses a personal torment—"an accusing conscience" owing to a trust she betrayed: "Listen. . . . I had a Friend—one to whom I owed everything. He trusted me implicitly. I was disloyal. In a weak moment I betrayed His trust. He forgave me but I never forgave myself. It happened many years ago but the thought of it is an ever-present pain. It keeps nagging—nagging—nagging" (University Archives, Irish Collection, 1.2.50b, JJBL). The added material reveals that mother and son feel a similar spiritual dissatisfaction.

In their second major conversation, Brian discloses to Christina that he is leaving Ardcullen to enter the Trappist Abbey of Mount Melleray. Incredulous, she warns Brian of his father's parental claim. In an added speech that gives the play its title, Brian insists that the attraction drawing him to the monastery is not a delusion: "It springs from the light of cold reason and—I dare to think—of divine illumination. My way is set as the stars in their courses" (University Archives, Irish Collection, 2.62, JJBL). Brian's resolution is markedly different from the ambivalence of Maurice Harte and Myles O'Regan. Brian also reveals to Christina that at one point in his life, he had longed "for a regard deeper than your friendship" (2.64). Stunned with surprise, she, in turn, declares her love for him and calls this turn of events "a cruel prank life was about to play on us" (2.64; Murray 1998, 2.255). In the 1946 revision Brian insists there is a love stronger than human love: "something that changes us so utterly that we become as if recreated" (2.65); in the original he calls this power "something which changes us so utterly that a universe lies between what we were and what we are" (Murray 1998, 2.256). Christina's response evokes great pity for her: "I shall remember you've killed in me every atom of pride, of self-respect I've ever had. You've left me to be a mockery to myself" (2.66; Murray 1998, 2.256).

The major character breakthrough in *Illumination*, Brian's emancipation, comes in the *scène-a-fâire*, the necessary confrontation between father and son. In asserting his decision as "a matter of conscience," Brian shows his kinship with Maurice Harte (University Archives, Irish Collection, 2.84, JJBL; Murray 1998, 2.266). Brian's steadfast pursuit of his happiness shatters Charles's plans. In the climax of the play, Charles resorts to threats. "If your Melleray denies me justice I go to the Bishop. . . . Let him fail me and—by Heaven—Rome itself shall hear my cause" (2.87–88; 2.267–68). Alone with his mother, Brian hesitantly asks how she feels about his decision. Quite to Brian's surprise, she discloses *her* secret: that she had once desired to become a nun, but that her family was so upset that, like Maurice Harte, she had acceded to their wishes. She tells him she is pleased to see Brian's greater strength: "You have redeemed my own unhappy fault. This is the most grateful moment in my life" (2.90; 2.269).

This ending may earn ÓhAodha's comment, "all's sweetness and light here" (1958, 190). *Illumination* is an imperfect play dramaturgically. Squarely within the tradition of the well-made play extending from Scribe to Ibsen, it is tightly structured. Murray clearly and carefully crafts the play from the exposition through the complication and rising action to the secret revealed at the climax. Indeed the machinery of the plot seems all too obvious; the melodramatic explosion during the father-son confrontation, recalling the similar scene in *The Serf*, is expected. Of the typical conflict in a Murray play, Fitzgibbon says, "[T]here is no simple alignment of situations and persons with positive or negative values" (1975, 61). But in *Illumination* the lines are clearly drawn. Brian and Mrs. Egan are aligned with the impulses toward growth and light; Christina, her father, and Charles are aligned with the conventional code of life. Murray notes that these characters are "treated very predictably and defined more by their function within the drama as a play of ideas than as evolving sensibilities" (1998, 219). This lack of complexity weakens *Illumination,* making it a less satisfying play. Conlin's claim (1961, 129) that neither character nor dialogue rings true in Murray's urban plays is an apt comment on *Illumination.*

Regarding character delineation, there are places where Murray dodges the truth to avoid offending Catholic Dublin audiences. For example, Christina says, "O, my dear, what a cruel prank life was about to play on us." Christina's line would read more accurately, "what a cruel prank God was about to play on me." The cruelty is not Murray's for he has not so much created this situation of unnecessary pain for the woman character; rather he has depicted the Irish Catholic reality of the time. In his choice, Brian also experiences pain in excluding the option of a life with Christina. Here, too, another dimension of the harshness of Irish life is evidenced, located this time, not in the land or the family but in the Church's monastic order which valued vowed religious chastity more highly than vowed sexual union in matrimony. At the expense of Brian's free choice, another person is placed in torment. Though this may be an accurate depiction of Christina's suffering, one does not sense that Murray is critical of the structures that occasioned it.

Though it is imperfect, *Illumination* is yet Murray's most mature play philosophically and spiritually. Brian's struggle to be free of the community yet responsible to it echoes the essential conflict in Ibsen's plays where the central characters experience the conflict between attaining self-fulfillment and establishing a responsible role within the community, living according to its code. When Brian leaves home, he will leave on a note of personal victory, not after eight years of marriage like Nora in *A Doll's House,* but after only eight months of indenture or "marriage" to his father's firm. Noticeable, too, in Brian's departure, is the break from family responsibilities that was central to the heated controversy surrounding *A Doll's House.* Christina's reminding Brian of his duty to his father signals that in 1939 responsibility to family was still a living issue in the Irish mind, though not so scandalous as a mother deserting her children in nineteenth-century Norway.

The second Ibsenite strain is seen in the dénouement where the life lie is revealed in Mrs. Egan. She confesses to Brian her aborted desire to become a nun and the hidden pain of this lost vocation that she has suffered all her life. Recalling *Ghosts,* another Ibsenite touch is Murray's double twist on the sins of the father being visited upon the children. In this case it is, rather, the *graces* of the *mother* visited upon the son. Using the ancient language of the Catholic Church, Mrs. Egan refers to her failure of will as a "happy fault"—*felix culpa.* It is not a sin but a grace that is passed on to the son. Mrs. Egan's religious vocation has been transmitted through her natural temperament *supernaturally* to her son—grace building on nature. Richard McBrien explains the Roman Catholic understanding of grace, nature, and human freedom: "Human freedom is never to be conceived totally apart from grace, because it is always modified and qualified by grace, so, too, the grace of God is operative only insofar as it interacts with, and radically transforms, the natural order of the human person" (1981, 161). We see this dynamic operative in Brian when he tells Christina, "One can never tell what new force may transfigure a man's life" (University Archives, Irish Collection, 2.63, JJBL).

The final moment of *Illumination* holds two literary allusions. Mrs. Egan's speech, recounting her desire to become a nun, is similar to Mary Tyrone's speech in Eugene O'Neill's *Long Day's Journey into Night* (1940). Mrs. Egan recalls, "From the time I could think I felt that the Convent was my natural home. All my thoughts seemed to turn that way. . . . A quiet steady flame. Constant as the altar lamp. . . . then came your father asking me to marry him" (University Archives, Irish Collection, 2.89–90, JJBL). Mary Tyrone similarly recalls her attraction to James Tyrone (1973, 3.105).

This same scene of consoling understanding between mother and son also alludes to an occurrance in *Confessions*, by Augustine of Hippo: a moment of closeness between Augustine and his mother Monica in the scene known as "The Vision at Ostia," in which they "touched" Eternity (1979, Book 9:196–98). It is this fleeting moment of Eternity experienced in these scenes—by Monica, Augustine, Helen, and Brian—that Brian seeks to enjoy. This moment reveals Murray's play as Augustinian in its theology of spirit and its philosophy of knowing. In Augustine's understanding, God, acting as a friend, sheds light upon the person's intellect, enabling him or her to know ultimate truth. Augustine says: "With the eye of my soul . . . I saw the Light that never changes casting its rays over the same eye of my soul, over my mind. What I saw was something quite, quite different from any light we know on earth" (1979, Book 7:146–47). Augustine's doctrine of illumination gives Murray's play its title. In Brian, Murray finally broke free of the restrictions of the family by enlisting, as Augustine did, the help of a supernatural partner.

*Illumination* both departs from the main body of Murray's work and returns to develop further themes introduced in *The Pipe in the Fields*. *Illumination* qualifies Thomas Hogan's comment that "frustrated sensitive souls do not revolt" against oppressive forces (1950, 47). Brian, sensitive soul that he is, does revolt from the forces marshalled against him, and he achieves autonomy. The conflict in *Illumination* is essentially the same as in Murray's earlier works. Fitzgibbon describes the conflict of *Birthright* as: "The struggle of the individual to possess his own soul and destiny in the face of pressure from family and from tribe; the conflict between romantic ideals of self-fulfillment and the hard actualities of farming poor and broken land; the conflict of hope with embittered wisdom; the conflict between the wider world of books or travel and the narrower one of ignorance, the village, the family" (1975, 62). One only needs to substitute "law firm" for "land" and Fitzgibbon's remarks apply perfectly well to *Illumination*. The same word substitution can be made with Maurice Harmon's comment regarding *Birthright*—that a "domineering parent fights to hold both land and son" (1977, 154). Likewise Ellis-Fermor's description of Bat Morrissey in *Birthright,* as a man "who is slave himself to the land he has mastered and would make his children serve it with the same fanatic ardour as his own" (1939, 189), could apply equally well to Charles Egan and his law firm in *Illumination*.

Contrary to the observations of Thomas Hogan and Gerald Fitzgibbon regarding Murray's heroes, Brian is not defeated. Unlike the heroes of *Birthright, Maurice Harte,* and *Aftermath,* Brian prevails in the struggle against his father. Unlike Hugh Morrissey, Maurice Harte, and Myles O'Regan, Brian succeeds in self-possession and self-determination. He follows the allure of the wider world of books. Brian also has a far more defined sense of what he wants than Murray's earlier heroes do. He follows his own dream and his *true* love, pursuing what Fitzgibbon rightly calls "romantic ideals" against the narrow view of the community. He sheds the lifeless duty of taking over his father's law firm, a new equivalent of barren land. Brian does not cower; he does not surrender. His is not a Myles O'Regan revolt after the fact. It is a revolt in the first, full heat of battle, accomplished with composure and grace under pressure.

Brian is able to choose the Good, which is what Dorothy Macardle calls in Murray's work "the claim of each new generation to free, sweet, natural life" (1925, 394). He is able to make a choice consonant with his particular human nature. Murray painstakingly demonstrates that Brian possesses a sensitive, introspective nature, attuned to spiritual movements. Brian led an active social life, enjoying companionship, music, and sports, not unlike Hugh Morrissey in *Birthright,* lover of drinking, fiddling, and versifying. Brian's breakthrough to his contemplative dimension is occasioned by his discovery of the theological books which lead him to his true self and puncture the social formation derived from family and society. Hugh Morrissey and Maurice Harte were never given such opportunities for self-discovery, let alone self-possession. Whether the monastic life Brian chooses to pursue is more or less restrictive than a career in his father's firm is beside the point: Brian has made a free choice, consonant with his unique person, based on reason and faith—and has succeeded in maintaining it in the face of obstacles.

Brian Egan completes the progressive march toward the exercise of free will in Murray's plays begun with the submission of Maurice Harte and continued in the bitter freedom of Myles O'Regan in *Aftermath*. In *Illumination* Brian moves beyond family oppression to freedom. Although Brian experiences pain in his conversation with Christina, one senses that he actually enjoys the combat with his father. Robert Hogan says Murray's plays "suggest the lawless artist trying to escape from lawful authority" (1967, 28). Certainly in *Illumination* Brian's breakthrough to freedom is not without cost, either to him or to the tribe. Fitzgibbon takes issue with those who would seek to limit Murray's achievement to that of a realist, reproducing accurately the surface features of reality. Fitzgibbon convincingly argues, rather, that Murray's awareness of the human spirit "pushing towards growth, knowledge, achievement, emotional completion could equally suggest that he is, in some senses, a romantic" (1975, 65).

The play's noteworthy feature lies in Murray's accurate depiction of religious experience, a spiritual occurrence in which a person apprehends the presence of God, as distinct from religion with its focus on rituals, rubrics, and dogmas. Religious conversion—or saying a radical "yes" to God—lies at the heart of *Illumination*. Murray's rendering of the spiritual movements in the conversion process is remarkable. Brian moves beyond the oppression of religion seen in *Maurice Harte* and *The Briery Gap*; his spiritual transformation is a conversion from religion to the presence of God (Conn 1986, 225). Unlike Peter Keville in *The Pipe in the Fields*, Brian needs no priests to mediate his way to liberation or to God. *Illumination* is not about religion. Rather, it is about the action of the transcendent God upon a cooperative human person. Brian achieves his liberation without human intervention; he is assisted only by God's grace working through his particular human nature, or personality. Walter Conn states that in religious conversion a person first discovers that the self is insufficient for survival, and surrenders an illusory sense of autonomy

(1986, 227). Brian's dissatisfaction with the life offered in his father's law firm renders him vulnerable to the message of à Kempis.

In *Illumination*, Murray depicts a religious "call" characterized by absorption beyond the self, in God. William Barry and William Connolly discuss a person's contemplative absorption in God: "When it is a person who is being contemplated, he lets that person, with his personality, concerns, and activity take his attention. He lets himself be absorbed, for a moment at least, and at some level, in the other person" (1982, 48). Connolly presents the example of a man sitting on a park bench gazing into the blue sky as he begins to experience a contemplative drawing into the beyond: "Gradually the blue, the depth, and the peace of the sky begin to hold his attention, and he feels his attention being drawn deeper, then thousands of miles deep, into the sky. A few minutes later he beings to feel that his attention is being drawn even beyond the sky" (1981, 41). Murray has revealed these qualities in Brian Egan. Christina speaks of his capacity for contemplative absorption.

Murray's accurate depiction of religious experience, together with the central character's break from the heritage of family oppression, makes *Illumination* his richest play philosophically and spiritually. Although it is weak dramaturgically, in its paleness of language and in sketchy development of supporting characters, the play is still noteworthy in Murray's dramatic corpus for the growth of the central character.

The extensive press coverage for the premiere of *Illumination* on 31 July 1939 makes clear that this new Murray play was an important event in Dublin's theatrical year. *The Irish Times* reported on 1 August that "one of the theatre's most honoured dramatists had an enthusiastic reception for his new play" ("Abbey Theatre: *Illumination*" 1939). In "Mr. T. C. Murray's New Play," another reviewer, noting that "all the old Murray 'fans' were present," observed, "It was like one of the great Abbey days of old, and the stalls were crowded, many of the old habitués being present" (Ms. 23,513, 2:82, TCM, NLI). The production showcased F. J. McCormick and Eileen Crowe, husband and wife in real life, as Charles and Helen Egan; it also featured Joseph Linnane as Brian, Phyllis Ryan as Christina, and Michael J. Dolan as Dr. Moore. Joseph Holloway's diary offers evidence that something was amiss with the star performer; after the final Sunday rehearsal, F. J. McCormick sent word to Murray that "he was at his lowest ebb . . . seemed not to have off his words and was in a real nervous . . . state" (qtd. in Conlin 1952, 21). Holloway, in his diary entry for opening night, documented: "F. J. McCormick as 'Charles Egan' . . . was speaking so rapidly and clipping his words so badly that what he was saying rarely crossed the footlights and the prompter was often heard" (1968, 3:32–33). The *Irish Times* reviewer also noted that McCormick was "not perhaps at the top of his form" ("Abbey Theatre: *Illumination*" 1939), while the *Irish Independent* critic stated that he was "almost inaudible at times" ("D. S." 1939). Holloway claimed, however, that Linnane and Ryan, as Brian and Christina, saved the evening, capturing the audience when they disclosed their true feelings for each other. The scene, he says "was as delicate and beautiful as any such scene could possibly be, and one felt as they spoke the stillness of intense interest that came over the audience and told that great acting was taking place on the stage" (1968, 3:32–33).

The press reviews showed great respect for Murray, both as a person and as the author of *Maurice Harte* and *Birthright*. Nevertheless, *The Irish Times*, while speaking respectfully of the play, could not hide its disappointment: "One may say at once that it is a play in Mr. Murray's later, slighter manner. The rugged strength of *Birthright* and *Maurice Harte* has gradually given place to accomplished playwrighting and his themes seem to lose somewhat through the ease with which he handles them" ("Abbey Theatre: *Illumination*" 1939). "D. S." in the *Irish Independent* championed the play's unique subject matter: "It was a bold experiment to attempt to express convincingly something so essentially intimate, personal, and spiritual as a vocation" (1939). Gabriel Fallon was so impressed by *Illumination*, that he wrote two reviews of it in *The Standard*. In his first review, on 11 August 1939, he hailed it as Murray's "greatest play" (Fallon 1939a, 20). His next piece, on 18 August, indicates public acceptance of the play: "So many people have written to me and spoken to me about the work, I feel that three issues of *The Standard* could hardly exhaust the subject so far as they are and I am concerned" (Fallon 1939b). In this review, Fallon also examines Murray's ability to view life with distinction: "What is it, one wonders, that urges a distinguished member of an Abbey audience to say of *Illumination*: 'The pity of it that our theatre gives us so few plays like this'?"

All the first night reviewers mention the great ovation at the end of the performance and note that Murray made a speech from the stage in response to repeated audience calls for "author." A photo caption in a press cutting suggests brisk box office business: *"Illumination,* Mr. T. C. Murray's new play, is playing to crowded audiences at the Abbey Theatre this week" (1939). In a lecture on Murray delivered in Dublin on 17 November 1982, Mathew O'Mahony claimed that from the outset, it was clear that there was no likelihood of an extension of the run into the following week (Ms. 23,976:19, MOM, NLI). After its initial run from 31 July to 5 August 1939, *Illumination* was presented again from 9 to 14 October 1939, for a total of twelve performances (*Abbey Theatre Playbook* n.d., 35). On 1 January 1940, the critic for *The Irish Times,* in evaluating the fourteen new plays that had opened in Dublin in 1939, named *Illumination* "the most important contribution to drama" ("The Dublin Stage: A Varied Year" 1940).

Until 1998 *Illumination* remained one of T. C. Murray's few unpublished plays. At first, publication by the London house of Allen and Unwin, Murray's steady publisher, was delayed by the paper shortage occasioned by the outbreak of World War II. Later, Allen and Unwin cancelled publication plans, arguing that publishing any play was commercially risky. Murray's letter of 10 December 1946 to Terence Connolly discussed publication by a Dublin house: "Much against the grain I arranged yesterday with Duffy's to publish the play. Their books are turned out crudely but I felt I have had so many requests for the script from Catholic Colleges & amateurs, that it was best to get it into print" (Cat. 112, MJMC, JJBL). A year later, however, Murray was frustrated by another long delay. In 1948, out of exasperation and perhaps wounded pride, he asked Duffy's to return the script.

When in 1949 O'Mahony wrote Murray to request permission to perform scenes from *Illumination,* Murray was overjoyed: "Your letter of this morning excited me so pleasantly," he wrote back on 30 April 1949, "that I felt I *had* to write to you. *Illumination* has been to me rather a neglected child & to find its being brought into the limelight even in a restricted way pleased me mightily" (Ms. 24,902, folder 9, MOM, NLI). Interest in *Illumination* in amateur circles continued high as Murray began to doubt the play's merit. On 14 November 1949 he confided to O'Mahony: "I begin to feel that the play isn't as good as I once felt it was. Yet it must have struck a spark in some stray souls, for some time ago I got a request for the script from Cornwall. The writer, it appears, chanced to be in Dublin during its [presentation] and it was on his mind all those years. Radio Éireann is to give it a broadcast—but when I've no idea" (Ms. 24,902, folder 9, MOM, NLI). According to a letter to Connolly written 8 December, the broadcast was to have occurred mid-December 1949 (Box 13, folder 17:27–28, TLC, JJBL). In the last letter exchanged between Murray and O'Mahony, dated 29 December 1956, Murray lamented—almost twenty years later—his untimely retrieval of the script from Duffy's: "It bore the marks of its just being in the printer's hands!" (Ms. 24,902, folder 10, MOM, NLI). One can sense Murray's long-held hopes dashed.

One may wonder why this play was so important to Murray and why he was so fascinated with monasticism. He wrote to Connolly on 8 December 1949: "I've been reading with intense interest Thos. [Thomas] Merton's *Elected Silence* [*The Seven Storey Mountain*] as his autobiography has been entitled here. It has been for me not only the book of the year but of many years" (Box 13, folder 17:27–28, TLC, JJBL). One suspects that this "intense interest" preceded both Thomas Merton's book and his play of 1939. The obvious reason is his deep religious instinct. Two years after Pauline entered the Poor Clares in 1932, Murray was deeply moved by the ceremony of her first vows. Later he described the life of the nuns in "I Go to Nun's Island," one of his regular columns for the *Irish Press*, published on 20 July 1945 (Ms. 23,513, 2:153, TCM, NLI). In this article, Murray wondered why the nuns seemed so peace-filled. It is worth noting that in the true account upon which Murray based *Illumination*, the son, a graduate of Clongowes (a Jesuit secondary school), entered not the Trappists of Melleray but the Society of Jesus (Conlin 1952, 20). Murray may have altered the venue because a Trappist monastery evokes more mystery for a lay audience. However, his fascination with his daughter's life-choice may also have provoked the change of setting. Not surprisingly, then, Murray wrote to Connolly on 19 January 1950: "I find myself becoming almost a publicity agent for Thos. [sic] Merton. Willy nilly I have to introduce the extraordinary appeal of his *Elected Silence* in conversation with any friend whom I chance to meet" (Box 13, folder 17:27–28, TLC, JJBL).

Given Murray's demonstrated interest in monasticism, one wonders if Murray himself felt called to the enclosed life as a youth. One also wonders if *Illumination* is not somewhat autobiographical. The image of Brian Egan, rummaging through theological books at the canon's auction, recalls Murray delighting as a schoolboy in the thought of the bookstalls of medieval Leipzig. In "The First National Book Fair," a 1940 piece for *The Irish Press,* Murray imagined perusing the volumes in these stalls and "coming away with an armful of treasure" (Ms. 23,513, TCM, NLI). Both images appear in *Aftermath.* Clearly these cast-off books proved to be Brian's "treasure in the field" (Matthew 13:44), for which he surrendered all else. One may muse further whether Murray stands in like relation to his daughter Pauline as Mrs. Egan is to Brian, passing on to her, with grace working upon nature, the grace of the vocation to the enclosed life. Other points of similarity exist. On 19 January 1950 Murray described Pauline, then mother vicaress of the Poor Clare Convent in Galway, to Connolly: "Yet [she] was—and still is—a girl of bubbly spirits, and her coming into a room always meant some brightening influence on the company" (Box 13, folder 17:27–28, TLC, JJBL). Thus Pauline Murray seems cousin to the outgoing Brian Egan in the ingratiating manner he is said to have displayed in social situations.

As *The Serf* of 1920 proves revelatory of Murray's exterior life, recounting the strain of the schoolmaster's lot, so *Illumination* of 1939 reveals the landscape of Murray's interior life. Treating a very rare subject, it does not appear a play for popular consumption. Only in the Dublin of 1939, one imagines, could a play like this win a presentation. Yet Murray's correspondence reveals that *Illumination* did win something of an afterlife, as evidenced by requests for the text from college and amateur theatrical groups. The 1990s witnessed a resurgence of popular interest in spiritual questing and questioning. Murray's play of ideas, though dated in its dramaturgical style, might provoke discussion, as it is less about Catholicism than about pursuing spiritual growth and wholeness.

Among Murray's Irish dramatic successors, Brian Friel, Thomas Murphy, and Thomas Kilroy have all dramatized the struggle for faith in conflict with the opposing standards of spirit and world. Shortly after Murray's death, Friel depicted a monastic environment in *The Enemy Within* (1962), a treatment of Columba, a sixth-century Irish Cistercian monk. Friel differs from Murray, however, in showing us Columba's inner torment, the cost of his choice. Columba does not live his choice with placid conviction as Brian does. Friel dramatizes a soul in conflict. Though Columba perseveres in his role as abbot of a remote island monastery, he does not forswear his kinsmen so easily as Brian rebuffs his father (University Archives, Irish Collection, 3.70, JJBL). Had Murray dramatized the torment of his hero, as Friel does, he might have enlisted greater sympathy for Brian.

Thomas Murphy's *The Sanctuary Lamp,* originally published in 1976 and revised in 1984, is a play about Harry's struggle for faith amid the competing influences of Maudie, who supports him, Francisco, who challenges him, and Monsignor, who is unable to minister to him in any effective way. A quasi-expressionistic drama, it is set in "a church in a city" (1994,98). Thomas Kilroy's *Talbot's Box* (1977) depicts Matt Talbot (1856–1925), Dublin laborer and reformed alcoholic. "I wanted to write a play," says Kilroy in the Author's Note to his play, "about the mystic and the essentially irreducible division between such extreme individualism and the claim of relationship, of community, society" (1979). Though the theme is similar to that found in Murray's work, Kilroy's dramatic style is of the symbolist rather than the realist school. The effect is like a medieval miracle or morality play. All three plays deal with the dynamic of conversion, treated first by Murray in *Illumination.* Their dramatic methods, however, point to one of Murray's difficulties as a dramatist. Ever the realist, Murray was unable to adapt to a dramaturgical world changing before him. In his characters and his themes, however, he pointed the way ahead.

"I thought *Illumination* was to be my swansong," wrote Murray to O'Mahony on 11 February 1942, "but I've just sent to Niall for typing a little tragic play of peasant life entitled *Gentlefolk.* Some day I can see your players putting it across—for its message should go right to the heart of country people. At the moment nobody wants a play, long or short, with a tragic theme. So I feel I shall pigeon-hole it till minds are more tuned to a serious note in the theatre" (Ms. 24,902, folder 6, MOM, NLI). In a later letter to O'Mahony, written 22 February 1942, Murray says that he decided to send it on to the Abbey, having been prompted by his family. "It moves slowly and its note lacks the intensity of *The Briery Gap* and *Spring.* I have only the faintest hope that the Abbey will accept it but it is so trifling a study at its best that I shall not mind. I wrote it, or I should say more truthfully, that it wrote itself in a few weeks" (Ms. 24,902, folder 6, MOM, NLI).

Eventually retitled *The Green Branch* (1943), this one-act tragedy concerns the effects of environment and heredity on a rural family whose children succumb to tuberculosis. Though Murray's suspicions were correct and the Abbey directors rejected it, *The Green Branch* shows Murray returning to his strength, writing a naturalistic peasant play about the people he knew, which, in many ways, sums up his career. In his end, in effect, was his beginning. The scene opens on a note of worry as Humphrey and Mary Dalton are debating the cost of the bill for their son Diarmuid's recent funeral. Themes of death and poverty immediately converge, recalling *Spring* as well as *Maurice Harte* and *The Briery Gap*. The conversation also reveals that the Daltons are well acquainted with loss and, like Jude and Seumas in *Spring*, are keenly aware of the cost of funerals, having lost three sons to tuberculosis. A litany of the dead sons—Diarmuid, Maurice, and Sean—likewise cannot fail to evoke memories of Synge's *Riders to the Sea*. When we learn that Diarmuid was a hurling champion, we are reminded of Hugh Morrissey in *Birthright*. When Humphrey speaks of Una as the one child left to them, "and she as healthy as any one of them young apple trees in the garden outside" (Murray 1943, 17), the contrast creates an ironic tone suggesting that Una will be death's next victim.

Una is a tragic hero who grows in stature as the play progresses. Fully aware of the lot that is to befall her, she breaks off her imminent marriage to Owen. Possessing a strength defying belief, she not only sacrifices her present fulfillment for Owen's future happiness, but she also insists that they keep this news from her parents, who could not bear it at the present time. Instead they discuss everyday matters like the autumn harvest and the empty milk jug, suggestive of the desolation to come. As Una and Owen leave, Mary and Humphrey still anticipate the marriage, as the curtain falls:

> HUMPHREY: (*Hopefully.*) I like to think of a young man in this house again—and little children, maybe. The marriage will make up to us for many things.
>
> MARY: (*Kindling.*) It will—it will, Humphrey. Deep down in my heart I feel 'twill be the beginning of a new life for us. A new, life, Humphrey, by the grace of God. (34)

The play ends on an intensely painful note. Mary and Humphrey's talk of marriage and children creates an irony more bitter than that evoked at the conclusion of *Spring*. It is easy to see why this play did not suit the Abbey directors' need for material suited to an audience demanding lighter fare. But in an earlier era, this play would no doubt have been featured on Abbey tours of America, as was *Spring* and Murray's other successes. Indeed, Gerald Fitzgibbon ranks *The Green Branch* with *Birthright, Maurice Harte,* and *Autumn Fire,* saying, "[Murray] has explored deeper patterns and tensions among his characters" (1975, 61). Though marred by coincident and, perhaps, by an excess of sentiment, it is as strong as any play Murray wrote. The language, in the peasant idiom, is beautiful. The characters evoke great sympathy for their plight. Indeed, it is a pity that *The Green Branch* was never produced, for a production of the play at the time of its submission to the Abbey might have gone a long way toward rehabilitating Murray's declining reputation. Though ÓhAodha, writing in 1961, regarded it as one of the few Murray plays to have become dated, because of the cure for tuberculosis (30), the subsequent resurgence of some strains of that disease, and, indeed, persistant outbreaks of other virulent diseases such as AIDS still give resonance to the play's message.

When Murray sent the text to Holloway, he revealed in the accompanying letter of 9 May 1942 his own awareness of the play's shortcomings: "It is, as I told you, very slight—indeed little more than a trifle—but I set out to give a little study of a peasant group who were as the doctor in the play observes 'gentlefolk in the true sense of the word.' Its lack of action is redeemed somewhat I think by the closing scene between the boy Owen & the young star crossed girl, Una. Some good angel may yet enlighten me as to how I could give more body and strength to the play but I have never found it easy to view a piece of work from an angle different from that which I saw it originally" (Ms. 13,267, folder 16, NLI). A year later, on 5 May 1943, Murray disclosed to Holloway revisions he made to the text before releasing it for publication in *The Dublin Magazine*. The development of the doctor's character was, in fact, a response to comments made by the Abbey directors in their written critique of the play. "I sent that little play of mine (as you suggested) to *The Dublin Magazine*. Seamus O'Sullivan liked it very much and it is to be published in the next issue. . . . I've rewritten the doctor's part slightly—representing him as having been asst.[sic] for three years in a Sanatorium and therefore particularly qualified to draw inferences. I'll be glad to have the play in permanent form" (Ms. 13,267, NLI). *The Green Branch* was duly published in *The Dublin Magazine* in July to September 1943 (Murray 1943). The Abbey directors' decision to reject the play smarted. Three years after the rejection, a sense of bitterness shows through in Murray's letter of 7 May 1945 to Frank O'Donnell: "They [the Directorate] pleaded that during the emergency— blessed word!—they couldn't fit in a one-acter with the regular full length show but that when things returned to normal they wo[uld] reconsider it. But this, of course, was merely a diplomatic way of easing the sharp edge of rejection. The little play was published in *The Dublin Magazine* & I must confess that I am rather fond of it" (Ms. 21,715, folder 10, NLI). Thus ended T. C. Murray's playwriting career.

# 6

## Cloistral Quiet

### *Critical Evaluation*

"I LIVE VIRTUALLY a cloistered life and this is a hermitage." According to Larry Morrow in "T. C. (don't call me Dr.) Murray"—published in Cork's *Sunday Press* on 6 November 1949—Murray spoke these words near the end of his life while living in self-described "cloistral quiet" (Box 13, folder 17:27–28. TLC, JJBL). In 1935, however, *The New York Herald Tribune* reported in an article from 24 March, "Abbey Theatre Widens Scope to Continent," that Murray was "now probably the best known [Abbey Theatre] dramatist throughout the world"—a statement underscoring the reach of Murray's reputation at one point in time (HTC). Murray's influence is recognized most readily when one looks beyond Ireland to England and America. Although Murray never traveled to America, his plays, regularly featured on the Abbey Theatre tours from 1911 to 1935, were well known to American theatergoers. By 1938, however, during the Abbey Theatre Festival of that year, Terence Connolly was complaining that Murray's work had been neglected in recent Abbey visits to America. Una Ellis-Fermor likewise contended that even in his lifetime, "Murray's work never achieved the esteem it deserved" (1967, 351).

Murray's stature as an Abbey Theatre playwright during the first three American tours (1911–1914) is indicated by the fact that three of his plays inaugurated these visits, sharing the opening night bills with plays by J. M. Synge and Augusta Gregory. By the time the Abbey company resumed its tours of America in the 1930s, however, several factors had undermined his stature with the critics and his popularity with the public.

One such factor was the changing temper of public taste, notably the movement away from the peasant plays in the mid-twenties and the growing popularity in the thirties of tragicomedies. When Teresa Deevy's new play was poorly received by critics and the public at the opening of the 1937–1938 tour in New York City, *Katie Roche* was withdrawn from the tour program, a victim of the change in the American entertainment climate; this change also affected Murray's reception. The serious strain in Murray's plays, so appreciated by O'Neill, became a reason for their lack of appeal. Some of Murray's plays were thought "unbearably tragic," a phrase used by Maurice Kennedy in "Fine First Night," his 25 March 1951 *Sunday Press* review of the revival of *Maurice Harte* (Ms. 23,510, TCM, NLI). In 1932 *New York Times* critic Brooks Atkinson touched on a key feature of Murray's art. In his review of 30 December, *"Autumn Fire* Acted by the Abbey Players," he complained that Murray's play displayed "few of the rollicking adornments of the favorite [Irish] plays" (HTC), for while Murray's subject matter was Irish, his dramaturgy was French, influenced by the psychological realism of Jansenist-educated Jean Racine (1639–1699) whose characters exist in a tightly confined psychosocial world.

According to Holloway, for example, O'Casey felt that Murray's plays "take too much out of him. Both *Birthright* and *Maurice Harte* distressed him very much in witnessing. . . . O'Casey loves Shaw's work because in the very kernel of tragedy he can introduce something to make one laugh its sting away. Murray never does this; his tragedy is ever unrelieved" (1967, 220). O'Casey, a man of the Dublin street, reflects the taste of the middle-class Dubliners who patronized the Abbey. It was O'Casey's genius to reflect their taste in his tenement plays as well. Murray was unsuited by temperament to create the mixed form of tragicomedy at which O'Casey excelled. The lack of comedy in Murray's work, his rural peasant subject matter, and the emergence of America's own realist playwrights (Dalsimer 1981, 86) all contributed to the elimination of his plays from the Abbey touring repertoire in America.

Murray's occasional outspokenness and refusal to engage in theatrical politics also affected his fortunes. The satirical poem Murray penned about Frank O'Connor in 1926 caused him some political damage, but worse damage was inflicted by his disagreement with the Abbey directors in 1936, expressed in *Guth na nGaedheal,* about what a National Theatre should be.

The programming of his work during this period may reflect Abbey reprisals for his views. Terence Connolly claimed that "for a year and a half after this incident, none of T. C. Murray's plays were done at the Abbey nor on tour" (1960, 364–65). Murray's letter refusing to retract his statement in *Guth na nGaedheal* is dated 3 April 1936. An examination of the *Abbey Theatre Playbook* reveals that *Autumn Fire* had just been performed at the Abbey the month prior, from 9 to 14 March 1936, for six performances. There was not to be another Murray play staged at the Abbey until 22–28 August 1937, when *Spring* was played for six performances. This is indeed a gap of almost "a year and a half," as Connolly asserted. After this, Murray's plays were performed less frequently than before 1936. A presentation of *A Spot in the Sun* followed, from 14 to 19 February 1938, for six performances, succeeded by a revival of *Maurice Harte* for six performances from 18 to 23 July of the same year. Murray's last premiere at the Abbey, that of *Illumination,* followed, receiving six performances from 31 July to 5 August 1939 (*Abbey Theatre Playbook* n.d., 6, 35, 51, 81).

Given the busy production schedule for Murray's plays in the 1920s and early 1930s, this marks a slowdown of staging activity. Holloway's assertion that the directors "practically closed down the Abbey Theatre on his work" may be accurate. It is difficult to substantiate this claim conclusively as there are no references to Murray regarding this situation in the correspondence of Ernest Blythe. Yet it appears that Murray paid a high price for his conviction and his honesty in the *Guth na nGaedheal* essay.

Murray's timidity also caused his reputation to suffer (Hogan 1996, 155–62). Malone wrote in the late 1920s: "Perhaps the greatest obstacle to the wider fame of Murray as a dramatist is his own incurable modesty. He is one of the shyest and most retiring of living writers shunning publicity of every kind" (1965, 185). Some literati judged that Murray's native diffidence would not dispose him to accept a vacant director's post at the Abbey in 1942 when Dr. Walter Starkie resigned (Holloway 1968, 3:77). On 25 January 1954, near the end of his life, he denied O'Mahony's request to publish a biographical note in a drama festival program for *Michaelmas Eve*: "Writing of myself & my 'career' always makes me wince. It is a self laudatory pat on the back—a hateful gesture" (Ms. 24,902, folder 10, MOM, NLI).

Though truthful, Malone's claim of Murray's shyness is exaggerated. Murray did not shrink from social situations when an occasion called for his presence. When he was required to officiate at a literary conference he carried the responsibility with ease. It is more accurate to say that Murray did not promote himself; he chose solitude rather than celebrity. Days before the Dublin premiere of *Maurice Harte,* an eager reporter tried to get Murray to speak; Murray declined the journalistic opportunity: "I tried all my persuasion towards him, but in vain. I gave him opening which he, with a smile, refused to take; but still I got some information out of him" (J. P. M. 1912).

Murray did not pursue publicity as did Frank O'Connor, Paul Vincent Carroll, or Sean O'Faoláin, and he was unsympathetic to any public display of ego, disapproving of O'Connor's and Carroll's vanity. Of O'Connor's resignation from the Abbey Board of Directors, Murray wrote in a letter to Connolly on 6 June 1939: "That will seem to you (as it did to all of us) a casual event. But to the author of *Times Pocket* it seemed such a world shaking event as to justify a special interview with the press to explain his motives. The public merely smiled and shook its head at this exhibition of childish vanity" (TLC, JJBL). Of Carroll and his *White Steed,* Murray wrote that the author "has become somewhat overheady with the strong brew that your critics so lavishly gave him." In the same letter, Murray singled out O'Faoláin as well. Although he found O'Faoláin's travel book, *An Irish Journey,* "intensely interesting," he observed that "it is marred by frequent displays of such egotism as to make one gasp" (Box 13, folder 17, TLC, JJBL). Although he failed to appreciate Carroll's play *The Old Foolishness* in its Gaiety Theatre premiere, he wrote in a letter to Joseph Holloway on 11 August 1942 that he was amused by Carroll himself and the evening was redeemed: "I felt from the moment the lady invaded the farmhouse that all the strings were false. I enjoyed very much the author's own performance at the end!!" (Ms. 22,404, folder 12, JH, NLI).

Murray refused to pamper his own ego. He did not even wish to have his photo taken. In a letter to Terence Connolly, written on 2 April 1959, Murray's daughter Eva explained: "We have very few photographs of him at all. He never liked sitting for them and avoided doing so at all costs" (Box 13, folder 17:27–28, TLC, JJBL). As it was, Murray's native diffidence and his determined solitude led him away from posterity's notice.

Murray realized in the 1950s that his dramatic day had passed. Yet Matthew Conlin recalls witnessing the revival of *Maurice Harte* at the Abbey in the 1951 season: "Three times in one week I saw the audience very much intrigued" (Conlin 1991). Though this presentation failed to draw throngs to the theater, it managed to captivate those who attended. According to Quidnunc's "An Irishman's Diary," which appeared that year in *The Irish Times,* American scene designer and playwright Mordecai Gorelick was among those so intrigued. Gorelick could not understand why Murray's plays were not "known more widely and ranked more highly in theatrical placings" (Ms. 23,514, TCM, NLI).

Although Murray was a limited dramatic artist with respect to theme and form, he helped popularize the realistic Irish peasant play. Richard Fallis asserts that Murray "helped define the norms of modern Irish drama" (1977, 112). Yeats recognized the importance of Murray's work in developing both a body of Irish plays and an audience for the Abbey in the years after Annie Horniman withdrew her subsidy in 1910. Yeats and Gregory realized that some of Murray's dialogue, characters, and dramatic situations were flawed. They also recognized his plays' native merit and consistently produced his work into the early 1930s.

Murray's forte was dramatic structure, although sometimes his plots may seem too well made. The best of the plays are true in language, character, and incident, although they are not flamboyant in language or electrifying in action like the plays of Synge and O'Casey. Abbey patrons of the period no longer lived in rural areas, but they were not far removed from life on the land. Thomas Hogan judged that Murray wrote "from within the people" (1950, 42). He definitely enriched the school of Irish dramatic realism with his singular studies of the religious dimensions of his characters. With few exceptions, the plays were apolitical, yet in mirroring a people, they contributed to the cause of cultural nationalism.

This study derives from Gerald Fitzgibbon's observation that beneath the surface realism of Murray's most important plays, the real issue is one of freedom versus oppression. Murray examined the actual situations in which his characters—the people he knew—lived; in doing so, he presented for critique the sources of oppression in their lives. Six of the plays, in particular, reveal a growth from domination to liberation in the central characters. This progression, though overtly apolitical, can suggest the nationalistic advance to an

Irish Free State. *Maurice Harte* depicts a family using religion to oppress its youngest son in order to achieve social status and economic security. Maurice represses his own desires to please his family and to placate his mother. He pays a high price to alert his family that their choice is not his choice. In *The Briery Gap*, a country priest uses his clerical office to tyrannize his congregation. Morgan's subsequent desertion of Joan and her resulting suicide demonstrate their lack of freedom; their "choices" are far from free. *The Serf* represents a new facet in Murray's work. Charles Drennan boldly questions the clerical abuse of power in uncharacteristically nationalistic tones. As Charles rises in defiance, so he also rises in self-esteem. His courage to confront clerical authority is a life-enhancing choice. In these three plays Murray dramatizes the exalted status of the priest in the Irish community. Murray is not afraid to demythologize priests by showing their failings and injustices. In *The Serf,* furthermore, Murray dares to preach a sermon on the manner in which a priest—or any governing power—ought to teach.

*Aftermath* begins a new movement in Murray's writing. In it Myles O'Regan achieves a hard-won, bitter freedom from his mother and his wife. Though devoid of substantive religious content, the play provides a link to two of Murray's later plays. Myles O'Regan is more free than Maurice Harte. Unlike Maurice, Myles knows what he wants and, after a sustained period of unhappiness, he chooses what he believes will be a life-enhancing path. In *The Pipe in the Fields* Murray uses the priest to promote the course of greater freedom in the life of Peter Keville. Murray depicts the priest as the person of wisdom in the community. He is able to interpret accurately Peter's near-religious experiences and encourage his artistic expression. More than just a symbol, art becomes a dynamic path to personal freedom.

*Illumination* precisely depicts religious experience and presents a character who breaks free of family restrictions decisively. With confidence derived from his conscious religious experience, Brian Egan repeatedly withstands his father's pressure tactics and reaches the threshold of liberation. Brian sees Mount Melleray Abbey as a life-enhancing environment, consonant with his nature and likely to nurture his interior growth.

The world of Murray's plays, therefore, is not quite so constricted and oppressive as some critics have indicated. Rather, these six plays show Murray's dramatic field as possessing a wider interior landscape. Three major characters—Charles Drennan, Peter Keville, and Brian Egan—follow the network of roads to freedom; of these, Brian Egan reaches a state of true liberation, allowing him to make free choices consistently. Murray's terrain is essentially a religious one. Murray's skill in dramatizing Ireland's socioreligious forces and omnipresent undercurrents constitutes the distinguishing feature of his dramatic corpus. It is his greatest contribution to Irish dramatic literature and cultural nationalism.

I wish to make some final observations on T. C. Murray's life and career. Hugh Hunt asserts that Murray failed to be sufficiently critical of the forces causing the unhappiness he dramatized (1979, 88). However, one must remember that in Murray's day, just to raise these issues by dramatizing them on the stage was a bold and critical action. Certainly the Cork priest who shunned Murray after the production of *Maurice Harte* in 1912 thought so. No doubt Murray wrote *The Serf* (1920) under the pseudonym of Stephen Morgan because he feared reprisals for his criticism of clerics. Indeed, considering the times in which Murray wrote, his depiction of the old priest is just short of incendiary.

Murray never broke from the tradition of the well-made play. Though he was aware of contemporary continental dramatic thought and form, he eschewed them. Temperamentally, he was unsuited to the challenge of dramatizing life in other than realistic treatments. In the mid-1960s, shortly after Murray's death, Brian Friel began transforming the realistic Irish peasant play by incorporating alter egos, a fluid use of space, and nonliner time patterns. But Murray was not alone among his contemporaries in his less than successful attempts to dramatize an expressionistic or symbolist element. Colum, Robinson, Carroll, and O'Casey all experimented with expressionistic or poetic forms of drama, but they are most remembered for their realistic studies. Even Synge floundered when he wandered away from peasant realism.

Far from being catholic in the widest sense, Murray's views and tastes suffered from a marked parochialism. He was a victim of a Jansenistic puritanical strain in Irish Catholicism; as a result, he was timid in his treatment of sexual material. Murray failed as a dramatist more from lack of nerve than of insight. The alternative endings to plays reveal a true initial vision that was self-censored. Although Murray's repression and self-censorship are lamentable, they are not insurmountable as far as production is concerned. Tomás MacAnna contends that if *Autumn Fire,* for example, were to be performed today, it would require "a director who would show us things we didn't know were in it" (1992). In this regard, the alternative endings should be studied by directors and used in productions if they are more truthful than the published versions.

Murray died in the spring of 1959 as the amateur dramatic societies around Ireland were preparing for competition. More than one regional festival noted his passing. P. Gunnigan, president of the Mayo festival, stated before the assembly that the works of T. C. Murray "probably more than any other playwright . . . had formed the backbone of the amateur drama movement" ("Festival Tribute to T. C. Murray" 1959). A Dublin obituary from 9 March stated: "New tensions in Irish life call for new treatments in dramatic form, but, despite the present neglect, Murray's position in the future seems assured. It is hardly likely that he will ever be surpassed in the genre of the peasant play that has been Ireland's distinctive contribution to world drama" (ÓhAodha 1959). Shortly after Mícheál ÓhAodha wrote these words, Brian Friel and John B. Keane came upon the Irish dramatic scene, harvesting the ground that Murray had broken and tilled. Martin McDonagh's *Beauty Queen of Leenane* (1996) is an Irish peasant play whose well-made structure and brutal realism reaches back to Murray. The film *This is My Father* (1998) likewise draws on this latter aspect of Murray's work.

In fewer than fifty years, Murray's tombstone in Glasnevin cemetery has suffered from neglect and weathering. The worn epitaph speaks of his neglected status in Irish theater history and dramatic literature. Yet he deserves to be remembered for the full range of his contributions to Irish dramatic literature and theater history, both at the professional and amateur levels. Given his duties as teacher and headmaster, husband and father, the steady flow of poems, articles, and book and drama reviews, together with the plays, form a significant Irish literary testament.

Unlike Colum and O'Casey, Murray remained in Ireland and faithfully supported the development of Irish drama, even when he disliked some of what he observed and read. He was most successful when he was treating the lives of the people he best knew; his achievement in the peasant play tradition was singular.

In the introduction to *Selected Plays: T. C. Murray,* which he edited, Richard Allen Cave points to the subtextual richness of Murray's work, allowing that his plays "demand the finest standards of *ensemble* acting that has been a continuing tradition in the Abbey's rich heritage from its past" (Murray 1998, xxii). Irish productions of his works in the 1990s, most notably *Spring* and *Autumn Fire,* demonstrate that T. C. Murray is not completely forgotten as an artist. The Abbey Theatre's 1992 and 2000–2001 options on the professional performance rights to *Autumn Fire* suggests that his memory remains alive in the historical mind of the National Theatre Society (Fahy 2001). In making seven of Murray's plays newly available to readers, *Selected Plays: T. C. Murray* should assist the more frequent production of his plays and the rehabilitation of his reputation.

In "Tested upon the Public," Gabriel Fallon cites English director W. Bridges Adams, who once asserted, "Anyone who has the Irish drama at heart must be grateful to the man who, with such understanding and such patient and unassuming artistry, kept that gentle flame burning when the first great years of the Abbey Theatre had passed (qtd. in Fallon 1954, 8). At the end of his life, Murray said with honesty, "The candle is burnt out." I hope that this study makes the people Murray knew, as well as his understanding, perseverance, and artistry, newly visible.

Works Cited

Index

# Works Cited

"The Abbey Players to Open Here Oct. 18." 1932. *The New York Times*. 15 September. Ms. 23,510, TCM, NLI.

Abbey Theatre. Papers. National Library of Ireland, Dublin.

"The Abbey Theatre." Review of *The Blind Wolf*. 1928. *The Evening Mail*. 1 May. Ms. 23,513, 2:31, TCM, NLI.

"The Abbey Theatre: Brilliant Production of *Michaelmas Eve*." 1932. *The Irish Times*. 28 June. Ms. 23,510, TCM, NLI.

"Abbey Theatre: *Illumination*." 1939. *The Irish Times*. 1 August. Ms. 23,513, 2:76, TCM, NLI.

"The Abbey Theatre: New Play by Mr. T. C. Murray." 1938. Review of *A Spot in the Sun*. *The Irish Times*. 15 February. Ms. 23,510, TCM, NLI.

"Abbey Theatre: Sensitive Acting in Revival." Review of *Spring*. 1937. *The Irish Times*. 24 August. Ms. 23,510, TCM, NLI.

*Abbey Theatre Authors' Fees*. Dublin: National Theatre Society.

*Abbey Theatre Playbook*. n.d. Dublin: National Theatre Society.

"Abbey Theatre's Two Plays." Review of *Spring*. 1937. *Dublin Evening Mail*. 24 August. Ms. 23,510, TCM, NLI.

*Abbey Tour Programmes*. 1911–1912, 1912–1913, 1914, 1931–1932, 1937–1938. Dublin: National Theatre Society.

Armstrong, Everhardt. "Irish Troupe Offers Synge's Masterpiece." Review of *Spring*. 1935. *Seattle Post Intelligence*. 12 April. Ms. 25,512, 23, AT, NLI.

Augustine of Hippo. [1961] 1979. *Confessions*. Books 7 and 9. Translated by R. S. Pine-Coffin. Harmondsworth, Middlesex, England: Penguin Books.

"Autumn Fire." Review of *Autumn Fire*. 1926. *Dublin Evening Mail*. 18 May. Ms. 23,510, TCM, NLI.

"Autumn Fire." 1933. Review of *Autumn Fire*. *Chicago Journal of Commerce*. 7 March. Ms. 25,511, 22:153, AT, NLI.

"*Autumn Fire* at the Abbey." Review of *Autumn Fire*. 1926. *Irish Independent*. 18 May. Ms. 23,510, TCM, NLI.

Barry, William A., and William J. Connolly. 1982. *The Practice of Spiritual Direction*. New York: Seabury Press.

Bennett, James O'Donnell. 1914. "Return of the Irish Players." Review of *Sovereign Love*. [Chicago] *Record-Herald*. 18 February. Ms. 25,502, 14:71, AT, NLI.

Berg Collection. New York Public Library.

"*The Blind Wolf*: Mr. Murray's New Play at Abbey Theatre." 1928. *The Irish Times*. 1 May. Ms. 23,510, TCM, NLI.

Browne, Robert, and F. Flannery. 1900–1906. School Inspector's Summary Reports. Archives of Rathduff National School, Grenagh, Rathduff, Co. Cork.

Brown, Terence. 1985. *Ireland, A Social and Cultural History: 1922–1985*. Hammersmith, London: Fontana.

Byrne, Dawson. [1929] 1971. *The Story of Ireland's National Theatre: The Abbey Theatre, Dublin*. New York: Haskell House Publishers.

Canfield, Curtis, ed. 1929. *Plays of the Irish Renaissance: 1880–1930*. New York: Washburn.

Casey, D. J., and Robert E. Rhodes, eds. 1977. *Views of the Irish Peasantry, 1800–1916*. Hamden, CT: Archon.

Chisholm, Gregory, S.J. 1993. Comment on *The Briery Gap*. Paper read on 2 May. Tufts University, Medford, MA.

Clarke, Brenna Katz. 1982. *The Emergence of the Irish Peasant Play at the Abbey Theatre*. Ann Arbor, MI: UMI Research Press.

Conlin, Matthew T., O.F.M. 1952. "T. C. Murray: A Critical Study of His Dramatic Work." Ph.D. diss., National Univ. of Ireland.

———. 1961. "T. C. Murray: Ireland on the Stage." *Renascence* 13: 125–31.

———. 1991. Interview with the author. Rye, NH, 22 February.

Conn, Walter. 1986. *Christian Conversion: A Developmental Interpretation of Autonomy and Surrender*. New York: Paulist.

Connell, K. H. 1968. *Irish Peasant Society: Four Historical Essays*. Oxford: Clarendon Press.

Connolly, Terence L., S.J. 1960. "T. C. Murray: The Quiet Man." *The Catholic World* 190 (March): 364–69.

Connolly, William J., S.J. 1981. "Exploring Relational Prayer." *Human Development* 2, no. 4 (winter): 40–44.

Corish, Patrick J. 1985. *The Irish Catholic Experience: A Historical Survey*. Dublin: Gill and Macmillan.

Corkery, Daniel. 1931. *Synge and Anglo-Irish Literature*. New York: Longman's Green and Co.

"Cork Playwright in London: Mr. T. C. Murray On His Writings—London Interview." 1926. Regarding *Autumn Fire*. *The Cork Examiner*. 16 April. Ms. 23,510, TCM, NLI.

Curran, C. P. 1927. *"The Pipe in the Fields."* Review of *The Pipe in the Fields*. *The Irish Statesman*. 8 October. Ms. 23,510, TCM, NLI.

Curran, Ita O'Donovan. Family Collection. Kiliney, Co. Dublin.

Dalsimer, Adele M. 1981. "Players in the Western World: The Abbey Theatre's American Tours," *Éire-Ireland* 16, no. 4 (winter): 75–93.

"D. S." 1938. *"Spot in the Sun*: New Play by T. C. Murray." Review of *A Spot in the Sun*. *Irish Independent*. 15 February. Ms. 23,510, TCM, NLI.

———. 1939. "Fine Acting in New Play: First Production of *Illumination*." *Irish Independent*. 1 August. Ms. 23,513, 2:74, TCM, NLI.

Donaghy, J. L. 1932. "New Play at the Abbey: Mr. Murray's *Michaelmas Eve*. A Drama of Youth and Age." 3 July. *Observer*. Ms. 23,510, TCM, NLI.

"The Dublin Stage: A Varied Year." 1940. Review of *Illumination*. *The Irish Times*. 1 January. Ms. 23,514, TCM, NLI.

Ervine, St. John. 1923. "At the Play: Three Irish Dramatists." *Observer*. 7 January. See also Ms. 23,510, TCM, NLI.

Ellis-Fermor, Una. 1939. *The Irish Dramatic Movement*. London: Methuen & Co.

———. 1967. "Thomas Cornelius Murray." In *The Oxford Companion to the Theatre*, edited by Phyllis Hartoll. London: Oxford Univ. Press.

Fahy, Martin. 2001. Letter. To Albert J. DeGiacomo, 30 April.

Fallis, Richard. 1977. *The Irish Renaissance*. Syracuse: Syracuse Univ. Press.

Fallon, Gabriel. 1939a. *"Illumination*—Murray's Greatest Play." *The Standard*. 11 August. Inserted in bound *Illumination* typescript. University Archives, Irish Collection, JJBL. Also in Ms. 23,513, 2:82, TCM, NLI.

———. 1939b. "More About a Play and a Dramatist." Review of *Illumination*. *The Standard*. 18 August. Ms. 23,513, 2:82, TCM, NLI.

———. 1954. "Tested Upon the Pulse." *Standard* 14 May. Ms. 23,510, TCM, NLI.

Farrell, Michael. 1940. "Plays for the Country Theatre." *The Bell* 1, no. 3 (December): 58–64.

"Festival Tribute to T. C. Murray." 1959. *Irish Press* (March). Archives of Macroom Museum and Historical Society.

Fitzgibbon, T. Gerald. 1975. "The Elements of Conflict in the Plays of T. C. Murray." *Studies* (spring): 59–65.

Fleischmann, Ruth. 1992. "Catholicism in the Culture of New Ireland: Cannon Shee-han and Daniel Corkery." In *Irish Writers and Religion,* edited by Robert Welch. Gerrards Cross, Buckinghamshire: Colin Smythe.

Friel, Brian. 1979. *The Enemy Within.* Dublin: Gallery Press.

Gelb, Arthur, and Barbara Gelb. 1965. *O'Neill.* New York: Dell Publishing Company.

Goldman, Emma. 1914. *The Social Significance of the Modern Drama.* Boston: Richard G. Badger.

Gregory, Augusta Isabella Perse. 1913. *Our Irish Theatre.* New York: G. P. Putnam's Sons, Knickerbocker Press.

Gregory, Augusta Isabella Perse. 1947. *Lady Gregory's Journals 1916–1930.* Edited by Lennox Robinson. New York: Macmillan. Quoted in Mícheál ÓhAodha, "T. C. Murray and Some Critics," *Studies* 47(summer 1958):187.

Gunning, G. Hamilton. 1912. "The Decline of Abbey Theatre Drama." *Irish Review* (February), 606–9.

Hall, O. L. 1912. "Irish Players in Triple Bill." *Chicago Daily.* 31 December. Ms. 25,502, 14:4, AT, NLI.

Hanifin, Ada. 1935. "Abbey Players in Murray's *Spring* on Curran Stage." 1935. *San Francisco Examiner.* 27 March. Ms. 25,512, 23, AT, NLI.

Harmon, Maurice. 1977. "Cobwebs Before the Wind." In *Views of the Irish Peasantry, 1800–1916,* edited by D. J. Casey and Robert E. Rhodes. Hamden, CT: Archon Books.

Harvard Theatre Collection. Nathan Marsh Pusey Library, Cambridge, Mass.

Hayes, J.J. 1927. "An Abbey Success: The Irish Seem Enthusiastic about T. C. Murray's New One-Acter." Review of *The Pipe in the Fields. New York Times.* 23 October. Ms. 23,510, TCM, NLI.

———. 1928a. "An Irish Play in New York." Review of *The Blind Wolf. The New York Times.* 23 June. Ms. 23,510, TCM, NLI.

———. [1928]b. "T. C. Murray, Ireland's Foremost Dramatist: Makes the Tragedies of Young Men the Theme of His Plays—Is Public School Teacher." *The New York Times.* Ms. 23,513, 2:29–30, TCM, NLI.

———. 1928c. "Tragedy At the Abbey: Dublin Sees T. C. Murray's New Play, Which Departs From the Irish Folk Field." Review of *The Blind Wolf. The New York Times.* 27 May. Ms. 23,513, 2:34, TCM, NLI.

Hogan, J. J. 1949. "Thomas Cornelius Murray." *Studies* 38: 194–96.

Hogan, Robert. 1967. *After the Irish Renaissance.* Minneapolis: Univ. of Minnesota Press.

———. 1996. "The Brave Timidity of T. C. Murray." *Irish University Review* 26, no. 1 (spring/summer): 155–62.

———, ed. 1980. *The Macmillan Dictionary of Irish Literature*. London: Macmillan.

Hogan, Robert, and James Kilroy. 1978. *The Abbey Theatre: The Years of Synge, 1905–1909*. Dublin: Dolmen Press.

Hogan, Robert, and Richard Burnham. 1984. *The Art of the Amateur, 1916–1920*. Atlantic Highlands, NJ: Humanities Press.

———. 1992. *The Modern Irish Drama: A Documentary History*. Vol. 6, *The Years of O'Casey, 1921–1926*. Newark: Univ. of Delaware Press.

Hogan, Robert, Richard Burnham, and Daniel P. Poteet. 1979. *The Abbey Theatre: The Rise of the Realists, 1910–1915*. Atlantic Highlands, NJ: Humanities Press.

Hogan, Thomas. 1950. "T. C. Murray." *Envoy* 3 (November): 38–48.

Holloway, Joseph. Papers. National Library of Ireland, Dublin.

Holloway, Joseph. 1967. *Joseph Holloway's Abbey Theatre: A Selection from His Unpublished Journal, Impressions of a Dublin Playgoer*. Edited by Robert Hogan and Michael J. O'Neill. Carbondale and Edwardsville: Southern Illinois Univ. Press.

———. 1968. *Joseph Holloway's Irish Theatre*. 3 vols. Edited by Robert Hogan and Michael J. O'Neill. Dixon, CA: Proscenium Press.

———. *The Diaries of Joseph Holloway, 1895–1944*. "Impressions of a Dublin Playgoer." Ms. 1857. JH, NLI.

Hooper, P. J. 1930. "Abbey Theatre Hit On Play Rejection: Dublin Admirers of T. C. Murray, Noted Dramatist, Defend Latest Work. But He Denies Bias Talk." *New York Evening Post*. 24 October. Ms. 23,513, TCM, NLI.

Hunt, Hugh. 1979. *The Abbey: Ireland's National Theatre, 1904–1979*. New York: Columbia Univ. Press.

"I was interested to read in the obituaries." [1959]. Ms. 23,510, TCM, NLI.

"*Illumination*, Mr. T. C. Murray's new play, is playing to crowded audiences at the Abbey Theatre this week." Photo caption. 1939. Unmarked news cutting. Week of 1 August. Ms. 23,513, 2:75 TCM, NLI.

"Irish Dramatic Movement: Lecture at National Literary Society" (unmarked news cutting). 1914. Ms. 23,514, TCM, NLI.

"Irish Players in Comedy and Tragedy: Three Plays by Lady Gregory and T. C. Murray at the Adelphi." Review of *Birthright*. 1912. *Philadelphia Press*. 12 January. Ms. 25,499, 2:329, AT, NLI.

"Irish Players to Show at Notre Dame School: Company to Give *Maurice Harte* and

*The Workhouse-Ward* at Roman Catholic Institution." 1913. *Chicago News.* 8 January. Ms. 25,502, 14:10, AT, NLI.

"Is this the *Daily Express?*" 1930. Cartoon about *A Flutter of Wings.* Unmarked cutting. Ms. 23,513, TCM, NLI.

Jacques. 1918. "Sobs and Snuffles." *The Evening Herald.* 9 January, 3. Quoted in Robert Hogan and Richard Burnham, *The Art of the Amateur, 1916–1920.* (Atlantic Highlands, NJ: Humanities Press, 1984), 140–41, 329n.

James, William. [1902] 1971. *The Varieties of Religious Experience.* New York: Collier Books.

J. W. G. 1928. "Mr. Murray's New Play: *The Blind Wolf* at the Abbey." *Irish Independent.* 1 May. Ms. 23,510, TCM, NLI.

Kavanagh, Peter. 1946. *The Irish Theatre.* Tralee: Kerryman.

———. 1950. *The Story of the Abbey Theatre.* New York: Devin-Adair.

Keane, John B. 1992. Letter to the author. 4 February.

Kennedy, Patrick. 1867. *The Banks of the Boro: A Chronicle of the County Wexford.* Dublin: M'Glashin and Gill. Quoted in Connell, K. H., *Irish Peasant Society: Four Historical Essays* (Oxford: Clarendon Press, 1968), 126–27.

Kenny, Linda. 1999. "T. C. Murray's Timeless Play Bridges Generation Gap." Review of *Autumn Fire. The Examiner.* 22 March.

Kenny, P. D. 1906. *Economics for Irishmen.* Dublin: Maunsell. Quoted in K. H. Connell, *Irish Peasant Society: Four Historical Essays* (Oxford: Clarendon Press, 1968), 146.

Kilroy, Thomas. 1979. *Talbot's Box.* Dublin: Gallery Press.

L. E. M. 1926. "Providence Opera House: Art From Erin." Review of *Autumn Fire. The Providence Evening Bulletin.* 19 October. Ms. 23,510, TCM, NLI.

Leslie, Amy. 1912a. "Four Fine Irish Plays: *The Jail Gate* [sic] at Grand a Dirge of Blunt Agony Written by Lady Gregory: Synge's Effort in Satire: *The Birthright* by T. C. Murray, a Melodramatic offering—*The Jackdaw* a Comedy." *The* [Chicago] *Daily News.* 22 February. Ms. 25,499, 2:412, AT, NLI.

———. 1912b. "Abbey Theater Company at Fine Arts Presents Three Plays, One a Novelty." *Chicago Daily News.* 31 December. Ms. 25,502, 14:4, AT, NLI.

———. 1914. "Irish Actors Here Draw Big Audience." [Chicago] *Daily News.* 18 February. Ms. 25,502, 14:71, AT, NLI.

Little, Richard Henry. 1912. "Irish Play Tugs Heart Strings: Art Holds Audience Spellbound." *Chicago Examiner.* 31 December. Ms. 25,502, 14:4, AT, NLI.

"M." 1927. *"Pipe in the Fields:* New Play by Popular Irish Author." Unmarked press cutting. n.d. Ms. 23,510, TCM, NLI.

MacAnna, Tomás. 1992. Interview with the author. Dublin, 2 July.

Macardle, Dorothy. 1925. "The Dramatic Art of Mr. T. C. Murray." *Dublin Magazine* 2 (January): 393–97.

MacManus, Francis. 1959. "Three First Meetings" (Daniel Corkery, T. C. Murray, and Padraic Colum). *The Capuchin Annual* 26:53–59.

MacManus, M. J. Collection. The John J. Burns Library, Boston College, Chestnut Hill, Mass.

MacNamara, Brinsley. 1933. "A Note on Peasant Drama." *The Dublin Magazine* (January-March):61–63.

Malone, Andrew E. [1929.] 1965. *The Irish Drama*. New York: Benjamin Blom.

Martin, Augustine. 1980. *Anglo-Irish Literature*. Dublin: Department of Foreign Affairs.

Matthews, James H. 1983. *Voices: A Life of Frank O'Connor*. New York: Atheneum.

"*Maurice Harte* A Clever Study: Audience Followed New Irish Play Last Night With Absorbed Interest." Review of *Maurice Harte*. 1913. *Montreal Gazette*. 29 January. Ms. 25,502, 14:22, AT, NLI.

Maxwell, Desmond E. S. 1984. *A Critical History of Modern Irish Drama, 1891–1980*. Cambridge: Cambridge Univ. Press.

———. 1988. "T. C. Murray." In *The Cambridge Guide to World Theatre*, edited by Martin Banham. New York: Cambridge Univ. Press.

McBrien, Richard. 1981. *Catholicism*. San Francisco:Harper & Row.

Metcalfe. 1926. "Hibernian Domestic Affair." Review of *Autumn Fire*. *The Wall Street Journal*. n.d. Ms. 23,510, TCM, NLI.

Morash, Christopher. 2002. *A History of the Irish Theatre: 1601–2000*. Cambridge: Cambridge Univ. Press.

Mr. Gossip. 1926. "Irish Playwright: T. C. Murray's Flying Visit For London Production." *Daily Sketch*. 15 April.

Murphy, Thomas. [1976] 1994. *The Sanctuary Lamp*. London: Methuen.

Murray, Christopher. 1997. *Twentieth-Century Irish Drama: Mirror Up to Nation*. Manchester: Manchester Univ. Press.

Murray, T. C. Papers. National Library of Ireland, Dublin.

———. 1898. "Our Primary Schools and their Inspectors." *New Ireland Review* 9, no.4 (June-August): 229–34 and 348–57.

———. 1899. "Our Primary Schools and their Inspectors." *New Ireland Review* 11, no.2 (April): 112–22.

———. 1905. "The Philosophy of Looking Eastward." *The Irish School Weekly*. 21 October. Ms. 24, 870, TCM, NLI.

———. 1909. "Fugitive Jottings" by "Ariel." *The Irish School Weekly.* 17 April. Ms. 24,881, TCM, NLI.

———. 1911. *Birthright.* Dublin: Maunsel and Co.

———. 1913. "Literary and Scientific Society: Lecture by Mr. T. C. Murray." *Cork Constitution.* 18 January.

———. 1914. "Irish Dramatic Movement: Lecture at National Literary Society." Unmarked news cutting. Ms. 23,514, TCM, NLI.

———. 1922. *Aftermath.* London: George Allen & Unwin.

———. 1926. *Spring and Other Plays.* 1917. Reprint, London: George Allen & Unwin.

———. 1928a. *The Blind Wolf.* Acting edition. Dublin: Authors' Guild of Ireland (Tom Mooney).

———. 1928b. *The Pipe in the Fields and Birthright.* London: George Allen & Unwin.

———. 1929. "Dramatic Criticisms" by Bricriu. *The Irish Statesman.* 30 November.

———. [1930]. *A Flutter of Wings.* Acting edition. Dublin: Authors' Guild of Ireland (Tom Mooney).

———. 1932. *Michaelmas Eve.* London: George Allen & Unwin.

———. 1933. "Another Writer Brings Fame to Kerry: Masterpiece from the Blaskets." Review of *Twenty Years A-Growing* by Maurice O'Sullivan. *Irish Independent.* 2 May. Ms. 23,511, TCM, NLI.

———. 1934. *Maurice Harte and A Stag At Bay.* London: George Allen & Unwin.

———. 1937a. *Michaelmas Eve.* Production Copy. Dublin: Authors' Guild of Ireland.

———. 1937b. *Spring Horizon.* London: Thomas Nelson and Sons.

———. 1938. *A Spot in the Sun. Dublin Magazine* 13, no. 2 (April-June): 14–36.

———. 1939a. "My Seven Stars of Memory." *Irish Digest* 5 (December): 58–61.

———. 1939b. "George Shiels, Brinsley MacNamara, etc." *The Irish Theatre,* edited by Lennox Robinson. London: Macmillan.

———. 1940. "The First National Book Fair." *The Irish Press.* 30 March. N.p.Ms. 23, 513. 2:133. TCM, NLI.

———. 1943. *The Green Branch. The Dublin Magazine* 18 (July-September), no. 3:15–34.

———. 1946. *Illumination.* University Archives, Irish Collection, JJBL.

———. 1948. "F. J. McCormick: A Symposium of Tributes." *The Capuchin Annual* 18:149–225.

———. 1950. "T. C. Murray Remembers Sara Allgood." *Irish Press.* 16 September. Ms. 23,513, 2:123, TCM, NLI.

————. 1951. Letter. To Matthew T. Conlin, 19 October. Quoted in Matthew T. Conlin, "T. C. Murray: Ireland on the Stage." *Renascence* 13 (1961, 126).

————. 1998. *Selected Plays: T. C. Murray.* Irish Drama Selections, no. 10. Edited by Richard Allen Cave. Gerrards Cross, Buckinghamshire: Colin Smythe.

"New Abbey Actors at the Peacock." 1948. Review of *The Briery Gap. Irish Independent.* Wednesday, 27 October. 2. Trinity University, Dublin. Microfilm.

"New Abbey Play: Mr. Murray's *Sovereign Love.*" Review of *Sovereign Love.* 1913. *Freeman.* n.d. Ms. 23,510, TCM, NLI.

"New One-Act Play by T.C. Murray." Review of *A Spot in the Sun.* n.d. unmarked. Ms. 23,510. TCM, NLI.

"New Play at the Abbey: Birthright." Review of *Birthright.* 1910. *The Irish Times.* 10 October. Ms. 23,510. TCM, NLI.

"A New Play at the Abbey: First Production of Mr. T. C. Murray's *Birthright.*" Review of *Birthright.* 1910. *Evening Telegraph.* 10 October Ms. 23,510, TCM, NLI.

Nowlan, David. 1973. "Double Bill At the Peacock." *The Irish Times.* 27 February. NLI. Microfilm.

O'Connor, Frank. 1929a. "At the Peacock." *The Irish Statesman.* 26 October:154–55.

————. 1929b. "Author and Review." *The Irish Statesman.* 7 December:271.

————. 1969. *My Father's Son.* New York: Alfred A. Knopf.

"Obituary: Frank J. Hugh O'Donnell." 1976. *The Irish Times.* 5 November. C 24.

O'Donoghue, David J. 1979. *The Life of William Carleton.* Vol. 1. 1896. Reprint, New York: Garland.

ÓhAodha, Mícheál. 1958. "T. C. Murray and Some Critics." *Studies* 47(summer):185–91.

————. 1959. "Obituary: Mr. T. C. Murray—Death of Co. Cork-born Playwright." n.p. Monday, 9 March. Archives of Macroom Museum and Historical Society.

————. 1961. *Plays and Places.* Dublin: Progress House.

————. 1974. *Theatre in Ireland.* Totowa, NJ: Rowman and Littlefield.

O'Leary, Con. 1918. "T.C. Murray's New Plays." *The Leader.* 2 February, 636. Quoted in Robert Hogan and Richard Burnham, *The Art of the Amateur, 1916–1920.* (Atlantic Highlands, NJ: Humanities Press, 1984), 141, 330 n.

O'Mahony, Mathew. Papers. National Library of Ireland, Dublin.

————. 1982. Lecture to Irish Theatre Archive at Newman House, Dublin. 17 November. Ms. 26,976, NLI.

————. 1992. Interview with the author. Dunshaughlin, Co. Meath, 22 June.

O'Neill, Eugene. [1955] 1973. *Long Day's Journey into Night.* New Haven: Yale Univ. Press.

O'Riordain, Dominic. 1973. *"Autumn Fire* In Irish." *The Irish Times.* 27 November. NLI. Microfilm.

O'Riordan, Patrick. 1996. Interview with the author. Rathduff, Co. Cork, 30 July.

O'Ryan, W. P. 1910. *The Plough and the Cross: The Story of the New Ireland.* Dublin: Irish Nation. Quoted in K. H. Connell, *Irish Peasant Society: Four Historical Essays* (Oxford: Clarendon Press, 1968), 146.

Owens, Cóilín and Joan N. Radner. 1990. "T. C. Murray: 1873–1959." *Irish Drama: 1900–1980,* edited by Cóilín Owens and Joan N. Radner. Washington, D.C.: The Catholic Univ. of America Press.

Parker, Henry T. 1913. "An Irish Tragedy, Murray's *Maurice Harte* Newly Acted." Review of *Maurice Harte. The Boston Evening Transcript.* 3 April. Ms. 25,502, 14:58, AT, NLI.

———. 1933. "The Irish at Peak In One More Play: Remarkable Performance of Murray's Tragi-Comedy *Autumn Fire.*" Review of *Autumn Fire. Boston Evening Transcript.* 6 May. Ms. 25,511 22:153, AT, NLI.

*"The Pipe in the Fields."* 1927. Review of *The Pipe in the Fields. Dublin Evening Mail.* 4 October. Ms. 23,510, TCM, NLI.

"Play Which the Abbey Rejected: Dublin's Welcome to *A Flutter of Wings.*" 1930. *The Daily Express.* 12 November. Ms. 23,513:24, TCM, NLI.

Plunkett, Horace. 1908. *Ireland in the New Century.* New York: E.P. Dutton.

Point, Jack. 1913. "At the Abbey: Mr. Murray's New Play." Review of *Sovereign Love. Evening Herald.* n.d. Ms. 23,510, TCM, NLI.

Quigley, Jack. 1932. "Dublin's Abbey Theatre Rediscovers America." *The New York Times.* 13 March. Ms. 25,510, 21:54, AT, NLI.

Robinson, Lennox. 1942. *Curtain Up: An Autobiography.* London: M. Joseph.

———. 1951. *Ireland's Abbey Theatre.* London: Sidgwick and Jackson.

Rushe, Desmond. 1973. "Murray's Plays Badly Neglected." *Irish Independent.* 23 November. NLI. Microfilm.

Sahal, N. 1971. *Sixty Years of Realistic Irish Drama (1900–1960).* Bombay: Macmillan.

Salem, James M. 1979. *Foreign Drama, 1909–1977.* Part 3 of *A Guide to Critical Reviews.* Metuchen, NJ: Scarecrow.

Shaughnessy, Edward L. 1998. *Eugene O'Neill in Ireland.* New York: Greenwood Press.

Shaw, Len G. 1935. "The Theater." Review of *Spring. Detroit Free Press.* Saturday, 26 January. Ms. 25,515, 26, AT, NLI.

Sheaffer, Louis. 1973. *O'Neill, Son and Artist.* Boston: Little, Brown.

Skelton, Robin. 1971. *J. M. Synge and His World.* New York: Viking Press.

Smith, Edward Doyle. 1966. "A Survey and Index of *The Irish Statesman* [1923–1930]." Ph.D. diss., Univ. of Washington.

"Sovereign Love." 1914. Review of *Sovereign Love. The Stage.* 11 June. Ms. 23,510, TCM, NLI.

Sternlicht, Sanford. 1985. *Padraic Colum.* Boston: Twayne Publishers.

Stevens, Ashton. 1914. "J. M. Kerrigan Diabolically Clever in Act: Characters of *Sovereign Love* Show Mean Spirit and Low Purpose." *Chicago Examiner.* 18 February. Ms. 25,502, 14:72, AT, NLI.

———. 1935. "Springboard For Irish Players' Fun is Sad Tragedy Entitled *Spring:* Ashton Stevens Is Reminded of Gloomy Plays Mentioned in *Drama At Inish.*" *The Chicago American.* Saturday, 9 February, 10. Ms. 25,512, 23, AT, NLI.

"A Strong Irish Play: *Maurice Harte* Proves Most Forceful of Present Repertoire." Review of *Maurice Harte.* 1913. [Philadelphia] *Public Ledger.* 21 March. Ms. 25,502, 14:49, AT, NLI.

"T." [1920]. "A New Play at the Abbey—and a Review." Review of *The Serf. Old Ireland.* Saturday, 30 October. Ms. 23,510, TCM, NLI.

"T. C. Murray Puts the Modern Irishman in a Play." 1939. Unmarked news cutting. n.d. Ms. 23,513, 2:75, TCM, NLI.

"Thomas Murray, Playwright, Dies." 1959. *The New York Times.* 9 March. Box 13, Folder 17:27–28, TLC, JJBL.

*Thom's Directory.* 1951. Dublin: A. Thom, Printer and Publisher.

"Three New Plays: Presented At the Peacock." Review of *The Briery Gap.* 1928. *Irish Independent.* 21 May. Ms. 23,513, 2:35, TCM, NLI.

Trinity College Library, Dublin.

Walsh, Seano. 1996. Interview with the author. Rathduff, Co. Cork, 30 July.

Waters, Arthur B. 1932. "New Irish Drama Given at Garrick by Abbey Players: T.C. Murray's *Autumn Fire* One of Series' Best." Review of *Autumn Fire.* [Philadelphia] *Public Ledger.* 21 December. Ms. 25,511, 22:153, AT, NLI.

Welch, Robert. 1999. *The Abbey Theatre 1899–1999: Form & Pressure.* Oxford: Oxford Univ. Press.

Weygandt, Cornelius. 1913. *Irish Plays and Playwrights.* Boston: Houghton Mifflin.

Wilmot, Séamus. 1929. "Gaelic Drama: To the Editor." *The Irish Statesman*. 9 November:190.

"Wintermute." 1926. *"Autumn Fire."* Review of *Autumn Fire*. *Variety*. 27 October. Ms. 23,510, TCM, NLI.

Yeats, W. B. [1912]. Letter to Abbey Theatre Directorate. n.d. W. B. Yeats Papers. Ms. 13,068, folder 27, NLI.

Yeats, W. B. 1914. Letter to T. C. Murray. 11 November. BC, NYPL.

———. [1905] 1961. "Introduction: Mr. Synge and His Plays." Preface to the first edition of *The Well of the Saints*, by J. M. Synge. London, A.H. Bullen. Reprinted in *Essays and Introductions*, by W.B. Yeats. New York: Macmillan.

# Index

Note: Fictional characters' names are not inverted and are identified by (fict.)